# CYBER INFLUENCE AND COGNITIVE THREATS

# CYBER INFLUENCE AND COGNITIVE THREATS

*Edited by*

VLADLENA BENSON
*University of West London, London, United Kingdom*

JOHN MCALANEY
*Bournemouth University, Fern Barrow, Poole Dorset, United Kingdom*

ELSEVIER

ACADEMIC PRESS
An imprint of Elsevier

Academic Press is an imprint of Elsevier
125 London Wall, London EC2Y 5AS, United Kingdom
525 B Street, Suite 1650, San Diego, CA 92101, United States
50 Hampshire Street, 5th Floor, Cambridge, MA 02139, United States
The Boulevard, Langford Lane, Kidlington, Oxford OX5 1GB, United Kingdom



**Notices**
Knowledge and best practice in this field are constantly changing. As new research and experience broaden our understanding, changes in research methods, professional practices, or medical treatment may become necessary.

Practitioners and researchers must always rely on their own experience and knowledge in evaluating and using any information, methods, compounds, or experiments described herein. In using such information or methods they should be mindful of their own safety and the safety of others, including parties for whom they have a professional responsibility.

To the fullest extent of the law, neither the Publisher nor the authors, contributors, or editors, assume any liability for any injury and/or damage to persons or property as a matter of products liability, negligence or otherwise, or from any use or operation of any methods, products, instructions, or ideas contained in the material herein.

**Library of Congress Cataloging-in-Publication Data**
A catalog record for this book is available from the Library of Congress

**British Library Cataloguing-in-Publication Data**
A catalogue record for this book is available from the British Library

ISBN: 978-0-12-819204-7

For information on all Academic Press publications visit our website at https://www.elsevier.com/books-and-journals

*Publisher:* Nikki Levy
*Acquisition Editor:* Joslyn Chaiprasert-Paguio
*Editorial Project Manager:* Barbara Makinster
*Production Project Manager:* Bharatwaj Varatharajan
*Cover Designer:* Mark Rogers



Typeset by TNQ Technologies

# Contents

## 4. 'Nothing up my sleeve': information warfare and the magical mindset

K. Scott



## 5. Digital hoarding behaviours: implications for cybersecurity

Nick Neave, Kerry McKellar, Elizabeth Sillence, and Pam Briggs



## 6. A review of security awareness approaches: towards achieving communal awareness

Azma Alina Ali Zani, Azah Anir Norman, and Norjihan Abdul Ghani

## 7. Understanding users' information security awareness and intentions: a full nomology of protection motivation theory

Farkhondeh Hassandoust and Angsana A. Techatassanasoontorn



## 8. Social big data and its integrity: the effect of trust and personality traits on organic reach of facebook content

Vladlena Benson and Tom Buchanan



## 9. The impact of sentiment on content post popularity through emoji and text on social platforms

Wei-Lun Chang and Hsiao-Chiao Tseng



## 10. Risk and social influence in sustainable smart home technologies: a persuasive systems design model

Nataliya Shevchuk, Harri Oinas-Kukkonen, and Vladlena Benson

# Contributors

**Vladlena Benson** Professor of Information Systems, Aston Business School, Aston University, Birmingham, United Kingdom

**Pam Briggs** Psychology and Communications Technology (PACT) Lab, Department of Psychology, Northumbria University, Newcastle upon Tyne, United Kingdom

**Tom Buchanan** School of Social Sciences, University of Westminster, London, United Kingdom

**Wei-Lun Chang** Department of Business Management, National Taipei University of Technology, Taipei City, Taiwan

**Norjihan Abdul Ghani** Department of Information Systems, Faculty of Computer Science and Information Technology, University of Malaya, Kuala Lumpur, Malaysia

**Stefanos Gritzalis** Information and Communication Systems Security Laboratory, Department of Information and Communications Systems Engineering, University of the Aegean, Samos, Greece

**Farkhondeh Hassandoust** Auckland University of Technology, Auckland, New Zealand

**Christos Kalloniatis** Privacy Engineering and Social Informatics Laboratory, Department of Cultural Technology and Communication, University of the Aegean, Mytilene, Lesvos, Greece

**Brian Keegan** Applied Intelligence Research Centre (AIRC), Technological University Dublin (TU Dublin), Dublin, Ireland

**Angeliki Kitsiou** Privacy Engineering and Social Informatics Laboratory, Department of Cultural Technology and Communication, University of the Aegean, Mytilene, Lesvos, Greece

**Andrei Queiroz Lima** Applied Intelligence Research Centre (AIRC), Technological University Dublin (TU Dublin), Dublin, Ireland

**John McAlaney** Associate Professor of Psychology, Department of Psychology, Bournemouth University, Poole, United Kingdom

**Kerry McKellar** Psychology and Communications Technology (PACT) Lab, Department of Psychology, Northumbria University, Newcastle upon Tyne, United Kingdom

**Nick Neave** Hoarding Research Group, Department of Psychology, Northumbria University, Newcastle upon Tyne, United Kingdom

**Azah Anir Norman** Department of Information Systems, Faculty of Computer Science and Information Technology, University of Malaya, Kuala Lumpur, Malaysia

**Harri Oinas-Kukkonen** Oulu Advanced Research on Service and Information Systems (OASIS), Faculty of Information Technology and Electrical Engineering, University of Oulu, Oulu, Finland

**K. Scott** Arts, Design, and Humanities, De Montfort University, Leicester, United Kingdom

**Nataliya Shevchuk** Oulu Advanced Research on Service and Information Systems (OASIS), Faculty of Information Technology and Electrical Engineering, University of Oulu, Oulu, Finland

**Elizabeth Sillence** Psychology and Communications Technology (PACT) Lab, Department of Psychology, Northumbria University, Newcastle upon Tyne, United Kingdom

**Angsana A. Techatassanasoontorn** Auckland University of Technology, Auckland, New Zealand

**Hsiao-Chiao Tseng** Department of Business Administration, Tamkang University, New Taipei City, Taiwan

**Eleni Tzortzaki** Information and Communication Systems Security Laboratory, Department of Information and Communications Systems Engineering, University of the Aegean, Samos, Greece

**Azma Alina Ali Zani** Department of Information Systems, Faculty of Computer Science and Information Technology, University of Malaya, Kuala Lumpur, Malaysia

# Preface

In the wake of fresh allegations that personality data from Facebook users have been illegally used to influence the outcome of the US general election and the Brexit vote, the debate over manipulation of social big data is gaining further momentum. This book addresses the social data privacy and data integrity vulnerabilities threatening the future of policy. Attackers exploit users' trust, breach their privacy, undertake industrial espionage and disrupt critical infrastructure.

Cyber criminals are using a wide range of methods, which are continuously evolving and increasingly motivated by financial gain on industrial scale. On one hand, machine learning is being integrated into many security solutions, so that the platform automatically learns, adjusts and adapts to the ever-changing Internet threat environment. The cyber security industry, policymakers, law enforcement, public and private sector organizations are yet to fully realize the impact emerging AI capabilities have or will have on security. On the other hand, researchers have addressed human behavior in online contexts for some time, though humans are still seen as the weakest link in cyber security chain. It is important that this gap is addressed.

Understanding human behaviors that have emerged and influence over social platforms in cyber security is critical and is an acute issue in ensuring security in personal, professional and organizational settings.

This book covers a variety of topics and addresses different challenges that have emerged. It discusses changes in the ways in which it is possible to study various areas of cognitive applications that relate to decision-making, behavior and human interaction in relation to cyber security.

These new challenges include phenomena such as the growth of hacktivism, the proliferation of open source hacking tools and social media-enabled social engineering strategies, which are worthy of attention.

This publication comprises chapters, which address social influence, cognitive computing and analytics as well as digital psychology, and the opportunities offered by cyber researchers. Academics contributing to this edited volume represent a wide range of research areas: information systems, psychology, sociology, strategy, innovation and others.

**Chapter 1. Cybersecurity as a social phenomenon** opens the debate on how individuals engage with technological systems, and how they may attempt to exploit both these systems and the others who are engaging with them. Gaining a greater understanding of these processes will enable researchers to develop more informed prevention and mitigation strategies in order to address the increasing challenges we face within cyber security.

**Chapter 2. Towards an integrated socio-technical approach for designing adaptive privacy aware services in cloud computing** highlights the increasingly complex nature of privacy preservation within cloud environments. The authors propose that the identification of users' social context is of major importance for a privacy aware system to balance between users' need for preserving personal information and the need for disclosing them. They propose a structured framework that incorporates both of social and technical privacy prerequisites for the optimal design of Adaptive Privacy Aware Cloud Systems.

**Chapter 3. Challenges of using machine learning algorithms for cybersecurity: a study of threat-classification models applied to social media communication data** focuses on how researchers and security experts are using forums and social media posts as a source for predicting security-related events against computational assets. The authors present an overview of the methods for processing the natural language communication extracted from social platforms. They provide an overview of the common activities that take place on these channels, for instance, the trade of hacking tools and the disclosure of software vulnerabilities on social media forums. The chapter concludes with a discussion regarding the challenges of using learning-based techniques in cybersecurity.

**Chapter 4. 'Nothing up my sleeve': information warfare and the magical mindset** outlines how human factors are leveraged as key strategic tools in information warfare and online influence in general. The chapter introduces the concept of a 'magical mindset' and addresses how it may help mitigate hostile influence operations and enable offensive capability.

**Chapter 5. Digital hoarding behaviours: implications for cybersecurity** explores the phenomenon known as 'digital hoarding' using a case study. The authors link digital hoarding behaviours with the aspects of Personal Information Management and explain how such behaviours may have negative impacts on an organization, particularly in relation to cybersecurity.

**Chapter 6. A review of security awareness approaches: towards achieving communal awareness** continues the discussion of the effectiveness of collaborative learning with the aim to change user behaviour communally to promote security awareness.

**Chapter 7. Understanding users' information security awareness and intentions: a full nomology of protection motivation theory** investigates the impact of users' cybersecurity awareness on their security protection intentions. The authors extend the PMT by investigating the role of fear and maladaptive rewards in explaining user behaviours.

**Chapter 8. Social big data and its integrity: the effect of trust and personality traits on organic reach of Facebook content** shares the insights on the fake content propagation through social platforms. In the light of recent content manipulation on Facebook influencing politics, the authors extend the fake news propagation attack scenario and address the strategies of manipulating the integrity of social big data. User personality characteristics are analysed in relation to content organic reach. Researchers discuss how social data privacy and data integrity vulnerabilities may be potentially exploited, threatening the future of applications based on anticipatory computing paradigms.

**Chapter 9. The impact of sentiment on content post popularity through emoji and text on social platforms** addresses content popularity on social platforms. The study presented in this chapter analysed posts by Clinton campaign vs Trump in the US election battle. The sentiment-based content post popularity was modeled using SentiStrength and Linguistic Inquiry and Word Count. The authors' analysis reveals post popularity and the direction of emotion. The results show that emoticons have positive relations with the number of post shares. The chapter therefore helps predict content popularity and the likelihood of its propagation through social platforms.

**Chapter 10. Risk and social influence in sustainable smart home technologies: a persuasive systems design model** focuses on influencing user behavior and guiding them to consider environmental sustainability. The chapter explores how persuasive systems design influences intention to continue using a smart metering system as well as how risk and self-disclosure affect the impact of the persuasive systems design on a smart-metering system. The chapter proposes a research model and forms hypotheses by drawing on Persuasive Systems Design (PSD) model and Adaption Level Theory. As smart home technologies are proliferating, persuasive techniques and social influence may present opportunities for fostering sustainable behavior and alleviating cyber security risks concerns.

This comprehensive and timely publication aims to be an essential reference source, building on the available literature in the field of security, cognitive computing and cyber psychology while providing for further research opportunities in this dynamic field. It is hoped that this text will provide the resources necessary for academics, policy makers, technology developers and managers to improve understanding of social influence and to help manage organizational cyber security posture more effectively.

CHAPTER

# 1

# Cybersecurity as a social phenomenon

*John McAlaney*[1], *Vladlena Benson*[2]

[1] Associate Professor of Psychology, Department of Psychology, Bournemouth University, Poole, United Kingdom; [2] Professor of Information Systems, Aston Business School, Aston University, Birmingham, United Kingdom

OUTLINE



## Social influence

Allport (1954) defined social psychology as an attempt to understand and explain how the thoughts and actions of individuals are influenced by the actual, imagined and implied presence of others. As digital technologies have continued to develop the lines between actual, imagined and implied have become blurred; yet the social psychological influences that shape our behaviour remain as powerful as ever. Humans have


https://doi.org/10.1016/B978-0-12-819204-7.00001-4

evolved to be social creatures; our existence and survival is dependent on our interactions with others. These basic drives are so deeply rooted in human nature that it may be difficult to change them, even when it is in our best interests to do so. For instance, it has been noted that people do not tend to alter their use of social network sites even if they have been hacked (O'Connell & Kirwan, 2014). It may be that the social benefits that social networking sites provide are, to the user, worth the risks inherent of using them, even when these risks are made explicit.

Despite these social influences on our behaviours and attitudes, people often like to see themselves as individuals, who oversee their own cognitions. This is especially pronounced in individualistic cultures, where the emphasis is on individual attainment and success (Hofstede, Hofstede, & Minkov, 2010). Nevertheless, as demonstrated in social psychological research, people will tend to alter their behaviour and cognitions to match the group (Kelman, 2006), whilst tending to underestimate how much they are being influenced by the group (Darley, 1992). Contagion effects can also be evident in groups, with emotions spreading through a group to an individual, even if the individual was not involved in the original situation that caused that emotion (Smith, Seger, & Mackie, 2007). As based on social identity theory, the subjective group dynamics model suggests that people may also derive self-esteem from the groups to which they belong (Marques, Abrams, & Serodio, 2001). This is an important consideration when it comes to preventing and mitigating cybersecurity incidents, both in relation to those who instigate cybersecurity attacks and those who are targeted by them. Attempting to dissuade young people from becoming involved in hacking groups, for instance, may be counterproductive if it threatens what, to them, is an important source of their social identity and self-esteem. Similarly, bringing about change within teams of cybersecurity practitioners may be risky if it is, even inadvertently, communicated to such teams that their current performance is somehow sub-par.

Whilst hacking may be technological in nature, this is only the means by which the end result is achieved — it is the how, but not the why. Seebruck (2015) identifies several motivations for hacking that include a social element, including hacking for prestige, ideologically driven activities such as hacktivism, and insider threats motivated by revenge. Even if the motivation for hacking is not primarily a social one, there may still be social influences that steer the actions of those involved in hacking groups. Individuals are known to make riskier decisions when in groups than when alone (Smith et al., 2007), which could be applicable to both the group who are behind attacks and the groups within organizations who make the decision on what actions to take when an attack does happen. Group dynamics and intra-group conflicts are evident in some of the more well-documented attacks by hacking groups, such as the conflicts that arose within Anonymous (Olson, 2012). It could be argued that these internal conflicts were a larger contributing factor in Anonymous reducing their activities than were the actions of the law enforcement agencies that were pursuing them. These group dynamics also impact on individual behaviour within organizations. Johnston and Warkentin (2010), for instance, note that social influence is a determinant of end-user intentions to take individual computer security actions. As based on the Theory of Planned Behaviour, it has also been observed that the intention someone has to perform a desired behaviour (such as updating software) is in part determined by whether they think influential others will support or condemn their actions (Venkatesh, Morris, Davis, & Davis, 2003). This demonstrates the need to understand how not only individuals perceive cybersecurity risks, but also how they think other people perceive those risks. An individual may fail to act to prevent or mitigate a cybersecurity attack if they think those actions will be judged harshly by senior managers.

Perceptions of others are important factor in cybersecurity. As individuals we continually attempt to explain, or attribute, the actions of others to their underlying motivations, characteristics and mental states. We tend to be somewhat inaccurate in doing so and come to simplistic conclusions based on observable actions. This known as fundamental attribution error (Jones & Davis, 1965). In much the same way that we make attributions at an individual level, it has also been suggested that we may make intergroup attributions (Hewstone & Jaspars, 1982), in which we try to explain the behaviours and attitudes of groups other than our own. As with individual attributions, however, we are prone to making errors. This could include attributing the success of our own group to the skills and abilities of the members, or attributing the success of the other group to external factors and luck (Hewstone & Jaspars, 1982). Within cybersecurity this could have several consequences, such as leading a group to overestimate their ability to either instigate or mitigate a cybersecurity attack. This phenomenon would appear to have been present in the case of several hacking groups, where, following several successful attacks, individuals underestimated the ability of FBI to identify and prosecute them (Coleman, 2014). These group processes may be unintentionally further enhanced by media reports and external organizations. The category differentiation model (Doise, 1978) suggests that identifying groups as being group (categories) can strengthen the sense of group membership. The infamous Fox News report on Anonymous that identified them as domestic terrorists and included footage of an exploding van, for example, only appeared to strengthen the identity of the group and emboldened them to take further action (Coleman, 2014). This highlights the need for responsible media reporting of hacking incidents, that avoid glamorizing the actions of hackers.

## Heuristics and biases

Humans have in the past been considered a weakness in cybersecurity. They make irrational decisions and fail to demonstrate an understanding of the risks of their actions. Despite the best efforts of the IT department and the directives from senior management, workers continue to display their passwords on post-it notes next to their office computer. To understand these behaviours, it is important to consider how people navigate their social worlds. Each day we encounter a myriad of social situations and instances where we must make decisions. However, our cognitive capacities are limited, and we are often under time constraints in which a decision must be made quickly. In order to do humans have evolved the use of heuristics. These heuristics are mental short-cuts that we employ to enable us to come to quick decisions based on limited information (Kahneman, 2011). For instance, if we see someone in a white coat, we may tend to assume that person is a medical doctor. These heuristics can result in counter-intuitive results. In one noted study Schwarz et al. (1991) asked participants to think of either 6 or 12 occasions in which they been assertive. Those participants who were asked to think of 12 occasions were subsequently more likely to rate themselves as lower in assertiveness than those who were asked to think of 6 occasions. Schwarz suggests that this is an example of a specific heuristic known as the availability heuristic (Tversky & Kahneman, 1973), in which our perception of the frequency or probability of an event is influenced by how easily we can think of examples of that event. Thinking of 12 separate occasions in which they have been assertive is something that many people may find challenging. As a result of being unable to do so, the availability heuristic leads participants in the study to conclude that they must not be a particularly assertive person. This heuristic has many applications within cybersecurity context. As opposed to kinetic attacks, for example, cyberattacks may lack readily visualized, tangible outcomes. It is easier for an employee of a typical organization to picture a bomb exploding than it is for them to picture a virus infecting a system. The availability heuristic may be connected to other heuristics and biases, such as the false consensus effect (Ross, Greene, & House, 1977), in which we assume that the majority of those around us share our opinion on a topic. These heuristics and biases may form obstacles to behaviour change strategies. A campaign to raise awareness of the danger of using easily guessed passwords, for instance, may be undermined if individuals within the target population believe (erroneously) that most peers believe this issue to be unimportant.

Whenever we decide based on a careful consideration of all the available information, we are being naïve scientists. If instead we make a quick decision based on limited information and with heuristics, then we are being cognitive misers. Kruglanski (1996) argues that which approach we employ in any situation is determined by how important our understanding of that situation is, and what we perceive the risks of coming to the wrong conclusion to be. In doing so we are being motivated tacticians. For example, if meeting someone for the first time at a party, we might not feel too invested in learning a lot about that person, and in turn may not feel that we need to impress that person. If instead we are meeting a new roommate or officemate, we are likely to be substantially more interested in understanding who that person is as our interactions with them are likely to become an important part of our daily lives. Similarly, we are more likely to put effort into trying to develop a positive relationship with that person.

This is not a perfect strategy. It has several points of failure, including misperceptions on our part as to how important the decision is, or misunderstandings as to the information on which we are basing our choice of approach. If we do choose a cognitive miser approach, then we may be giving ourselves very little margin for error. An analogy would be only filling up the gas tank of a car to exactly the point needed to travel between one petrol station and another, distant petrol station along a long and empty road. Whilst the strategy may work most of the time, it can become easily disrupted due to unanticipated factors, or miscalculations of what is required. When a heuristic leads us to come to an incorrect decision, it may be considered a cognitive bias. The distinction between heuristics and biases is not consistent or clear. What may be an appropriate heuristic in one situation can be a cognitive bias in another situation. This creates challenges for strategies that aim to change bias in decision making in relation to cybersecurity – in some scenarios such cognitive biases may be helpful.

Even though heuristics and biases can lead people to come to an incorrect decision, it is important to acknowledge that such cognitive processes are not a weakness of humans. They are not a design flaw, or a deficit to be solved through engineering solutions. Instead they are a fundamental characteristic of human psychology that have evolved as a method of allowing us to function and survive in an environment where we are faced for more information than it would ever be feasible for us to fully and carefully process. By changing perceptions of risk and importance, it may be possible to alter how individuals approach decision making towards cybersecurity behaviours – that is, moving them from a cognitive miser approach to a naïve scientist approach. However, when doing so we have to acknowledge that this may result in an unintended move away from the naïve scientist approach to a cognitive miser approach in other areas of their lives or workplace activities. This is because balance must be reached in how we make use of our limited cognitive resources. As such we recommend that stakeholders within cybersecurity design systems in a way that acknowledges and accepts the cognitive processes of humans, do not treat the human element as a necessary evil that has to be fixed.

## Exploitation

As social influence and heuristics have evolved, so have strategies to exploit them. Existing in a social network increases our own chances of surviving and thriving. In other words, as argued by Cialdini et al. (1987), every apparently social act is in fact motivated by self-interest. Considering this, it is perhaps not surprising that we have developed ways of attempting to exploit the social influences and heuristics of those around us. Such practices are exemplified within marketing and advertising strategies (Cialdini et al., 1987). For instance, providing a consumer with a free sample draws upon the norm of reciprocity, in which we feel compelled to return the favour to someone who has given us something. Similarly, presenting an item as being scarce can increase the demand for it, as scarcity is interpreted as meaning that the item must be valuable. Examples of this can be seen throughout marketing campaigns, such as in trading cards or toys distributed with fast food meals that are produced in differing amounts so that some variants are less available than others. These manipulations by marketing and advertising are a form of behaviour change; in terms of principles and underlying processes they are not dissimilar from behaviour change techniques used within psychology.

There is one group within cybersecurity that already demonstrates a strong understanding of the characteristics and quirks of human decision making, and how this is often steered by social influence – cyber criminals. The basis of many social engineering attacks is to push the target towards being a cognitive miser. For example, phishing emails that contain some form of urgency appeal (e.g. 'Your account will be locked unless you respond immediately') are designed to encourage the target to feel they must make a quick decision. Similarly, the inclusion of a bank logo in a phishing email is intended to lead the target to come to a quick conclusion that the email must be genuine. This is perhaps a conflict between the idea of social manipulation by hackers and the concept of a hacker as someone who lacks social skills – the stereotypical teenage boy operating from his parents' basement. Whilst there would appear to be certain demographic characteristics of people who engage in hacking, there is a greater degree of diversity within the hacking community in terms of age, gender and background than may be anticipated (Thackray, Richardson, Dogan, Taylor, & McAlaney, 2017). In addition Rogers (2010) points out that social skills can take many forms, and that people who may not be socially skilled offline can be extremely socially skilled online. In order to prevent and mitigate cybersecurity incidents, we need to think beyond stereotypes, and to develop a deeper understanding of the human factors of all of the actors involved.

## Conclusion

Cybersecurity is a sociotechnical phenomenon. For us to address the challenges within cybersecurity, we need to consider how individuals engage with technological systems, and how they may attempt to exploit both these systems and the others who are engaging with them. To do so we must recognize that the apparent irrationality of humans is not a weakness to be solved but is instead a characteristic that has evolved to serve a function. By doing so we can develop new avenues of prevention and mitigation approaches that can be applied to everyone who has a stake in cybersecurity – those who would seek to instigate attacks, those who are the targets of attackers and those who protect systems.

## References

Allport, G. (1954). *The nature of prejudice*. Reading, MA: Addison-Wesley.

Cialdini, R. B., Schaller, M., Houlihan, D., Arps, K., Fultz, J., & Beaman, A. L. (1987). Empathy-based helping – is it selflessly or selfishly motivated. *Journal of Personality and Social Psychology, 52*(4), 749–758. https://doi.org/10.1037/0022-3514.52.4.749.

Coleman, G. (2014). *Hacker, Hoaxer, Whistleblower, Spy: The many faces of anonymous*. London: Verso.

Darley, J. M. (1992). Social organization for the production of evil. *Psychological Inquiry, 3*(2), 199–218. https://doi.org/10.1207/s15327965pli0302_28.

Doise, W. (1978). *Groups and individuals: Explanations in social psychology*. Cambridge: Cambridge University Press.

Hewstone, M., & Jaspars, J. M. F. (1982). Intergroup relations and attribution processes. In H. Tajfel (Ed.), *Social identity and intergroup relations* (pp. 99–133). Cambridge: Cambridge University Press.

Hofstede, G. H., Hofstede, G. J., & Minkov, M. (2010). *Cultures and organizations: Software of the mind: Intercultural cooperation and its importance for survival* (3rd ed.). New York: McGraw-Hill.

Johnston, A. C., & Warkentin, M. (2010). Fear appeals and information security behaviors: An empirical study. *MIS Quarterly, 34*(3), 549–566.

Jones, E. E., & Davis, K. E. (1965). From acts to dispositions – the attribution process in person perception. *Advances in Experimental Social Psychology, 2*(4), 219–266.

Kahneman, D. (2011). *Thinking, fast and slow* (1st ed.). Penguin.

Kelman, H. C. (2006). Interests, relationships, identities: Three central issues for individuals and groups in negotiating their social environment. *Annual Review of Psychology, 57*, 1–26. https://doi.org/10.1146/annurev.psych.57.102904.190156.

Kruglanski, A. W. (1996). Motivated social cognition: Principles of the interface. In E. T. Higgins, & A. W. Kruglanski (Eds.), *Social psychology: Handbook of basic principles*. New York: Guilford Press.

Marques, J. M., Abrams, D., & Serodio, R. G. (2001). Being better by being right: Subjective group dynamics and derogation of in-group deviants when generic norms are undermined. *Journal of Personality and Social Psychology, 81*(3), 436–447. https://doi.org/10.1037/0022-3514.81.3.436.

O'Connell, R., & Kirwan, G. (2014). Protection motivation theory and online activities. In A. Power, & G. Kirwan (Eds.), *Cyberpsychology and new media: A Thematic reader.* New York: Psychology Press.

Olson, P. (2012). *We are anonymous.* New York: Back Bay Books.

Rogers, M. K. (2010). The psyche of cybercriminals: A psycho-social perspective. In G. Ghosh, & E. Turrini (Eds.), *Cybercrimes: A Multidisciplinary Analysis.*

Ross, L., Greene, D., & House, P. (1977). The "False Consensus Effect" an egocentric bias in social perception and attribution processes. *Journal of Experimental Social Psychology, 13,* 279–301.

Schwarz, N., Bless, H., Strack, F., Klumpp, G., Rittenauerschatka, H., & Simons, A. (1991). Ease of retrieval as information – another look at the availability heuristic. *Journal of Personality and Social Psychology, 61*(2), 195–202. https://doi.org/10.1037//0022-3514.61.2.195.

Seebruck, R. (2015). A typology of hackers: Classifying cyber malfeasance using a weighted arc circumplex model. *Digital Investigation, 14,* 36–45. https://doi.org/10.1016/j.diin.2015.07.002.

Smith, E. R., Seger, C. R., & Mackie, D. A. (2007). Can emotions be truly group level? Evidence regarding four conceptual criteria. *Journal of Personality and Social Psychology, 93*(3), 431–446. https://doi.org/10.1037/0022-3514.93.3.431.

Thackray, H., Richardson, C., Dogan, H., Taylor, J., & McAlaney, J. (2017). *Surveying the hackers: The challenges of data collection from a secluded community.* Paper presented at the 16th European Conference on cyber Warfare and security, Dublin.

Tversky, A., & Kahneman, D. (1973). Availability: A heuristic for judging frequency and probability. *Cognitive Psychology, 5*(2), 207–232. https://doi.org/10.1016/0010-0285(73)90033-9.

Venkatesh, V., Morris, M. G., Davis, G. B., & Davis, F. D. (2003). User acceptance of information technology: Toward a unified view. *MIS Quarterly, 27*(3), 425–478.

CHAPTER

# 2

# Towards an integrated socio-technical approach for designing adaptive privacy aware services in cloud computing

*Angeliki Kitsiou*[1], *Eleni Tzortzaki*[2], *Christos Kalloniatis*[1], *Stefanos Gritzalis*[2]

[1] Privacy Engineering and Social Informatics Laboratory, Department of Cultural Technology and Communication, University of the Aegean, Mytilene, Lesvos, Greece; [2] Information and Communication Systems Security Laboratory, Department of Information and Communications Systems Engineering, University of the Aegean, Samos, Greece

OUTLINE



*Cyber Influence and Cognitive Threats*
https://doi.org/10.1016/B978-0-12-819204-7.00002-6

## Introduction: privacy as a socially constructed phenomenon

The ubiquitous usage of Information and Communication Technologies (ICT) has brought dynamic social transformations, which have led to an increasing dependence of the social systems on the informational infrastructure, as well as to the intensification of individual and social action complexity within ICT (Abowd, 2016; Lahlou, 2008; Pinter, 2008). The personalization and the customized services are the basic characteristics of ICT usage, which enable social outlet (Fortunati & Taipale, 2016). Nevertheless, apart from the several advantages deriving from the personalized ICT and the Internet prevalence, plenty of privacy issues have arised, concerning users' social life both online and offline. These issues are addressed through the utilization of a variety of privacy policies and issues, which are based on individuals' detailed and extensive preferences and interests (Chang, 2015). Thus, privacy aspects that need to be protected are not clearly identified. This occurs due to the fact that the definition of privacy does not reflect a sole reality (Acquisti, Brandimarte, & Loewenstein, 2015; Cohen, 2013; Lahlou, 2008; Wessels, 2012), but it constitutes a complex, socially constructed phenomenon (Acquisti et al., 2015; Wessels, 2012; Camp & Connelly, 2008), which is related to users' autonomy and control over their personal space and information and to their human dignity as well. Privacy, as a social phenomenon, is interpreted in several ways both individually and collectively, and even though it has been recognized as an important principle and a fundamental right in all modern democratic societies (Henderson, 2012), indistinct legal connotations are still used to define it (Ganji, Mouratidis, Gheytassi, & Petridis, 2015; Solove, 2008). Therefore, the concept of privacy is defined multi-dimensionally (Rossler, 2018) and is outlined by different terms in different contexts (Chang, 2015), focusing especially on three dimensions as follows (Chang, 2015; Rossler, 2018): (1) decisional privacy — *the right to autonomous decisions/actions and the protection of undesirable access to them*, (2) informational privacy — *the right to control and protect personal information* and (3) spatial/local privacy — *the right to the protection of undesirable intrusions to personal physical space.*

Accordingly, as far as online privacy is concerned, especially within Cloud Computing Environments (CCEs), plenty of terms and categories are utilized for its definition. Since individuals have easier access to communication and they are exposed to the 'information flood' (Eriksen, 2001), the boundaries among personal information and public accessible personal information become even more indistinct, lacking traditional borders and raising more privacy concerns (Chang, 2015). Smith, Dinev, and Xu (2011) support that the unwanted access to personal information, the over-collection of personal information, the unapproved secondary use of personal information, as well as the errors that are made regarding the collection of personal information constitute faces of the online privacy issues. UK Information Commissioners Office (2014) identified four dimensions of online privacy: (1) privacy of personal information, regarding data and information, (2) privacy of the person, (3) privacy of personal behaviour and (4) privacy of personal communication.

Moreover, new concepts of privacy have been suggested. Woo (2006) argues about individuals' right to remain anonymous and untraceable. More precisely, individuals do not provide personal information at all, but they also provide untrue information in order not to be visible while online (Chen, 2018). DeCew (1997) refers to the term 'expressive privacy', focusing on individuals' right to be protected by unwanted peer expression, so as to express freely their own identity. Richards (2008) maintains that privacy should be explored through its social aspect, pointing out the term 'intellectual privacy', namely the individuals' right to protect their free thoughts and to develop new ideas. Raynes-Goldie (2010) argues about the term 'social privacy', indicating the raising privacy issues within Internet users' social networks, which is differentiated from the term 'institutional privacy', which concerns privacy issues related to the communication access by enterprises and governments.

Additionally, apart from the several definitions of the concept of privacy, since privacy has specific and very often descriptive and measurable interactive functions within a society (Chang, 2015; Schoeman, 1984), literature also provides a variety of different definitions and terms for privacy issues, such as privacy concerns, privacy risks, privacy behaviors, privacy management (De Wolf, Willaert, & Pierson, 2014; Petronio, 2002; Xu, Dinev, Smith, & Hart, 2011), indicating once again the complexity of privacy and its dimensions, as a social phenomenon.

Therefore, privacy can be determined efficiently provided that its concept is related to specific social factors within a specific social context (Chang, 2015; Solove, 2008) and if the social value of it is explored. Certainly, the concept of the social value of privacy does not constitute a new dimension, but it often provides wider notions for the definition of privacy (Raynes-Goldie, 2010), without though substituting *the fundamental individual value of privacy* (Chang, 2015, p. 151). In this frame, as Nissenbaum (2009) maintains, privacy is valued even more when it is recognized as a fundamental principle within an organized social and political system. Baruh and Popescu (2017) also argue that when privacy is examined from a collective aspect, it is defined as a value (codependency) and as a social phenomenon (cooperation) as well.

Up to this point, it is important to note Gerstein's (1970) thesis regarding the interrelation between privacy and the development of meaningful social relationships, as well as Reiman's (1976) thesis, in which privacy constitutes a social ritual prerequisite for individuals' personhood development.

In this regard, privacy represents a collective value in a specific socio-economic and political context (Regan, 2015), determined both individually and institutionally, which indicates that the measures, the policies and the features used for its protection are not exclusively a matter of personal choice or individual responsibility, but a result of interactive actions among social systems and individuals (Steeves & Regan, 2014). Schoeman (1984) emphatically supports that privacy is an important social concept, the interpretation of which shapes the social outlet both in obvious and latent ways, by regulating choices, practices, activities and social action of both individuals and institutions.

Respectively, among all bounded definitions and approaches, it is crucial to note that privacy has been acknowledged as an important principle in all modern societies and it is in need of preservation, taking into consideration its social aspects (Cohen, 2013), while its protection rises to the level of public policy and social good (Chang, 2015).

Since privacy definitions and concepts are formed and shaped accordingly with the societal changes, it is important to comprehend how ICT usage alternates the essence of privacy in digital and real life (Acquisti, Gritzalis, Lambrinoudakis, & De Capitani di Vimercati, 2008). In this regard, the preservation of privacy, in an adaptive to users' needs way, cannot be designed and implemented without giving thought to both the technological advancements and its social aspects, especially as far as CCE concerns, where privacy risks and concerns are raising rapidly.

In this respect and in order for users' privacy to be preserved in changing socio-cultural contexts within cloud computing, this chapter aims to point out the Adaptive Privacy Aware Cloud-based Systems (APACS) as an emerged research area, where an interdisciplinary approach is considered of great importance. Therefore, technical and social aspects of privacy are identified and explored. Both social and technical factors, which are critical for the successful design of APACS, are considered and examined within a unified framework. Therefore, an integrated conceptual model is proposed, which aims at highlighting the emerged need for Adaptive Privacy Aware Cloud-based Systems and at establishing solid theoretical and methodological structures between the social and technological aspects of privacy.

The rest of the chapter is organized as follows: Privacy risks within Cloud Computing Environments section briefly presents the CCEs' involvement and the privacy risks that emerge within it. Social aspects of privacy in Cloud Computing Environments section addresses work regarding the social aspects of privacy within CCE, focusing on users' social identity and social capital, while the technical aspects of privacy and its emerged requirements within CCE are presented in Technical aspects of privacy in Cloud Computing Environments section. The emergence of the adaptive privacy aware systems section focuses on the emerging of the Adaptive Privacy

Aware Systems. Towards an integrated socio-technical approach section discusses the interrelated social and technical privacy requirements that should be taken into consideration for the design of the Adaptive Privacy Aware Cloud-based Systems under a novel conceptual model. Finally, Conclusion section concludes our approach and raises future research directions.

## Privacy risks within Cloud Computing Environments

Nowadays an increasing number of ICT providers look for new services and solutions within the Internet, in order to reduce their operational costs and technical support on one hand and to increase the scalability of their systems on the other (Takabi, Joshi, & Ahn, 2010). Thus, it is a common practice for ICT industry to outsource some of their services to third parties, paying the respective cost. The efforts made in order for such new ways of services provided to users to be found led to cloud computing architecture (Lovell, 2011), namely to the ability of instant customization of computer resources as an external service through the Internet. The main objective of cloud computing consists in its usage by the society as a utility service, which is made possible due to the wide variety of services provided to users at low cost. On a technical level, this objective translates into (Mel & Grance, 2011): (1) *Five essential characteristics: On-demand self-service, Broad network access, Resource pooling regardless location, Rapid elasticity, Measured service provision*; (2) *Three fundamental service distribution models*: *Infrastructure as a Service,* where consumers use provider's infrastructure to install and run software, having no control over the underlying cloud infrastructure but only over operating systems, storage and applications. *Platform as a Service,* where consumers can develop and control their own applications using the infrastructure and the deployment tools of the provider. *Software as a Service,* where consumers can make use of all the aforementioned abilities including provider's applications and databases, neither controlling nor managing the infrastructure or the applications; and (3) *Four Deployment models: Public cloud, Community cloud, Private cloud and Hybrid cloud.* Within this framework, users can use private cloud in order to increase security and public cloud to store non-sensitive data and applications.

It thus becomes clear that CCE can provide enormous capabilities for increasing interaction between social actors and service providers (Farnham & Churchill, 2011). In this way, CCE overcomes geographical boundaries and limitations of the past, leading to the diffusion and disclosure of even more personal and sensitive information of users (Toch, Wang, & Cranor, 2012) and raising consequently privacy circumvention risks. This occurs due to the potential dynamic change and combination of the services, deriving from both providers and customers, as well as due to the different privacy features utilized in each service distribution and deployment model (Pearson, 2009). Additionally, since the provision of services includes the access, collection, storage, edit and disclosure of personal information, often by third parties as well, data loss and data breaches have been acknowledged as the most essential risks that should be addressed (Liu, Sun, Ryoo, Rizvi, & Vasilakos, 2015). The loss of direct control from local to remote cloud servers, the multiple legal jurisdictions, the virtualization that brings new challenges to user authentication and authorization, the non-technical issues related to the technical solutions (Liu et al., 2015), the low degree of transparency and privacy assurance provided into customers operations (Takabi et al., 2010), the sharing of platforms between users and the non-compliance with enterprise policies and legislation, leading to the loss of reputation and credibility (Pearson, 2009), are important issues that raise privacy risks within CCE.

In particular, even more privacy issues are expressed regarding the social network sites (SNSs), as the most widespread CCE, which provide a technological field for users' social interaction, communication and resources, replacing many forms of social practices in order for numerous psychological and social needs to be satisfied (Utz, 2015). Thus, their structural function enhances several privacy concerns and risks both in personal and social level. In many cases, in order for a user to utilize the services of an SNS, he/she has to make disclosures due to system's privacy settings, so as disclosure to become a common practice within it (Stutzman, Gross, & Acquisti, 2013). Disclosure happens either in full publicity towards unknown users or towards specific individuals within the users' network (Taddicken, 2014). In both cases, information can be easily sought, copied, expanded and shared (Papacharissi & Gibson, 2011), since the generation of big data enabled cheap data collections and analysis (Liu et al., 2015). As Taddicken (2014) argues, it is often unclear who and how many people are included in the audiences to which disclosures have been made. Furthermore, it is unclear who accesses and stores customers' data, which are often analysed by unauthorized parties (Liu et al., 2015). Therefore, it is an undeniable fact that CCEs, which are still evolving (Takabi et al., 2010), have introduced a number of privacy challenges. Despite the several disclosures and privacy risks, especially SNSs users are multiplying (Stutzman, Vitak, Ellison, Gray, & Lampe, 2012), while privacy solutions are lagging behind (Liu et al., 2015). Consequently, in order for the privacy solutions to be evolved accordingly to users' needs and requirements both in social and technical level, privacy requirements need to be redefined and changed, taking into consideration both of these aspects (Pearson, 2009).

## Social aspects of privacy in Cloud Computing Environments

As it was argued in the Introduction section, privacy has been recognized as a fundamental individual and social principle in contemporary societies, without, though, reflecting a standard social reality (Acquisti et al., 2015; Cohen, 2013; Wessels, 2012), and consequently it is defined as multifaceted. Within CCE, and in particular within SNSs, a solid and clear definition of privacy becomes an even more complex procedure. Besides legal and technical requirements, its notions are interrelated with individuals' personal interpretations and values about privacy, which are respectively formatted according to users' context (Patkos et al., 2015) both online and offline. Therefore, privacy in SNSs is not just a personal matter, which depends on users' options, but it constitutes of a social dynamic and ongoing process (Marwick & boyd, 2014), by which users balance between their social needs and their needs for privacy. However, these social needs related to privacy have not been thoroughly examined, identified or correlated (Wessels, 2012), especially in ways that could be helpful to produce privacy software that focuses on social well-being. Therefore, the great challenge lies in the elicitation of privacy requirements within CCE related to users' actual social needs and their distinctive social characteristics. Social identity theory and social capital theory related to CCE is of great importance in order for this matter to be addressed and for further understanding to be promoted.

## Social identity

Social identity constitutes the basis on which an individual constructs their taxonomies and discriminations about themselves and others who may either belong or not in a social group (Jekins, 2008). Accordingly within CCE, social identity is shaped by the two same notions, the feeling of belonging to an online community and the identification of self-concept within it (Wang & Shih, 2014).

The main characteristics of the social identity are (1) multiplicity (Baym, 2010), since individuals belong to and participate in several social groups either since birth or by choice and (2) intersectionality, as identity is changing and overlapping, affecting the way individuals perceive their experiences in relation to power and privileges within the context they live (Nario-Redmond, Biernat, Eidelman, & Palenske, 2004).

Individuals are characterized by multiple and intersectional social identities that define their behaviours within a context of action (Nario-Redmond et al., 2004) and respectively within CCE. Although several studies have been conducted to correlate social actors' identity with the acceptance and adoption of personalized ICT (Arbore, Soscia, & Bagozzi, 2014; Guegan, Moliner, & Buisine, 2015; Wu & Lin, 2016), only a few thorough studies associate social identity with privacy management and the utility of existing privacy aware systems. Especially, the multiplicity and intersectionality of social identity constitute factors that have not been adequately taken into consideration, in particular within SNSs.

As Steeves and Regan (2014) argue, these environments lack privacy, leading users to adapt their feelings, beliefs and choices to the expected norms within them. Thus, if privacy can be ensured, multiple users' identities may emerge, enabling them to be social interactive and to address social groups' reactions to them (Steeves & Regan, 2014). The complexity of the social identity is a very important parameter for the optimal identification of the concept of privacy within SNSs (Farnam & Churchill, 2011; Wessels, 2012), since individuals are acting within a web of relationships with other social actors and determine privacy through the performance of roles and identities both of themselves and others (Steeves & Regan, 2014). Post (2001) also supports that privacy does not exist as a concept, if individuals are not socially situated and their identity and self-concept does not depend on social norms. Up to this point Marwick and Boyd's (2011) research is indicative, since it demonstrates that many users' privacy breaches within SNSs arise because of the users' multiple identities. Additionally, Nissenbaum (2009) emphatically argues that the protection of privacy within SNSs is strongly depended on the way information is disseminated among different social contexts where individuals belong, which respectively determine how, when and why the dissemination of information takes place or not.

In this regard, privacy should be explored as a *dialectical* and ongoing procedure, since *it cannot be given away once and for all* (Steeves & Regan, 2014, p. 309), while the further understanding of the correlation of privacy and social identity will enable privacy preservation.

Moreover, besides privacy definition, social identity can be an interpretative tool, showing how belonging to an online social group influences users' behaviour (Hsu, Fan, Chen, & Wang, 2013) and is related to their privacy practices. In this regard, researchers (Tufecki, 2012; Wessels, 2012) argue that users manage privacy settings in SNSs, affected by the behaviour of the other members of their groups. Steeves and Regan's research (2014) also points out that young individuals recognize social dimensions of privacy related to identity issues, such as boundaries, expectations, responsibilities and trust towards themselves and others.

Therefore, as shown in previous literature, the concept of privacy can be interpreted in relation to people's different perspectives and their connections with society (Cohen, 2013). A key tool for the better understanding of privacy and for people's social identity interpretation, in order to set specific technical and functional requirements for privacy aware systems, is to record the number of individuals' different identities and their overlapping degree (Grant & Hogg, 2012). The most central variables to address that issue, regarding particularly online identities mentioned in previous literature (Balicki, 2014; Jenkins, 2008), are as follows: gender, age group, national group/identity, permanent address, religious beliefs, political orientations, education and field of study, free time activities, hobbies, branding, likes, mentions and traffic flows. Although previous research examines these variables separately, even more parameters and variables regarding social the interrelation of identity and privacy interrelation should be explored, the combination of which has not been taken into consideration, such as social capital that follows.

## Social capital

According to Chen (2018), social capital has been explored within CCE, and in particular within SNSs, due to the numeral features of the latter that enable social interactions and enhance the development of social relationships. Previous research (Ellison, Vitak, Steinfield, Gray, & Lampe, 2011; Stutzman et al., 2012; Tzortzaki, Kitsiou, Sideri, & Gritzalis, 2016) also shows that users' social capital constitutes a significant factor to a further understanding of their privacy management in SNSs. Regardless of users' privacy concerns and their ability to manage their privacy through SNSs features effectively, users are willing to share personal information and sacrifice their privacy within it (Stutzman et al., 2012). Users' need to obtain social capital benefits is a major factor for this paradoxical choice (Bohn, Buchta, Hornik, & Mair, 2014; Steinfield, Ellison, Lampe, & Vitak, 2012). Previous studies (Bohn, Buchta, Hornik, & Mair, 2014; De Wolf et al., 2014; Stutzman et al., 2012) have shown that the two most important social capital categories claimed by SNSs users are those of bonding and bridging social capital. These categories refer to multiple resources provided by different types of relationships (Ellison, Vitak, Gray, & Lampe, 2014). Bonding social capital refers to resources derived from tight relationships, such as close friends and family, while bridging social capital concerns resources that derive from more diverse networks that cultivate common interests and connective ties (Lin, 2017).

On the other side, Trepte and Reinecke (2013) focus on social capital correlation with self-disclosure, rather than with privacy. Nevertheless, literature underlines that this complex and interactive interrelation between the notions of social capital and those of privacy (Bazarova & Choi, 2014; Rains & Brunner, 2018; Spiliotopoulos & Oakley, 2013; Walton & Rice, 2013) has not been explored adequately (Stutzman et al., 2012) in order for technological solutions to be found that will permit users to utilize CCE without endangering their privacy. Consequently, although considerable attention has been given to social capital, it has not been embedded in the privacy calculus model so as to better comprehend the privacy paradox (Chen, 2018). Chen's (2018) research builds on the privacy calculus model to revisit the privacy paradox within SNSs, by extending it with the privacy self-efficacy notion related to social capital. However, the privacy paradox is not adequately revisited. As Dienlin and Trept (2015) support, in order for the privacy paradox to disappear, the different privacy dimensions (informational, social, individual, technical) should be identified. Therefore, in order for the concept of social capital to be helpful for a better understanding of privacy within CCE, it should be examined in correlation with all these dimensions.

## Technical aspects of privacy in Cloud Computing Environments

From a technical aspect, in order for a system to protect users' privacy, the concept of privacy can be defined, based on a series of technical requirements, as following (Pfitzmann & Hansen, 2007): *Authentication, Authorization, Identification, Data protection, Anonymity, Pseudonymity, Unlinkability, Unobservability.* Anthonysamy, Rashid, and Chitchyan (2017) support that privacy requirements are usually determined as instances of requirements pertaining to compliance, traceability, access control, verification or usability, while Winograd-Cort, Haeberlen, Roth, and Pierce (2017) argue that during the years more privacy guarantees have been suggested, namely randomization, k-anonymity and l-diversity. Thus, as Kalloniatis, Kavakli, and Gritzalis (2008) suggest, privacy requirements should be determined as organizational goals, following specific privacy process patterns in order to enable the recognition of the structure of the system which supports adequately organizations' privacy processes. In this regard, Mouratidis, Islam, Kalloniatis, and Gritzalis (2013) maintain that the comprehension of organizations' functions facilitates the identification and elicitation of privacy risks, threats, constraints, goals and requirements within CCE.

Nonetheless, privacy requirements within CCE have not been developed efficiently in order to identify their distinctive features (Kalloniatis et al., 2014); established encryption methods are not adequate to address the needs of privacy protection (He et al., 2017), while privacy leaks may be widely differentiated according to the CCE that is utilized (Pearson & Benameur, 2010).

Up to this point, a methodical approach that enables software engineers to identify which privacy requirements should be prioritized and to choose the proper cloud service provider pursuant to these, is lacking (Kalloniatis et al., 2014).

This failure may come up due to the insufficient design of systems (Omoronyia, 2016) and due to limited privacy choices offered by cloud providers to users (Mouratidis et al., 2013). In particular, usability issues are one of the main causes for most of the incidents that compromise users' privacy protection, revealing that the design of user-friendly and secure systems needs further attention and appropriate research. In this context, as Ruan, Carthy, Kechadi, and Crosbie (2011) support, cloud providers face a number of great challenges due to the following reasons: (1) There is a sheer volume of big data residing in cloud data centers that require time and cost to be accessed, thus resulting in the need for new methods and techniques development so that big data can be managed. (2) The legal framework of the countries that host cloud services differs, which results in various definitions of privacy protection and in multiple jurisdictions within the framework of privacy's protection applicability. (3) Data and resources distribution to users in cloud environments needs to be improved because it complicates resource segregation. (4) The development of processes in cloud computing virtual machines is monitored and operated through hypervisor usage. Despite the existing strategy for addressing malware in virtual machines, a severe lack of policies, procedures and techniques is being recorded, in order to facilitate, for example, an investigation for a user's privacy breach in cloud forensics (Poisel & Tjoa, 2012).

Therefore, it is of major importance for researchers to clearly define the privacy issues within CCE. Towards this, Kalloniatis (2015), pp. 115–117 identified and proposed the following privacy-related properties that are affected by each threat or vulnerability within the cloud: (1) *Isolation*, which refers to the complete seal of user's data inside CCE, in order to address data disclosure from a purpose limitation point of view and secondly from the aspect of the proper technical implementation techniques. (2) *Provenance ability*, which refers to the provenance of the data related to the authenticity or identification, the quality of the results of certain procedures, modifications, updates and vulnerabilities, the provenance of certain actions inside the cloud, the detection of origins of security violations of an entity, the auditability of client's data and matters that are related to the cloud's subsystem geographical dispersion which refers to the legal issues, regulations, policies and each country's rules as far as data processing and protection is concerned. (3) *Traceability*, which aims at providing the user with the ability to trace their data and verify that they are processed according to their collection purpose. Thus, privacy is protected through the ability of tracing them among the data repositories and reassuring that the data have been completely deleted or maintained invisible and anonymized after their deletion. (4) *Intervenability*, which refers to the fact that the users should be able to have access and process their data despite the service architecture of the cloud. A cloud provider may rely on other provider's subcontractor services in order to offer their services. That should not be an obstacle for the user to intervene with their data in case they suspect that their privacy is violated by the subcontractors. In fact, cloud providers must be able to provide all the technical, organizational and contractual means for accomplishing this functionality for the user, including all respective subcontractors with which the provider cooperates and interrelates. (5) *Compliance, Safety, Accountability (CSA) Accountability*, which refer to the fact that cloud providers should be able to provide information about their data protection policies and procedures or specific cloud incidents related to users' data at any given time, especially in the case of privacy violation. (6) *Anonymity*, which refers to the user's ability to use a resource or service to operate online without being tracked and without disclosing their identity. (7) *Pseudonymity,* which refers to the user's ability to use a resource or service by acting under one or many pseudonyms, thus hiding their real identity. However, under certain circumstances, the possibility of translating pseudonyms to real identities exists and therefore pseudonymity is used for protecting the user's identity in cases where anonymity cannot be provided. (8) *Unlinkability,* which refers to the inability to link related information, and it is successfully achieved when an attacker is unable to link specific information to the user that processes that information or between a sender and a recipient. In that second case unlinkability means that though the sender and recipient can both be identified as participating in some communication, they cannot be identified as communicating with each other. Ensuring unlinkability is vital for protecting the user's privacy. (9) *Undetectability* and *Unobservability,* where the concept of undetectability expresses the inability to detect if a user uses a resource of service. Pfitzmann and Hansen (2015) define undetectability as the inability of the attacker to sufficiently distinguish if an item of interest exists or not. In previous work, undetectability was absent as a privacy concept and the gap was fulfilled by unobservability. However, since 2010 undetectability is used as the concept of defining the inability of data, processes or user detection from an attacker's perspective. Undetectability is usually used to satisfy steganographic systems where the concealment of information plays a crucial role. Thus, unobservability is defined as the undetectability that uninvolved subjects have in a communication together with anonymity even if items of interest can necessarily be detected by the involved subjects.

The aforementioned privacy properties, even though they can be used as a starting point to address privacy issues within CCE since cloud systems, organizations' features and users' personal needs and preferences are acknowledged, are still not adequate enough as they do not take into consideration the role of privacy social aspects. In order to meet the needs of all stakeholders within CCE, privacy requirements should be extended by including privacy properties and techniques which derive from users' personal and social needs. Thus, they capture the dynamical concepts and notions of privacy within it, as well as to be suitable to the openness and the fluidity of these environments, through which user data and information disseminate rapidly (Anthonysamy et al., 2017).

## The emergence of the adaptive privacy aware systems

Given the aforementioned issues, the inability of the existing privacy systems and the software engineers to provide an efficient privacy framework according to users' social needs has been highlighted. It is also clear that wider users' privacy issues in CCE emerge whenever social and legal norms are ignored or technical privacy safeguards are circumvented (Netter, Herbst, & Pernul, 2013). In this regard, users' personalized privacy in CCE is essential. In order for this necessity to be achieved and targeted services according to users' social context, needs and preferences to be provided (Bennaceur et al. 2016; Lahlou, 2008), the design of Adaptive Privacy Aware Systems (Abwod, 2016; Cerf, 2015; Poslad, Hamdi, & Abie, 2013) is required. These systems have the ability to maintain users' privacy in changing contexts, either by providing users with recommendations or by proceeding to automated actions based on users' decisions for personal information disclosure or not, within a context (Schaub, Könings, Dietzel, Weber, & Kargl, 2012). In order for the Systems to meet the needs mentioned previously, standards of specific functions must be satisfied, as those briefly outlined in the next paragraphs. According to Schaub, Könings, and Weber (2015), classified interaction strategies concerning privacy protection to user should be applied, which facilitate the connection of the system (through three phases: (1) privacy awareness, (2) justification and privacy decision, (3) control capabilities) with user's cognitive processes for their privacy settings. Users should be provided with adequate opportunities to express preferences and give feedback in relation to the justification and the findings of privacy settings adjustment. According to Omoronyia (2016), the users should be offered the possibility of selective information disclosure, by providing the context and the control level over the information the user wants to reveal. Therefore, four operations should be performed: (1) monitoring, (2) analysis, (3) design and (4) implementation, utilizing framework models (*identifying user's environment and interconnections as well as their role in the system*) and behavioral models, in order to identify features to control, detect threats before data disclosure and calculate users' benefit in comparison to data disclosure cost. According to Bennaceeur et al. (2016), they should be adapted to the interoperability of technologies, to the structure of systems and behaviour within users' natural environment and to their ambiguous behaviour. They should also be capable of determining privacy requirements and the values of the involved groups, diagnosing threats based on these values, determining sensitive information that should not be revealed, balancing between privacy choices automation and users' choices and demanding short time investment regarding their operation training, as well.

Therefore, for the successful design of the Adaptive Privacy Aware Systems, it is essential to take into account empirical data related to users' social characteristics within interacting frameworks in and out of the information systems (Schaub et al., 2015). This becomes more essential within CCE. JagadeeshKumar and Naik (2018) proposed an Adaptive Privacy Policy framework to protect users' pictures within cloud, taking into consideration users' social settings, the content of pictures and metadata as well. Nevertheless, several studies related to the appliance of Adaptive Privacy Aware Systems in SNSs (Calikli et al., 2016) and mobile services of social networks (Bilogrevic, Huguenin, Agir, Jadliwala, & Hubaux, 2013; Hoang Long & Jung, 2015), taking into consideration users' social characteristics, specify them only on the basis of systems usage and the groups in which users appear to participate in. Therefore, they have not succeeded in meeting users' complex social reality and needs efficiently. As Munoz (2018) supports for all the self-adaptive software systems, in order for them to be developed with the appropriate techniques and methods, the requirements phase is crucial. Accordingly, for the Adaptive Privacy Aware Cloud-based Systems the elicitation of both social and technical privacy requirements is rather essential so as to be optimally designed.

## Towards an integrated socio-technical approach

Privacy constitutes a dynamic concept and a collective procedure that is formatted, not isolated, by changing circumstances (Baruh & Popescu, 2017; Chang, 2015), from both a social and technical aspect.

In particular, users' privacy within CCE can be defined only through a thorough examination of both social and technical aspects of privacy, since its management is directly associated with the physical, social, cultural, spatial, time and technological boundaries set by users themselves (Nissenbaum, 2009). Thus, there is a growing need to redefine the interaction between users and privacy aware systems in order to increase the usability of systems and the users' satisfaction as well, and therefore the necessity for the Adaptive Privacy Aware Cloud-based Systems has emphatically emerged.

Summarizing findings from previous literature, the necessity of the Adaptive Privacy Aware Cloud-based Systems can be justified as follows:

- To the new emerging privacy risks associated with users' personalization in social and spatial level and the delineation of their behaviour within CCE (Toch et al., 2012).
- To the users' choices with reference to personal information disclosure level, direct or indirect, through CCE usage (Lahlou, 2008).
- To the design of privacy protection systems, without taking into consideration empirical data concerning users' preferences and needs (Lahlou, 2008).
- To the stationary and complexity of privacy protection software that make the adoption and applicability by users a hard case (Acquisti, John, & Loewenstein, 2013).

- To the functionality and design of systems that have low safety standards and make access to users' data without their consent easy (Poslad et al., 2013).
- To users' failure to read or understand privacy policies or to anticipate downstream data uses (Solove, 2013).
- To the failure of correlating users' privacy concerns with the privacy choices provided that leads to the dissatisfaction of privacy technical requirements (Omoronyia, 2016).
- To the lack of the identification of users' social context that affects their determination for privacy (Chang, 2015).
- To the fact that technical privacy requirements within CCE have not been developed efficiently (Kalloniatis et al., 2014; Mouratidis et al., 2013)
- To software non-correspondence to integration and interoperability challenges in cloud computing in order for the digital, social and natural users' needs to be satisfied (Bennaceeur et al., 2016).

Focusing on these needs and challenges regarding adaptive privacy within CCE, several research questions are posed, such as 'How do users define their privacy within CCE based on their particular social characteristics and needs?', 'Which users' privacy behaviors within CCE are affected by their social and technical needs?', 'Which privacy technical requirements within CCE are related to users' social characteristics, social needs and privacy perceptions?', 'How technical privacy requirements within CCE affect users' privacy management?'. Even though a number of studies have been conducted to correlate social and technological perspectives of privacy (Spiliotopoulos & Oakley, 2013; Taddicken, 2014; Tufekci, 2012), these are fragmentary exploring specific social aspects (e.g. nationality, age, social influence) and their correlation with users' privacy concerns and needs, which fail to interpret the complexity of users' social reality both online and offline. Thus, the identification of social parameters and criteria that affect the elicitation of technical, functional and non-functional requirements is a critical step for an Adaptive Privacy Aware Cloud-based System to be designed.

As it is shown in previous literature, individuals' social identity and social capital are central social aspects that affect privacy issues within CCE, and in particular within SNSs. However, distinct features of users' social identity – multiplicity and intersectionality – and the correlation of users' social capital with a plethora of privacy dimensions and issues (concerns, risks, behaviours, management) should be more thoroughly and multifariously explored. This exploration should be elaborated for these factors not only separately, as it is suggested in previous research, but in combination as well. Social capital and social identity constitute interactive concepts that reinforce one another (Lin, 2017). Therefore, their combination will enable researchers to better understand how individuals' privacy interests and preferences are formatted and shaped according to their technological conceptual frameworks for action[1] and therefore it will allow a more specific elicitation of its technical privacy requirements.

Consequently, for a clearer definition of privacy within CCE and the optimal design of APACS, the key issue is to establish a solid interrelation between the social and technical requirements of privacy. To address that issue from a starting point of view, the following interdisciplinary conceptual model (Fig. 2.1.) is demonstrated, guided by the existing theoretical approaches for social identity and social capital, as well as the privacy properties for cloud-based services that Kalloniatis (2015) proposed in his work.

The model consists of a major entity 'Adaptive Privacy Aware Cloud-based System design' and three minor entities, 'Privacy definition', 'Social Aspects of Privacy within CCE' and 'Technical Privacy Properties within CCE', where major and minors are differentiated by level. The attributes of minor entities are also demonstrated. The relationships among entities are represented by directional and bidirectional bows, indicating their complex interrelations.

Our approach aims at making visible the important networks and variables between the two fields, leading to the elicitation of integrated privacy requirements for the optimal design of APACS, while it indicates the necessity for the adoption of an established interdisciplinary theoretical and methodological approach as the key to the efficient analysis and documentation of adaptive privacy design within CCE. Further analysis and specification of the proposed social and technical privacy requirements will allow researchers to capture the continuing changes within CCE and enable the adaptability of privacy aware systems to users' needs. Enhancing Chang's (2015) thesis, according to which privacy should be examined under the specific social context of each individual, we also suggest that this context is shaped, not only by social factors, putting special emphasis on social identity and social capital, but also by the technological frame within a user act. Therefore, our approach, incorporating both of social and technical privacy requirements, lays the ground for a wider determination of privacy within CCE, leading to further understanding of the utility of users' disclosure despite the privacy risks, so as the adaptive privacy software engineering activities for cloud to be supported.

[1] Iacono (2001) combined the sociological notion of 'conceptual framework for action' of Snow and Benford (1992) with the concept of technology and introduced the term 'technological conceptual framework for action'. This term refers to the way in which individuals give meaning to specific types of technology in order to serve their actions' framework, and according to these interpretations, they invest time and money so as to use them.

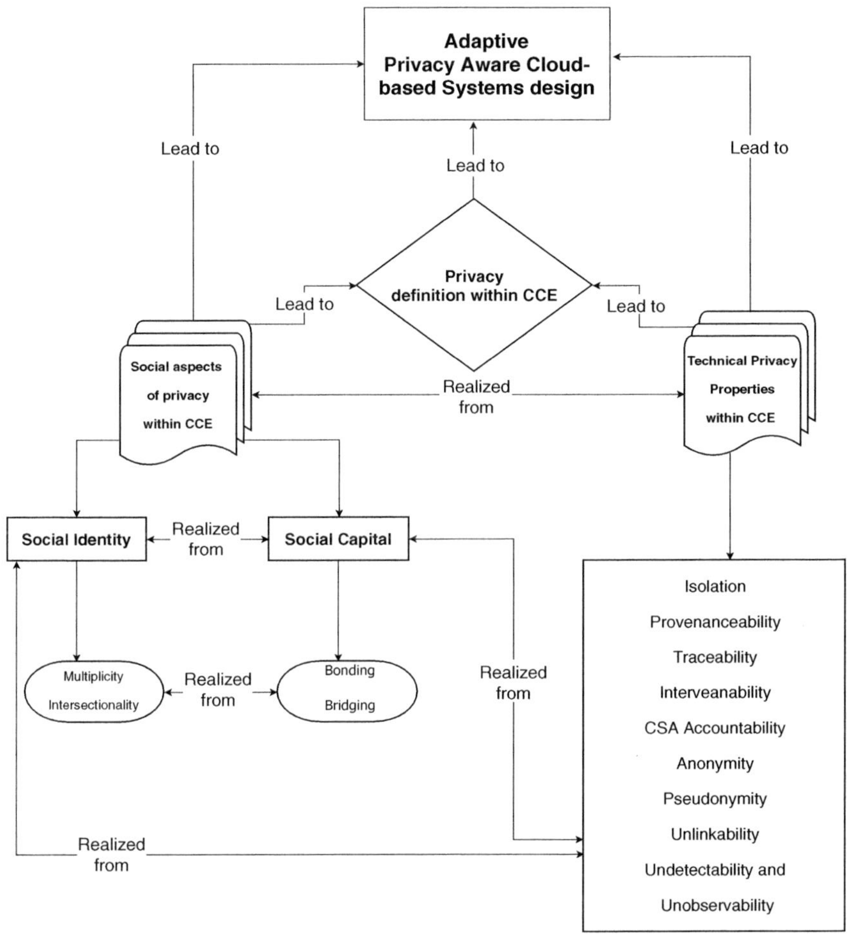


**FIGURE 2.1** Conceptual model towards an integrated socio-technical approach for adaptive privacy within CCE.

## Conclusion

Cloud Computing Environments, as emerged technologies, have made privacy risks, threats and leaks more difficult to be identified, while privacy preservation within CCE becomes even more complicated. The identification of users' social context is of major importance (Chang, 2015) in order for a privacy aware system to balance between users' need for preserving personal information and the need for disclosing them. Martin (2015) supports that even though individuals' privacy issues may differentiate, their privacy expectations should not be restricted. Consequently, sufficient privacy should have the ability to address privacy issues within CCE, deriving from social and legal dimensions as well as technological possibilities and limitations. Therefore, the need for the Adaptive Privacy Aware Cloud-based Systems in order to preserve users' privacy in changing sociocultural contexts within cloud computing is indicated. Despite the fact that research has paid attention to the development of privacy cloud-based engineering methodologies so as to fulfill these criteria, literature – to our best knowledge – has not achieved the provision of a structured framework that incorporates both social and technical privacy prerequisites for the optimal design of APACS. Towards this, in our approach, we present a novel conceptual model to highlight the emerged need for Adaptive Privacy Aware Systems and to support the identification and interrelation of social and technical privacy requirements within CCE, taking into consideration the new emerging privacy risks within CCE, the need for functional and applicable privacy protection software and the need for users' digital, social and natural interests and boundaries to be met with technical privacy affordances. The incorporation of social identity and social capital notions within our model provides further understanding for users' privacy interpretation and management; moreover, the demonstration of the technical privacy properties enhances fundamental understanding of the existing privacy methodologies within CCE in contrast to traditional systems. Their interactive relationship between these aspects leads towards the elicitation of cloud socio-technical privacy requirements in order for all the stakeholders' contemporary needs to be satisfied.

Despite the fact that we acknowledge several limitations regarding our conceptual model, such as the fact that the model may be not applicable in all deployment or service models, the technical privacy requirements may be updated due to the rapid evolvement of CCE, the social identity and social capital features may be multiplying due to the dynamic nature of the notions, our model goes beyond existing literature by bringing forward an integrated socio-technical approach that specifies not only distinct but also correlated social and technical privacy requirements within CCE. In this regard, the main contribution of this study is that, by encapsulating the emerging requirements, it sheds light on factors that affect the successful design of the Adaptive Privacy Aware Cloud-based Systems and can be beneficial to both the scientific community and the IT industry. Our approach, based on the theoretical and methodological background of both Social and Computer Sciences, reconstructs the existing knowledge regarding the social and technical privacy requirements within CCE, leading to interdisciplinary developments for both disciplines, by making visible the networks between them and by offering a starting point for further assessments. Our approach lays also the ground for socio-technical oriented appliances in the industrial field, in order for future adaptive privacy technologies to be developed.

Finally, our study provides a foundation for further research on several aspects of this field, such as the privacy perspectives of all stakeholders within CCE, the users' specific social groups and variables according to their specific social identity (e.g. parent, employee) and how these are associated with privacy in CCE, or how can users' social data be deployed for optimizing the design of APACS.

## References


Abowd, G. D. (2016). Beyond Weiser: From ubiquitous to collective computing. *Computer, 49*(1), 17–23.

Acquisti, A., Brandimarte, L., & Loewenstein, G. (2015). Privacy and human behavior in the age of information. *Science, 347*(6221), 509–514.

Acquisti, A., Gritzalis, S., Lambrinoudakis, C., & De Capitani di Vimercati, S. (Eds.). (2008). *Digital privacy: Theory, technologies and practices*. New York: Auerbach Publications.

Acquisti, A., John, L. K., & Loewenstein, G. (2013). What is privacy worth? *The Journal of Legal Studies, 42*(2), 249–274.

Anthonysamy, P., Rashid, A., & Chitchyan, R. (2017). Privacy requirements: Present & future. In *Proceedings of the 39th international conference on software engineering: Software engineering in society track, ICSE-SEIS '17, Buenos Aires, Argentina, May 20–28, 2017* (pp. 13–22). Piscataway, NJ, USA: IEEE Press.

Arbore, A., Soscia, I., & Bagozzi, R. P. (2014). The role of signaling identity in the adoption of personal technologies. *Journal of the Association for Information Systems, 15*(2), 86–110.

Balicki, J., Bieliński, T., Korłub, W., & Paluszak, J. (2014). Volunteer computing system comcute with smart scheduler. In J. Balicki (Ed.), *Applications of information systems in engineering and bioscience, proceeding of 13th international conference on software engineering, parallel and distributed systems, SEPADS, 15-17 May 2014* (pp. 54–60). Gdansk, Poland: WSEAS Press.

Baruh, L., & Popescu, M. (2017). Big data analytics and the limits of privacy self-management. *New Media and Society, 19*(4), 579–596.

Baym, N. K. (2010). *Personal connections in the digital age*. USA: Polity Press.

Bazarova, N. N., & Choi, Y. H. (2014). Self-disclosure in social media: Extending the functional approach to disclosure motivations and characteristics on social network sites. *Journal of Communication, 64*(4), 635–657.

Bennaceur, A., McCormick, C., Galán, J. G., Perera, C., Smith, A., Zisman, A., et al. (2016). Feed me, feed me: An exemplar for engineering adaptive software. In *Proceedings of the IEEE/ACM 11th international symposium on software engineering for adaptive and self-managing systems, SEAMS, Austin, TX, USA, May 16-17, 2016* (pp. 89–95). IEEE.

Bilogrevic, I., Huguenin, K., Agir, B., Jadliwala, M., & Hubaux, J. P. (2013). Adaptive information-sharing for privacy-aware mobile social networks. In *Proceedings of the 2013 ACM international joint conference on pervasive and ubiquitous computing, UbiComp, Zurich, Switzerland, September 08-12, 2013* (pp. 657–666). New York, USA: ACM.

Bohn, A., Buchta, C., Hornik, K., & Mair, P. (2014). Making friends and communicating on facebook: Implications for the access to social capital. *Social Networks, 37*, 29–41.

Calikli, G., Law, M., Bandara, A. K., Russo, A., Dickens, L., Price, B. A., et al. (2016). Privacy dynamics: Learning privacy norms for social software. In *Proceedings of the IEEE/ACM 11th international symposium on software engineering for adaptive and self-managing systems, SEAMS, Austin, TX, USA, May 16-17, 2016* (pp. 47–56). IEEE.

Camp, J., & Connelly, K. (2008). Beyond consent: Privacy in ubiquitous computing (ubicomp). In A. Acquisti, S. Gritzalis, C. Lambrinoudakis, & S. De Capitani di Vimercati (Eds.), *Digital privacy: Theory, technologies and practices* (pp. 327–343). USA: Auerbach Publications.

Cerf, V. G. (2015). Prospects for t he internet of things. *XRDS: Crossroads, The ACM Magazine for Students, 22*(2), 28–31.

Chang, C. H. (2015). New technology, new information privacy: Social-value-oriented information privacy theory. *NTU Law Review, 10*(1), 127–175.

Chen, H. T. (2018). Revisiting the privacy paradox on social media with an extended privacy calculus model: The effect of privacy concerns, privacy self-efficacy, and social capital on privacy management. *American Behavioral Scientist, 62*(10), 1392–1412.

Cohen, J. E. (2013). What privacy is for. *Harvard Law Review, 126*(7), 1904–1933.

De Wolf, R., Willaert, K., & Pierson, J. (2014). Managing privacy boundaries together: Exploring individual and group privacy management strategies in facebook. *Computers in Human Behavior, 35*, 444–454.

DeCew, J. W. (1997). *In pursuit of privacy: Law, ethics, and the rise of technology.* Ithaca, New York: Cornell University Press.

Dienlin, T., & Trempte, S. (2015). Is the privacy paradox a relic of the past? An in-depth analysis of privacy attitudes and privacy behaviors. *European Journal of Social Psychology, 45*(3), 285–297.

Ellison, N. B., Vitak, J., Gray, R., & Lampe, C. (2014). Cultivating social resources on social network sites: Facebook relationship maintenance behaviors and their role in social capital processes. *Journal of Computer Mediated Communication, 19*(4), 855–870.

Ellison, N., Vitak, J., Steinfield, C., Gray, R., & Lampe, C. (2011). Negotiating privacy concerns and social capital needs in a social media environment. In S. Trepte, & L. Reinecke (Eds.), *Privacy online* (pp. 19–32). Berlin, Heidelberg: Springer.

Eriksen, T. H. (2001). *Tyranny of the moment*. London: Pluto Press.

Farnham, S. D., & Churchill, E. F. (2011). Faceted identity, faceted lives: Social and technical issues with being yourself online. In *Proceedings of the ACM 2011 conference on computer supported cooperative work, CSCW, Hangzhou, China, March 19 – 23 2011* (pp. 359–368). New York, NY, USA: ACM.

Fortunati, L., & Taipale, S. (2016). Mobilities and the network of personal technologies: Refining the understanding of mobility structure. *Telematics and Informatics, 34*(2), 560–568.

Ganji, D., Mouratidis, H., Gheytassi, S. M., & Petridis, M. (2015). Conflicts between security and privacy measures in software requirements engineering. In H. Jahankhani, et al. (Eds.), *Proceedings of international conference on global security, safety, and sustainability, ICGS3, London, UK, September 15-17 2015* (pp. 323–334). Switzerland: Springer International Publishing.

Gerstein, R. (1970). Privacy and self-incrimination. *Ethics, 80*(2), 87–101.

Grant, F., & Hogg, M. A. (2012). Self-uncertainty, social identity prominence and group identification. *Journal of Experimental Social Psychology, 48*(2), 538–542.

Guegan, J., Moliner, P., & Buisine, S. (2015). Why are online games so self-involving: A social identity analysis of massively multiplayer online role playing games. *European Journal of Social Psychology, 45*(3), 349–355.

He, D., Kumar, N., Zeadally, S., Vinel, A., & Yang, L. T. (2017). Efficient and privacy-preserving data aggregation scheme for smart grid against internal adversaries. *IEEE Transactions on Smart Grid, 8*(5), 2411–2419.

Henderson, S. E. (2012). Expectations of privacy in social media. *Mississippi College Law Review, 31*, 227–247.

Hoang Long, N., & Jung, J. J. (2015). Privacy-aware framework for matching online social identities in multiple social networking services. *Cybernetics and Systems, 46*(1–2), 69–83.

Hsu, F. M., Fan, C. T., Chen, T. Y., & Wang, S. W. (2013). Exploring perceived value and usage of information systems in government context. *Chiao Da Management Review, 33*(2), 75–104.

Iacono, S. (2001). Computerization movements: The rise of the internet and distant forms of work. In J. A. Yates, & J. V. Maanen (Eds.), *Information technology and organizational transformation: History, rhetoric and practice* (pp. 93–135). Newbury Park, CA: Sage Publications.

ICO, Act, D.P. 20140225. (2014). *Conducting privacy impact assessments code of practice.* Technical report. Information Commissioners Office (ICO). https://www.theabi.org.uk/assets/uploads/Policies%20and%20Guidance/GDPR/pia-code-of-practice.pdf.

JagadeeshKumar, R., & Naik, M. V. (2018). Adaptive privacy policy prediction system for user-uploaded images on content sharing sites. *International Research Journal of Engineering and Technology, 5*(7), 148–154.

Jenkins, R. (2008). *Social identity.* United Kingdom: Routledge.

Kalloniatis, C. (2015). Designing privacy-aware systems in the cloud. In S. Fischer-Hübner, et al. (Eds.), *Proceedings of 12th international conference on trust and privacy in digital business. TrustBus, 1-2 september 2015, Valencia, Spain* (pp. 113–123). Switzerland: Springer International Publishing, LNCS 9264.

Kalloniatis, C., Kavakli, E., & Gritzalis, S. (2008). Addressing privacy requirements in system design: The PriS method. *Requirements Engineering, 13*(3), 241–255.

Kalloniatis, C., Mouratidis, H., Vassilis, M., Islam, S., Gritzalis, S., & Kavakli, E. (2014). Towards the design of secure and privacy-oriented information systems in the cloud: Identifying the major concepts. *Computer Standards and Interfaces, 36*(4), 759–775.

Lahlou, S. (2008). Identity, social status, privacy and face-keeping in digital society. *Social Science Information, 47*(3), 299–330.

Lin, N. (2017). Building a network theory of social capital. In R. Dubos (Ed.), *Social capital. Theory and research* (pp. 3–28). New York: Routledge.

Liu, Y., Sun, Y., Ryoo, J., Rizvi, S., & Vasilakos, A. V. (2015). A survey of security and privacy challenges in cloud computing: Solutions and future directions. *Journal of Computing Science and Engineering, 9*(3), 119–133.

Lovell, R. (2011). *White paper. Introduction to cloud computing. Think grid.* http://www.thinkgrid.com/docs/computing-whitepaper.pdf.

Martin, K. (2015). Privacy notices as Tabula rasa: An empirical investigation into how complying with a privacy notice is related to meeting privacy expectations online. *Journal of Public Policy and Marketing, 34*(2), 210–227.

Marwick, A., & boyd, d. (2011). I tweet honestly, I tweet passionately: Twitter users, context collapse, and the imagined audience. *New Media and Society, 13*(1), 114–133.

Marwick, A., & Boyd, d. (2014). Networked privacy: How teenagers negotiate context in social media. *New media & society, 16*(7), 1051–1067.

Mel, P., & Grance, T. (2011). *The NIST definition of cloud computing.* NIST Special Publication 800-145. U.S.A: Department of Commerce.

Mouratidis, H., Islam, S., Kalloniatis, C., & Gritzalis, S. (2013). A framework to support selection of cloud providers based on security and privacy requirements. *Journal of Systems and Software, 86*(9), 2276–2293.

Muñoz-Fernández, J. C., Mazo, R., Salinesi, C., & Tamura, G. (2018). 10 Challenges for the specification of self-adaptive software. In *Proceedings of 12th international conference on research challenges in information science, RCIS, Nantes, France, May 29-31, 2018* (pp. 1–12). IEEE.

Nario-Redmond, M. R., Biernat, M., Eidelman, S., & Palenske, D. J. (2004). The social and personal identities scale: A measure of the differential importance ascribed to social and personal self-categorizations. *Self and Identity, 3*(2), 143–175.

Netter, M., Herbst, S., & Pernul, G. (2013). Interdisciplinary impact analysis of privacy in social networks. In Y. Altshuler, Y. Elovici, A. Cremers, N. Aharony, & A. Pentland (Eds.), *Security and privacy in social networks* (pp. 7–26). New York: Springer.

Nissenbaum, H. (2009). *Privacy in context: Technology, policy and the integrity of social life.* USA: Stanford University Press.

Omoronyia, I. (2016). Reasoning with imprecise privacy preferences. In *Proceedings of the 2016 24th ACM SIGSOFT international symposium on foundations of software engineering, FSE, Seattle, USA, November 13 – 18, 2016* (pp. 952–955). ACM.

Papacharissi, Z., & Gibson, P. (2011). Fifteen minutes of privacy: Privacy, sociality &publicity on social network sites. In S. Trepte, & L. Reinecke (Eds.), *Privacy online* (pp. 75–90). Berlin, Heidelberg: Springer.

Patkos, T., Flouris, G., Papadakos, P., Casanovas, P., Ioannidis, G., Gonzalez-Conejero, J., et al. (2015). Privacy-by-Norms privacy expectations in online interactions. In *Proceedings of 2015 IEEE international conference on self-adaptive and self-organizing systems workshops, SASOW, Cambridge, MA, USA, September 21-25, 2015* (pp. 1–6). IEEE Computer Science.

Pearson, S. (2009). Taking account of privacy when designing cloud computing services. In *Proceedings of workshop on software engineering challenges of cloud computing, CLOUD, Vancouver, BC, Canada, May 23, 2009* (pp. 44–52). IEEE Computer Society.

Pearson, S., & Benameur, A. (2010). Privacy, security and trust issues arising from cloud computing. In *Proceedings of second international conference on cloud computing technology and science, Indianapolis, USA, November 30- December 3, 2010* (pp. 693–702). IEEE.

Petronio, S. (2002). *Boundary of privacy: Dialectics of disclosure*. New York: State University of New York Press.

Pfitzmann, A., & Hansen, M. (2015). *A terminology for talking about privacy by data minimization: Anonymity, unlinkability, undetectability, unobservability, pseudonymity, and identity management*. White Paper, v.0.34. http://dud.inf.tu-dresden.de/Anon_Terminology.shtml.

Pfitzmann, A., & Hansen, M. (2007). *Anonymity, unlinkability, undetectability, unobservability, pseudonumity and identity management-A consolidated proposal for terminology v.029*. Dresden: TU Dresden, ULD Kiel.

Pinter, R. (Ed.). (2008). *Information society. Studies on the information society. From theory to practice*. Thessaloniki: Technological Educational Institute of Thessaloniki.

Poisel, R., & Tjoa, S. (2012). Discussion on the challenges and opportunities of cloud forensics. In G. Quirchmayr, J. Basl, I. You, L. Xu, & E. Weippl (Eds.), *Multidisciplinary research and practice for information systems, CD-ARES 20–24 August 2012, Prague, Czech Republic* (pp. 593–608). Berlin, Heidelberg: Springer, Lecture Notes in Computer Science, 7465.

Poslad, S., Hamdi, M., & Abie, H. (2013). Adaptive security and privacy management for the internet of things. In *Proceedings of the 2013 ACM conference on pervasive and ubiquitous computing adjunct publication, ASPI, Zurich, Switzerland, September 08 – 12, 2013* (pp. 373–378). New York, USA: ACM.

Post, R. C. (2001). *Three concepts of privacy.* Faculty Scholarship Series. Paper 185. https://digitalcommons.law.yale.edu/fss_papers/185.

Rains, S. A., & Brunner, S. R. (2018). The outcomes of broadcasting self-disclosure using new communication technologies: Responses to disclosure vary across one's social network. *Communication Research, 45*(5), 659–687.

Raynes-Goldie, K. (2010). Aliases, creeping and wall-cleaning: Understanding privacy in the age of facebook. *First Monday, 15*(1–4).

Regan, P. M. (2015). Privacy and the common good: Revisited. In B. Roessler, & D. Mokrosinska (Eds.), *Social dimensions of privacy: Interdisciplinary perspectives* (pp. 50–70). Cambridge: Cambridge University Press.

Reiman, J. H. (1976). Privacy, intimacy and personhood. *Philosophy and Public Affairs, 6*(1), 26–44.

Richards, N.M. (2008). Intellectual privacy. *Texas Law Review, 87*(2), 387–445.

Rossler, B. (2018). *The value of privacy.* Cambridge: Polity Press.

Ruan, K., Carthy, J., Kechadi, T., & Crosbie, M. (2011). Cloud forensics. In G. Peterson, & S. Shenoi (Eds.), *Digital forensics 2011. IFIP advances in information and communication technology: Vol. 361. Advances in digital forensics VII.* Berlin, Heidelberg: Springer.

Schaub, F., Könings, B., Dietzel, S., Weber, M., & Kargl, F. (2012). Privacy context model for dynamic privacy adaptation in ubiquitous computing. In *Proceedings of the 2012 ACM conference on ubiquitous computing, UbiComp, pittsburgh, Pennsylvania, September 05 – 08, 2012* (pp. 752–757). New York, USA: ACM.

Schaub, F., Könings, B., & Weber, M. (2015). Context-adaptive privacy: Leveraging context awareness to support privacy decision making. *IEEE Pervasive Computing, 14*(1), 34–43.

Schoeman, F. (1984). *Philosophical dimensions of privacy: An anthology.* Cambridge: Cambridge University Press.

Smith, H. J., Dinev, T., & Xu, H. (2011). Information privacy research: An interdisciplinary review. *MIS Quarterly, 35*(4), 989–1016.

Snow, D., & Benford, R. (1992). Master Frames and Cycles of Protest. In A. Morris, & C. McClurg Mueller (Eds.), *Frontiers in Social Movement Theory.* New Haven: Yale University Press.

Solove, D. J. (2008). *Understanding privacy.* Cambridge, MA: Harvard University Press.

Solove, DJ. (2013). Privacy Self-management and the consent dilemma. *Harvard Law Review, 126,* 1880–1903.

Spiliotopoulos, T., & Oakley, I. (2013). Understanding motivations for facebook use: Usage metrics, network structure, and privacy. In *Proceedings of the SIGCHI conference on human factors in computing systems, CHI, paris, France, April 27 – May 02, 2013* (pp. 3287–3296). New York, USA: ACM.

Steeves, V., & Regan, P. (2014). Young people online and the social value of privacy. *Journal of Information, Communication and Ethics in Society, 12*(4), 298–313.

Steinfield, C., Ellison, N., Lampe, C., & Vitak, J. (2012). Online social network sites and the concept of social capital. In F. L. Lee, L. Leung, J. S. Qiu, & D. Chu (Eds.), *Frontiers in new media research* (pp. 115–131). New York: Routledge.

Stutzman, F., Gross, R., & Acquisti, A. (2013). Silent listeners: The evolution of privacy and disclosure on facebook. *Journal of Privacy and Confidentiality, 4*(2), 7–41.

Stutzman, F., Vitak, J., Ellison, N. B., Gray, R., & Lampe, C. (2012). Privacy in interaction: Exploring disclosure and social capital in facebook. In *Proceedings of the sixth international AAAI conference on weblogs and social media, ICWSM, Dublin, Ireland, June 4–7, 2012* (pp. 330–337). AAAI.

Taddicken, M. (2014). The 'privacy paradox in the social web: The impact of privacy concerns, individual characteristics, and the perceived social relevance on different forms of self disclosure. *Journal of Computer-Mediated Communication, 19*(2), 248–273.

Takabi, H., Joshi, J. B., & Ahn, G. J. (2010). Security and privacy challenges in cloud computing environments. *IEEE Security and Privacy, 8*(6), 24–31.

Toch, E., Wang, Y., & Cranor, L. F. (2012). Personalization and privacy: A survey of privacy risks and remedies in personalization-based systems. *User Modeling and User-Adapted Interaction, 22*(1–2), 203–220.

Trepte, S., & Reinecke, L. (2013). The reciprocal effects of social network site use and the disposition for self-disclosure: A longitudinal study. *Computers in Human Behavior, 29*(3), 1102–1112.

Tufekci, Z. (2012). Facebook, youth and privacy in networked publics. In *Proceedings of the sixth international AAAI conference on weblogs and social Media, ICWSM, Dublin, Ireland, June 4–7, 2012* (pp. 338–345). AAAI.

Tzortzaki, E., Kitsiou, A., Sideri, M., & Gritzalis, S. (2016). Self-disclosure, privacy concerns and social capital benefits interaction in FB: A case study. In V. Verykios, et al. (Eds.), *Proceedings of the 20th pan-hellenic conference on Informatics. PCI, 10 – 12 November 2016, Patras, Greece.* New York: ACM Press. Article No. 32.

Utz, S. (2015). The function of self-disclosure on social network sites: Not only intimate, but also positive and entertaining self-disclosures increase the feeling of connection. *Computers in Human Behavior, 45,* 1–10.

Walton, S. C., & Rice, R. E. (2013). Mediated disclosure on Twitter: The roles of gender and identity in boundary impermeability, valence, disclosure, and stage. *Computers in Human Behavior, 29*(4), 1465–1474.

Wang, W. I., & Shih, J. F. (2014). Factors influencing university students' online disinhibition behavior – the moderating effects of deterrence and social identity. *International Journal of Social, Behavioral, Educational, Economic and Management Engineering, 8*(5), 1477–1483.

Wessels, B. (2012). Identification and the practices of identity and privacy in everyday digital communication. *New Media and Society,* 14(8), 1251–1268.

Winograd-Cort, D., Haeberlen, A., Roth, A., & Pierce, B. C. (2017). A framework for adaptive differential privacy. *Proceedings of the ACM on Programming Languages, 1*(10). ACM Press, New York.

Woo, J. (2006). The right not to be identified: Privacy and anonymity in the interactive media environment. *New Media and Society, 8*(6), 949–967.

Wu, P. H., & Lin, C. P. (2016). Learning to foresee the effects of social identity complexity and need for social approval on technology brand loyalty. *Technological Forecasting and Social Change, 111*, 188–197.

Xu, H., Dinev, T., Smith, J., & Hart, P. (2011). Information privacy concerns: Linking individual perceptions with institutional privacy assurances. *Journal of the Association for Information Systems, 12*(2), 798–824.

CHAPTER

# 3

# Challenges of using machine learning algorithms for cybersecurity: a study of threat-classification models applied to social media communication data

*Andrei Queiroz Lima, Brian Keegan*

**Applied Intelligence Research Centre (AIRC), Technological University Dublin (TU Dublin), Dublin, Ireland**

OUTLINE



*Cyber Influence and Cognitive Threats*
https://doi.org/10.1016/B978-0-12-819204-7.00003-8

## Introduction

Social media is being used for gaining knowledge into a variety of subjects through social cooperation and communication among peers. There are a variety of social media tools such as blogs, social network sites, wikis and forums where people are searching for topics of interest for interacting and exchanging knowledge. As a result, a massive amount of information in the form of unstructured textual data is produced and put available to the world. The massive quantity of accessible content in social media has drawn the attention of the industry and scholars to find the real value of the produced information.

Similarly, computer security researchers, commonly called white hats, are making use of social media as part of the coordinate disclosure system. In a coordinate disclosure model, security experts report vulnerabilities found in software to a software-maker (vendor). Both parties agree over a period, which the vendor will release a fix for the software. At the end of the period, it is expected that the vendor releases a vulnerability patch, or the security experts will make the vulnerability public, through disclosing on social media channels. This model has two main goals: (1) alert software users regarding software that can put at risk their privacy and (2) enforce the big companies to develop and release secure software or to fix the security flaw in their software. The collection of this information provides value for cybersecurity in terms of planning security actions.

In this chapter, the following sections are an overview of the learning-based techniques used for proactive defence, including algorithms and approaches needed to make textual communication interpretable by machine learning algorithms. Moreover, there is a discussion on applications that use these learning-based models to extract insights from social media communities, such as Hacker forum, blogs and microblogs. Nowadays, social media has been seen as main source for acquiring prior information regarding recent software threats and cyberattack attempts. However, there are some challenges on using them as source of valid information, especially with regard to the creation and deployment of machine learning models. In the end is given an overview about a not-well-discussed subject regarding the ethical considerations of using the content of hacker forums and online communities for cybersecurity research.

## Cybersecurity using social media as open source of information

Regardless of its popularity among the young people, social media has been used widely. The easy spread and long reach of messages posted on social media is a valuable tool for mass communication. Considering this situation, researchers are producing several studies. An interesting one is from Sakaki, Okazaki and Matsuo (2010), who studied how the message posted on Twitter social network is useful for alerting a population in a city in Japan regarding coming earthquake incidents. The result shows that Twitter posts were able to communicate to people faster than announcements broadcasted by Japan Meteorological Agency (JMA). With this study, we see an example of the change in human behaviour with respect to the use of such tools for obtaining information.

In a different way, social media communication can be used for disseminating illegal activities. One common activity is the sharing of malicious software products and hacker services. These products are commonly related to exploiting tools that take advantage of a system's vulnerability allowing hackers to break into networks and perform the exfiltration of private data, distributed denial-of-service attacks and espionage (Benjamin & Chen, 2012). According to Ponemon Institute LLC (2017), in 2017, the favourite target of hacker was the Financial, Energy, Aerospace and defence, Technology and Healthcare sectors, respectively. In the same year, the security events that have caused significant loss within companies were malicious insiders, denial-of-service attacks and malicious code/software. It is the big companies who are facing the majority of the cybersecurity incidents. According to Roumani, Nwankpa and Roumani (2016), technology companies with significant financial records are more susceptible to security incidents. This study is based on financial records from 89 technology companies over a 10-year period, among them are Facebook, Oracle, Google, LinkedIn, LogMeIn, Nokia and Microsoft. The result shows a positive correlation between the firm's financial performance, the size and the number of sales with the number of vulnerabilities found in their software assets.

For this reason, companies are prone to invest more in security defence. The total number of investments in this area has been growing each year as the new businesses are shifting to online platforms. Besides, these investments are moving away from traditional/local security to outsourced services providers. According to Juniper Research (2017), the estimative of investment in cybersecurity is $135 billions by 2022, with a growth rate of 7.5%.

In Ponemon Institute LLC (2017), the report confirms that companies are investing more extensively in cybersecurity. Moreover, the majority of the investments are still on local security team of experts, but with a growing movement to outsourcing. The annual spend of small/middle companies in cybersecurity was about $11.7 millions on average in 2017. However, this study shows that companies, which have invested in security intelligence systems using machine learning and analytics, saved $2.8 million from their total expenditures with cybersecurity. Cyber analytics and other data-driven approach are still a new area. However, it has been pushing the computer security research to a new paradigm, the proactive defence. The goal now is to anticipate any attack attempt by using intelligent models and analytics to detect threats before it happens. This new concept is seen as opposed to the current security approach, which is mostly reactive to the known threats.

## Why is social media communication important for cybersecurity?

Social media has become a valuable tool for sharing information, understanding the current computer threats and solving security problems. It is accessible to anyone who has an interest in the subject. According to Algarni and Malaiya (2014), forums and specialized blogs are the entrance place for those who want to acquire knowledge of hacking techniques. On the one hand, some social media forums are the suitable tool for people who want to make money by selling malicious products, for instance, exploits, private data and stolen credit card numbers. These tools are sold in deep web forum, where the anonymity and privacy of its users is the primal concern. Some hacker exploit tools and services are around $100,000, depending on the damage capacity or novelty of the flaw discovered (Security Focus, 2013). Software vulnerabilities are sold on black market and have the price regulated according to its novelty and criticality. There are companies which hire these high-skilled people to find security breaches in their system, offering them a reward payment. However, the black market in deep web is still the most attractive path for those who want to profit more with software vulnerabilities and malicious products (Algarni & Malaiya, 2014).

On the other hand, there are other uses of social media within the security domain which is not related to malicious or illegal activities. It has been used by security researchers who want to alert people regarding security problems found in software. As seen in Sabottke, Suciu and Dumitras (2015), it is very common that security researchers finding new software vulnerabilities disclose them on social media such as Twitter. The disclosure of vulnerabilities is aimed to expose the software, which is putting the users' data and privacy at risk. Twitter's users often use the retweet feature to highlight these problems to their peers. This situation brings bad reputation to the companies which have their software under the spotlight. A study by Syed, Rahafrooz and Keisler (2018) shows that security professionals are prone to use social media to share technical analysis regarding software vulnerabilities to convince the vendor to fix and improve their development process to avoid vulnerable software being released.

Knowing that social media is part of the hacker ecosystem for sharing expertise and selling products, cybersecurity companies and researchers have been using these communities as an object of investigation and research (Portnoff et al., 2017). For instance, the authors Sabottke et al. (2015) created a model that uses Twitter post related to software vulnerabilities, where the main goal is to predict exploitation of vulnerabilities in software products. In the work of Lippmann, Campbell, Weller-Fahy, Mensch and Campbell (2016), the authors used posts from three social media, Twitter, Stack Overflow and Reddit, to train a classification model that would further distinguish posts regarding cyber/malicious communication from the other general communication. With a similar goal, although in social media content from deep web forum, Nunes et al. (2016) have used the posts of hacker forums to train a classification model to detect the commerce of malicious artefacts within the forums. The techniques to build these models that learn the current data to infer/classify instances of data will be part of this chapter.

## Learning-based approaches and processing techniques applied to textual communications

The primary goal of this section is to overview the methods and techniques used in cybersecurity data-driven research. Firstly, the conventional approaches for starting a learning-based model will be introduced: supervised, unsupervised and semisupervised approaches.

Afterwards, we are going to overview an essential step of data-driven research, which is the preprocessing of textual data. In the end, we will briefly discuss some metrics for evaluation of the model, which is an essential phase of the decision-making process.

***Supervised approach***

According to Russell and Norving (2010), supervised learning is 'the machine learning task of learning a function that maps an input to an output based on example input-output pairs'. It means that we are required to have the data that will fit our learning model already mapped (commonly called labelled) to the final output (result). There are two types of problem that supervised learning approach can solve, one is the regression and the other is classification. The difference between both approaches is concerned to its output value, where the former generates a continuous output and the latter a discrete output. In cybersecurity research, it is found more often that security problems require a classification model with a categorical output. For instance, in Lippmann et al. (2016), the author created a classifier model that marks the post sentences found in hacker communication as malicious or nonmalicious. While in Sabottke et al. (2015), the authors have created a model that labels the outputs as exploited or nonexploited to known software vulnerabilities. To make models that classify unseen data, they need to be 'taught' with set representative examples. This phase is usually called either building or, more commonly, training the model. For creating them, a wide range of supervised learning algorithms are available, each one with its characteristics and strengths. As examples of the commonly used algorithm, we see the support vector machine (SVM), decision tree and maximum entropy. It is important to notice that with different types of learning algorithm, the type of input data we have (continuous or discrete) is a factor that should be considered. Sometimes it requires a preprocessing of these inputs to meet the algorithm specification. For instance, SVM, linear/logistic regression and neural network algorithms use continuous data as input, as decision tree—based algorithm can use discrete data.

Some rules for using a supervised learning approach:

- The training dataset needs to be labelled.
- The sample instances on the training set should represent the population of every class in our experiment.
- Determine the features as a way to form the input representation.
- Determine the algorithm to define the learning function. The user should want the algorithm to be based on some of the learning paradigms: information gain, similarity and Bayes theory.

- Train the model and adjust the parameters using separate data (validation set).
- Evaluate the model on an independent data (test set).

***Unsupervised and semisupervised approach***

The other conventional method is the unsupervised learning. It differs from the previous one on the fact that the labelled dataset for training the model is not required. Instead, unsupervised-based algorithms will differentiate the instances by discovering the similarities through the underlying structure of the given data. Unsupervised learning approaches can be associated with the following tasks:

- Clustering, where the algorithm automatically splits the dataset into groups according to similarity. However, cluster analysis sometimes overestimates the similarity between the individual instances of the dataset, for example, grouping instances from group A as being from group B.
- Anomaly detection, where it can automatically discover unusual data points in the dataset. This approach is useful in detecting fraudulent transactions or determining failure on pieces of hardware/machinery. It can still be used for identifying an outlier from a normal distribution of events.
- Association mining, where it identifies sets of items that frequently occur together in the dataset. It is mostly used in retail businesses. This approach allows discovering clients purchase patterns to drive a better strategical development of marketing and merchandizing.
- Latent variable models, which are commonly used for data preprocessing, such as reducing the number of features in a dataset (dimensionality reduction) or decomposing the dataset into multiple components and sometimes for data visualization.

The commonly used unsupervised algorithms are K-means, principal component analysis and one-class SVM. In cybersecurity research, this unsupervised approach was used for anomaly detection (or outlier detection) tasks, more specifically applied to network intrusion detection systems as seen in Giacinto, Perdisci, Rio and Roli (2006). In this study, the authors are trying to detect any attempt of hacker intrusion within their network. The algorithm needs to learn all common behaviour of the system to differentiate such acts that might be a hacker attempt to break into the network.

Not as common as the first two previously discussed approaches, we have the semisupervised. The main benefit for choosing this approach is the possibility of using these unlabelled and labelled data for building a learning model. As in some cases, it is not a straightforward task to produce the label of the data because it is time-consuming and expensive; the semisupervised is an option. We can train the model using the unlabelled data with few labelled ones and achieve good results. It means that using both types of data during the training process tends to improve the accuracy of the final model while reducing the time and cost spent to label them. As we see in Nunes et al. (2016), they reached good results with classification of malicious products being offered on online forums using a semisupervised approach with slightly better results compared with supervised method.

The final considerations for choosing the right plan for creating our model are as follows: (1) The type of output we need to use (regression or classification), (2) a set of representative data related to the problem we want to solve, (3) the type of the input data (discrete or continuous) to fit our machine learning algorithm and (4) a critical evaluation of the entire process with respect to data, algorithm and computational resources. This is a fundamental part of an efficient model creation workflow.

### *Preprocessing social media content*

Before building (or training) a learning model, we need to clean and organize the social media content posts to use them as input for the chosen machine learning algorithm. These are the essential steps in data-driven research, and it is the phase in which data scientists spent more time. According to CrowdFlower (2016), this phase requires 60% of the time spent in data science workflow. The processing is necessary for attending specification of algorithms which involves the transformation of the textual into continuous or discrete input vector. In this section, the natural language processing (NLP) techniques and practises for manipulation of textual data will be discussed. Techniques such as tokenization, normalization, stemming, stop words removal and noise removal are frequently used in data-driven researches as well as in applications for cyber intelligence. In this section, we will discuss a typical workflow in Fig. 3.1 used for processing textual data.

### *Noise removal*

This step is generally associated with the removal of HTML/XML tags of the raw data. Fortunately, some tools can be used for dealing with this situation. In Python programming language, we have the NLTK framework, which can be used to extract the textual content from JSON and HTML formats. Those are usually the first step of the preprocessing workflow.

### *Tokenization*

Tokenization, for information retrieval domain of knowledge, is the process of delimiting each word or symbols of a sentence in tokens. These

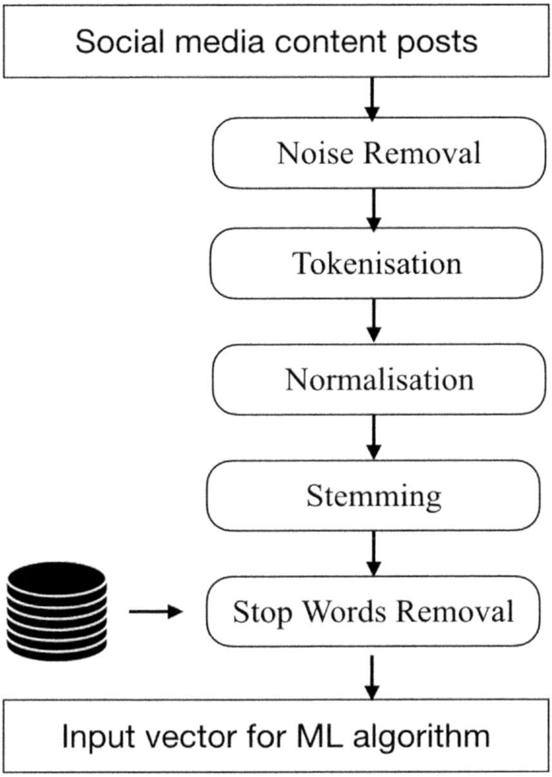


**FIGURE 3.1** Preprocessing workflow.

tokens will be the input for further machine learning algorithms. Tokenization is a useful technique for linguistics and computer science domain, where lexical analysis is needed to solve problems. The process of tokenization might find obstacles in defining the word boundaries as well as the limits of symbols like punctuation marks such as brackets and hyphens. Another problem is abbreviations and acronyms, which need to be interpreted as in standard form.

The process of tokenization differs according to the type of idioms. Languages such as English and French have their words separated by delimited white spaces. In Asiatic languages such as Chinese, the words have no clear boundaries. These languages require more morphological information to define such aspects.

***Normalization***

This phase is related to the transformation of text (words, sentences) into a single standard. For instance, transforming the data to the same case (upper or lower), removing punctuation and converting numbers to their word equivalents are usually applied to textual data. This step is generally taken before any descriptive analysis of the data.

***Stemming***

This method is used to identify the root/stem term of a word by removing prefix and suffix. For instance, the words hacker, hacked and hacking can be stemmed to the word 'hack' by suppressing the suffix of the words. One good reason for using this method is the reduction of the number of words and the saving of memory space. The transformation of a word to its stem is done assuming each one is related, as seen in the case of the word 'hacker'.

***Stop words removal***

There are some cases where certain words do not bring any value to the text analysis. They are usually the articles, prepositions and pronouns, i.e., the, in, a, an, with. They are also known as the stop words procedure. Removing them is optional depending on the type of research; in Twitter content research, for instance, removing stop words is not a recommended because of the short number of words (maximum text approximately of 200 characters). By eliminating them, we reduce the dimensionality of the input vector, which means that we can save computational processing resource. Some known procedures are used to remove this stop words from a corpus of text. The most used technique for removing stop words is based on a database formed by precompiled list, as can be seen in Fig. 3.1, which consists of a previously created list of words to be excluded from the main corpus.

***Vector transformation***

The transformation of the textual data into input vector requires (1) the definition of the features of the algorithm and (2) the representation type (continuous or discrete). Some algorithms such as SVM, logistic regression and neural network require continuous data as the input vector. The bag of words approach, also known as vector space model, is a conventional approach used to form the input vector from textual data, where the frequency words are used as features for the model. As we see in Fig. 3.2, each document (or messages in a social media platform) is assigned to the frequency of the word n appearing in a text. Also, the term frequency–inverse document frequency (TF-IDF) is used instead of the frequency of the words. The TF-IDF is a weight used to measure essential words in a document, given by the following equation:

TF(t) = (Number of times term t appears in a document)/(total number of terms in the document).

| | hacker | and | social | media | post |
|---|---|---|---|---|---|
| Document 1 | 0 | 1 | 0 | 1 | 0 |
| Document 2 | 2 | 0 | 0 | 0 | 1 |
| Document 3 | 1 | 1 | 1 | 1 | 1 |
| Document 4 | 0 | 0 | 0 | 0 | 1 |

**FIGURE 3.2** Bag of words with the frequency of terms.

IDF(t) = Log_e (total number of documents/number of documents with term t in it).

The bag of words can be formed for a different number of words or N-grams. The standard bag of words can be seen as N-gram, with N = 1, and as a consequence, the number of grams can be any. As shown in Fig. 3.3, we see a representation of an N-gram model, with N = 2. As the number of grams increase, more local information of the sentence is stored on the model, as we can see in Fig. 3.3, which was captured in the N-gram 'social media', which brings more information than 'social' and 'media' separately (Fig. 3.2).

### *Model evaluation and metrics*

To create efficient and precise models, we need to know how to evaluate them. The last procedure in a data-driven workflow is the evaluation of the model, which is usually known as the testing phase. At this point, we use a different part of the dataset, the test set, to measure the performance of the model built. The metrics most commonly used are precision, recall and F1-score. In addition, a standard set of graphs is used to inform the performance of the model; for instance, the receive operation curve (Bradley, 1997) and detection error tradeoff curve (Martin, Doddington, Kamm, Ordowski & Przybocki, 1997) are frequently used in cybersecurity research.

According to Kelleher, Namee & D'Arcy (2015), there are three primary considerations for model evaluation:

| | Hacker and | and social | social media | media post |
|---|---|---|---|---|
| Document 1 | 0 | 0 | 1 | 0 |
| Document 2 | 1 | 0 | 1 | 1 |
| Document 3 | 1 | 1 | 1 | 2 |
| Document 4 | 0 | 0 | 1 | 1 |

**FIGURE 3.3** N-gram of two or Bigram model representation.

| | | Actual class | |
|---|---|---|---|
| | | Positive | Negative |
| Predicted Class | Positive | True Positive (TP) | False Positive (FP) |
| | Negative | False Negative (FN) | True Negative (TN) |

FIGURE 3.4 Confusion matrix.

- To determine which of the models that we have built for a particular task is most suited to that task.
- To estimate how well the model will perform after deployed.
- To convince the business for whom a model is being developed that the model will meet their needs.

The most used tool for accessing precision, recall and F1-score measures is the confusion matrix, Fig. 3.4. In this figure, the confusion matrix is showing an example of results of a binary classification model where, by convention, we refer them with two levels (positive and negative levels); for this reason, there are just four outcomes when the model makes a prediction:

- True positive: An instance in the test set that had a positive target feature value and that was predicted to have a positive target feature value.
- True negative: An instance in the test set that had a negative target feature value and that was predicted to have a negative target feature value.
- False positive: An instance in the test set that had a negative target feature value but that was predicted to have a positive target feature value.
- False negative: An instance in the test set that had a positive target feature value but that was predicted to have a negative target feature value.

With confusion matrix, there are few other frequently used measures we can extract: true positive rate, true negative rate, false negative rate and false positive rate.

Concerning the experiment design, we will describe some of the evaluation experiment designs used and its main purpose. The most used are hold-out sampling, k-fold cross-validation, bootstrapping and out-of-time sampling.

The hold-out sampling is probably the most used form of sampling in data-driven approaches. As we need a large set for training and test phase, this experimental design is most appropriate for massive datasets. In this approach, we can subdivide the samples to a third one, the validation set. The validation set is usually used for adjusting the parameter of an algorithm. For example, SVM has some hyperparameter which can be adjusted to improve the performance of the model. This adjusting is usually done in the validation set. At the end, when the values of the hyperparameter are set, we use the test set to evaluate the model.

The k-fold cross-validation is an option when we do not have a large dataset but want to perform a reliable evaluation. In this approach, the data is divided into k equal-sized folds (or parts), and k distinct evaluation experiments are done. In the first evaluation experiment, the data in the first fold is used as the test set, and the remaining data (k − 1) are used as the training set. The performance in this step is recorded. This process goes until the last fold (researchers have been using 10-folds, although any value can be set for k). In the end, all recorded performance is aggregated to give us a final score representing the performance of the model.

Leave-one-out cross-validation is similar to k-fold cross-validation; however, the number of folds is same as that of the training instances. In this approach, we have each fold of the test set containing only one case, and the training set includes the other part of the data. This experimental design is useful when the amount of data available is small for performing the k-fold cross-validation.

The sampling methods discussed previously rely on random sampling to create training and test sets. Therefore, for some applications, we can take advantage of the time dimension to form these sample sets. We can use a specific period to build the model and afterwards we use it to perform predictions on data collected in a subsequent period. Those design approaches are referred to out-of-time sampling because we use data for the training, which was gathered in 2016 for instance, and we are not mixing them with the data of the test set collected in 2017.

## Use cases for learning-based model in cybersecurity problems

This section overviews the applications of learning-based models and how data-driven approach has been used for protective defence in cybersecurity. The main goal is to compare the techniques used in social media data for decision-making, including algorithms, preprocessing methods and evaluation strategies. It is fair to know that, despite the experiments discussed here are using similar techniques, the major difference is on the data collected; thus, the social media channel tested is the same as the model they trained. At the end, all the challenges faced by this approach are discussed. To facilitate our analysis, we group the security problems into the following research categories:

- Detection of messages regarding vulnerabilities and exploitation of software products.
- Detection of hacker services and products offered on marketplaces.

- Detection of influential hackers.
- Sentiment analysis over hacker message.

### *Detection of messages regarding vulnerabilities and exploitation of software products*

This branch of research is aimed to detect software vulnerability mentions through user's communication posted on social media. As previously discussed, social media is part of the hacker ecosystem in a way they use to share information regarding security issues in software and computational assets. As a result, cybersecurity companies are using this information for adjusting and updating their software to avoid a likely security breach in the future (Juniper Research, 2017). This type of approach is followed by works done in Sabottke et al. (2015) and Mulwad, Li, Joshi, Finin and Viswanathan (2011). Both studies are focused on classification of messages regarding security vulnerabilities and prediction of software exploitation; however, their method differs in some points as (1) the features used into the model and (2) the source of information they have used to train the classification model, as former used Twitter social media and the latter have used blogs, technical news and forum discussions. Regarding the features, the authors of the former have used the words and numeric features such as the number of retweets and number of followers and those of the latter used just the words.

A similar approach was seen by Lippmann et al. (2016). Instead of using the frequency of the words, the authors have chosen TF-IDF of words and the logistic regression algorithm to train their classification model. In terms of classification output label, this work has been different. Instead of just classifying subjects related to vulnerabilities, their classification model is focused on an extensive range of security problem, with class categories of 'malicious conversation' or 'nonmalicious conversation'. The authors Lippmann et al. (2016), as well as Mulwad et al. (2011), have used just hacker vocabulary within the train set as features to the model; as they have more than 90% of precision for detecting malicious activities according to the results, we imply that they are useful features for this type of task.

### *Detection of hacker services and exploitation tools on marketplaces*

The other branch of the studies is the detection of malicious tools and services being traded within hacker communication, especially in deep web forums and marketplaces. The term deep web is related to the part of the internet not indexed by popular web searching engines such as Google, Bing and Baidu. In most cases, the deep web resources are protected by some authentication system, i.e., login and password. There is other fraction of the deep web which is called dark web, where, for having access to it, we need a special tool called The Onion Router (ToR). This tool allows the user to access '.onion' forums, which is not accessible by regular browsers. Moreover, the ToR hides the IP information of the users for privacy and anonymity. The dark web communities commonly used are for illegal activities as drug selling and trade of hacking services and exploitation tools.

Within this context, the author of Nunes et al. (2016) used dark web forums as a source for experimenting their learning-based model. The goal is to use the model to detect malicious conversation to anticipate a hacker attack or exploitation of hidden vulnerabilities software. The authors produce one of the first experiments which use machine learning classification algorithms to provide detection of hacker services and tools being traded in dark web forums. The work has provided a comparison between supervised and semi-supervised approaches. According to the results, the semisupervised approach has offered the best performance. The semisupervised approach is suitable when few labelled data are provided in the dataset, as it was the case in this experiment. Regarding the features used for this model, they used the N-gram words from users' posts, similar to those seen in the experiment of Mulwad et al. (2011).

Addressing the same problem in a different perspective, the authors in Portnoff et al. (2017) are looking for transaction mentions (currency numbers and symbols including cryptocurrencies) for detecting malicious products being sold. In this experiment, the use of machine learning algorithms and NLP techniques to extract the name of the products on those messages with transactions mentions was required. A technique from the information extraction field called name entity recognition was applied to detect malicious software products.

In both works, the input is the postcommunication of the hacker forums. However, the main difference in their approach is the expected output. While in Nunes et al. (2016) the expected output of the model is a binary label (malicious content or nonmalicious content), in the work done by the Mulwad et al. (2011) it is expected to have the name of the vulnerable software product.

### *The influential hackers of a forum are main topics*

There is another type of study that follows a parallel way with the studies discussed in this section. It is the study of the key hackers in social media and hacker forums. In this study, the goal is finding the main subject in a hacker forum. The author Benjamin and Chen (2012) provided a study of the characteristic of the key hackers in forums according to their contribution to such communities. Their work is considered one of the first attempts to model the hacker behaviour using the hacker participation related to the sharing of trustworthy tools and expertise within the forum community. As a result, they conclude that the number of topic discussion the user is involved in, the quantity of attachment they share with peers (scripts, tutorial and software) and the number of messages are the main characteristics for increasing their reputation and, as a consequence, to put him in a position of key person within the group. Security researchers and machine learning experts would benefit from these characteristics to create models that classify the leading hacker in these communities. Security agencies and government would have benefits from these models for detecting and tracking those leaders and resources shared within social media communities.

In another study of key hackers, the authors Marin, Shakarian and Shakarian (2018) have created a model which uses numeric features to identify the key hackers using posts from dark web forums. They compared genetic algorithm with SVM, random forest and linear regression. For features, they used a specially crafted and well-planned set, such as the number of topics, number of replies; degree centrality, betweenness, closeness centrality (social network analysis features) and interval between user's post on forum communities. As a result, the genetic algorithm outperformed the others. In addition, the experiment showed that a model trained with data from just one forum is able to classify information from other hacker forums.

Another social media commonly used by hackers and not well-studied in computer security research is the Internet Relay Chat (IRC). IRC is client/server protocol used for communication in real time. It allows a group conversation or one-on-one private communication. In Marin et al. (2018), the model was built to identify key hacker in an IRC chat using the duration modelling as features, which is popular model in fields such as medical health, economic and social science domain. In this case, the duration model was calculated using the time when messages are posted on the channel. This set of features was able to identify the key hackers within the deep web forums quickly. The conclusion in this experiment is similar to that found in Benjamin and Chen (2012) as both models rely on a significant quantity of the posts made by the user, situation where it is not always achievable.

### *Sentiment analysis of hacker of hacker message*

A sentiment analysis in hacker communication for detection of vulnerabilities discussion in social media was first considered by Queiroz, Keegan and Mtenzi (2017). However, an experimental study of this came a year later by authors Shu, Sliva, Sampson and Liu (2018). In this study, the authors noticed that the sentiment related to cybersecurity attack could be captured and measured to define whether a message posted on social media is correlated with the occurrences of cyber events. They are using emotional signals, such as emoticons or punctuation, as features for the learning-based model to correlate changes in sentiment to the probability of an attack.

Aligned with the previous work, the authors Deb, Lerman and Ferrara (2018) have used the same sentiment analysis approach for detecting three types of events: malicious software installation, malicious destination visits and malicious emails that surpassed the target organizations' defence. The model was applied to 100 hacker forums of surface and deep web. Both studies are using the message posts in forums to find solutions for well-known problems of cybersecurity.

## Challenges of data-driven research in cybersecurity and ethical considerations

After training, testing and evaluating the features of the model in a controlled environment, the next step would be using them in real-life situation. To do so, there are some aspects that need to be taken into consideration.

The first aspect to notice is the *changes in hacker vocabulary*. There are some nuances on the semantic meaning, abbreviation, misspelling and even the constant evolution of technical jargons, which require a retraining of model periodically. Another issue notice by Lippmann et al. (2016) is that the model trained within a specific social media does not necessarily have same performance in another social media channel because of the difference within the vocabulary. For instance, there is no guarantee that the model trained with Twitter security-related content will perform well on security-related content extracted from Reedit. However, there are some studies focused on solving this problem. Marin et al. (2018) used genetic algorithms and carefully crafted features for building models that can be trained and tested in different platforms.

The third aspect to consider is regarding *the lack of ground truth dataset* for performing an evaluation of models. The mains goal of a ground truth dataset is providing the cybersecurity researchers the possibility of comparing their findings and improving on that basis. In a data-driven approach, comparisons between models are essential for understanding the efficacy of features of the model. Some researchers are improvising the ground truth dataset with information from other sources. For instance, the authors of Sabottke et al. (2015) did not have a ground truth dataset at the time of the experiment, and as a workaround, they used aggregated information public vulnerabilities/exploit databases (ExploitDB and OS-VDB), vendors and antivirus advisories (Microsoft and Symantec). As in Marin et al. (2018), they used the reputation score metadata (extracted from specific hacker forum) for testing their study. In Benjamin, Zhang, Nunamaker and Chen (2016), they revealed that, because of the lack of ground truth, they needed to verify the output of the model manually to determine the efficacy of their method in finding the key hackers of an IRC chat room.

### *Ethical consideration for using social media in cybersecurity research*

Researchers are using social media as a natural form of collecting information from people and groups of people around the world. Such information, otherwise, would have taken a considerable amount of time and resource to be obtained through traditional methods such as survey and controlled experimentation.

This is not different in cybersecurity research, where researchers are collecting information from hacker forums and online communities. However, some ethical considerations of using this information are not well-discussed within cybersecurity research. The following two questions are used to guide us through this discussion.

In social media platforms such as Facebook and Twitter, there is an explicit agreement (commonly called as contract agreement) that explains to user that their data might be used by third-party companies and research institutions. However, in hacker forums and chat rooms, there is no explicit contract for informing the participants regarding the use of their data. However, in some cases, the agreement through social platform is not a sufficient ethical requirement for the researcher to proceed with its research. According to Boyd and Crawford (2012), researchers need to improve their judgement to decide where they can use this data; ethical compliance cannot be ignored just because the data seem to be public. Despite these issues, the cybersecurity research and the industry continue to use data without appropriated approval. In cybersecurity research, the data are accessed and analyzed without the informed consent of participants, and they are rarely aware of their participation. Acquiring informed consent becomes more problematic as it can be practically impossible with a dataset containing hundreds of data.

## Acknowledgements

Andrei Queiroz Lima would like to thank the scholarship granted by the Brazilian Federal Programme Science without Borders supported by CNPq (Conselho Nacional de Desenvolvimento Científico e Tecnológico), No 201898/2015-2.

## References

Algarni, A. M., & Malaiya, Y. K. (2014). Software vulnerability markets: Discoverers and buyers. World academy of science, engineering and technology. *International Journal of Computer, Electrical, Automation, Control and Information Engineering, 8*(3), 480–490.

Benjamin, V., & Chen, H. (2012). Securing cyberspace: Identifying key actors in hacker communities. In *2012 IEEE international conference on intelligence and security informatic* (pp. 24–29).

Benjamin, V. A., Zhang, B., Nunamaker, J. F., & Chen, H. (2016). Examining hacker participation length in cybercriminal internet-relay-chat communities. *Journal of Management Information Systems, 33*(2), 482–510.

Boyd, D., & Crawford, K. (2012). Critical questions for big data. *Information, Communication and Society*, 662–679.

Bradley, A. P. (1997). The use of the area under the ROC curve in the evaluation of machine learning algorithms. *Pattern Recognition*, 1145–1159.

CrowdFlower. (2016). *Data science report*. https://visit.figure-eight.com/rs/416-ZBE-142/images/CrowdFlower_DataScienceReport_2016.pdf.

Deb, A., Lerman, K., & Ferrara, E. (2018). Predicting cyber events by leveraging hacker sentiment. *arXiv: Computation and Language*.

Giacinto, G., Perdisci, R., Rio, M. D., & Roli, F. (2006). *Intrusion detection in computer networks by a modular ensemble of one-class classifiers* (pp. 69–82).

Juniper Research. (2017). *Cybercrime and the internet of threats 2017*. https://www.juniperresearch.com/resources.

Kelleher, J. D., Namee, B. M., & D'Arcy, A. (2015). *Fundamentals of machine learning for predictive data analytics*. The MIT Press.

Lippmann, R. P., Campbell, J. P., Weller-Fahy, D. J., Mensch, A. C., & Campbell, W. M. (2016). *Finding malicious cyber discussions in social media*. Defense Technical Information Center.

Marin, E., Shakarian, J., & Shakarian, P. (2018). Mining key-hackers on darkweb forums. In *1st international conference on data intelligence and security* (pp. 73–80). IEEE.

Martin, A., Doddington, G., Kamm, T., Ordowski, M., & Przybocki, M. (1997). *The DET curve in assessment of detection task performance*.

Mulwad, V., Li, W., Joshi, A., Finin, T., & Viswanathan, K. (2011). Extracting information about security vulnerabilities from web text. In *Proceedings of the 2011 IEEE/WIC/ACM international conferences on web intelligence and intelligent agent technology* (pp. 257–260). IEEE Computer Society.

Nunes, E., Diab, A., Gunn, A. T., Marin, E., Mishra, V., Paliath, V., et al. (2016). *Darknet and deepnet mining for proactive cybersecurity threat intelligence* (pp. 7–12). Ingénierie Des Systèmes D'information.

Ponemon Institute LLC. (2017). *Cost of cyber crime study*. https://www.ponemon.org/library/2017-cost-of-cyber-crime-study.

Portnoff, R. S., Afroz, S., Durrett, G., Kummerfeld, J. K., Berg-Kirkpatrick, T., McCoy, D., et al. (2017). Tools for automated analysis of cybercriminal markets. In *Proceedings of the 26th international conference on world wide web* (pp. 657–666). International World Wide Web Conferences Steering Committee.

Queiroz, A., Keegan, B., & Mtenzi, F. (2017). Predicting software vulnerability using security discussion in social media. In *European conference on information warfare and security, ECCWS, 2017, Dublin, Ireland*.

Roumani, Y., Nwankpa, J. K., & Roumani, Y. F. (2016). Examining the relationship between firms financial records and security vulnerabilities. *International Journal of Information Management*, 987–994.

Russell, S. J., & Norving, p. (2010). *Artificial intelligence: A modern approach*. Prentice Hall.

Sabottke, C., Suciu, O., & Dumitras, T. (2015). *Vulnerability disclosure in the age of social media: Exploiting twitter for predicting real-world exploits*. Retrieved 8 23, 2018, from https://usenix.org/system/files/conference/usenixsecurity15/sec15-paper-sabottke.pdf.

Sakaki, T., Okazaki, M., & Matsuo, Y. (2010). Tweet analysis for real-time event detection and earthquake reporting system development. *IEEE Transactions on Knowledge and Data Engineering*, 919–931.

Security Focus. (2013). *Bug brokers offering higher bounties*. Security Focus. Retrieved from http://www.securityfocus.com/news/11437.

Shu, K., Sliva, A., Sampson, J., & Liu, H. (2018). *Understanding cyber attack behaviors with sentiment information on social media*. Charles Rivers Analytics. Retrieved from https://www.cra.com/publications/2018sliva1.

Syed, R., Rahafrooz, M., & Keisler, J. M. (2018). What it takes to get retweeted: An analysis of software vulnerability messages. *Computers in Human Behavior, 80*, 207–215.

# Further reading

Almukaynizi, M., Nunes, E., Dharaiya, K., Senguttuvan, M., Shakarian, J., & Shakarian, P. (2017). Proactive identification of exploits in the wild through vulnerability mentions online. In *2017 international conference on cyber conflict (CyCon U.S.)* (pp. 82–88).

Bullough, B. L., Yanchenko, A. K., Smith, C. L., & Zipkin, J. R. (2017). Predicting exploitation of disclosed software vulnerabilities using open-source data. In *Proceedings of the 3rd ACM on international workshop on security and privacy analytics* (pp. 45–53). ACM.

CHAPTER

# 4

# 'Nothing up my sleeve': information warfare and the magical mindset

*K. Scott*

Arts, Design, and Humanities, De Montfort University, Leicester, United Kingdom

OUTLINE



## Introduction: welcome to the desert of the real

> There is nothing wrong with your television set. Do not attempt to adjust the picture. We are controlling transmission. *[Title Sequence,* **The Outer Limits***].*

On Sunday 19 August 2018, Rudy Giuliani, in his capacity as a member of President Trump's legal team, appeared on NBC's *Meet The Press.*


https://doi.org/10.1016/B978-0-12-819204-7.00004-X

Interviewed by Mike Todd about the President's unwillingness to testify to Special Prosecutor Robert Mueller, Giuliani claimed that any such meeting would descend into an argument about the relative veracity of different witnesses. The exchange continued:

> Truth is truth, Todd responded.
>
> No, no, it isn't truth, Giuliani said. "Truth isn't truth. The President of the United States says, "I didn't ..."
>
> A startled Todd answered: "Truth isn't truth"? ***Morin and Cohen (2018).***

Communication of all kinds in the contemporary world is continually challenged by the inability or unwillingness to agree on the nature of 'truth' and/or 'reality'. Giuliani's claim is the logical conclusion of a deliberate political strategy that can be traced back to the administration of George W Bush and Ron Suskind's conversation with an unnamed White House aide (named by Englehardt (2014) as Karl Rove). The staffer challenged Suskind's concern for data and fact-based government:

> The aide said that guys like me were "in what we call the reality-based community," which he defined as people who "believe that solutions emerge from your judicious study of discernible reality." [...] "We're an empire now, and when we act, we create our own reality" ***(Suskind, 2004).***

Dishonesty, in short, is policy. The current (as of time of writing) US administration's polemics against 'fake news' and lauding of 'alternative facts' (a phrase used by Kellyanne Conway on *Meet the Press* on 22 January 2017) should not be seen as an isolated moment, but as part of a continuum of informational disruption (accidental and deliberate) which is present throughout the modern world, above all in the online environment. The cyber domain is no longer an adjunct to everyday human experience; as Adam Greenfield puts it, "Networked digital information technology has become the dominant mode through which we experience the everyday" (Introduction: Paris Year Zero, para. 19). This mode of existence, like any other, is shaped and experienced through a wide range of filters (from the social and cultural to the individual and cognitive), and it is the nature of the distortion (above all the deliberate distortion of perception) which interests me here.

The creation of a global information network has not led to a monoculture, still less a utopia. As Marshall McLuhan said, "[w]hen people get close together, they get more and more savage, impatient with each other ... The global village is a place of very arduous interfaces and very abrasive situations". (McLuhan, 2003, p. 265) Many in established politics are seeking to win the battle for full-spectrum dominance of the information realm; crucially, the nature of the cyber domain is such that dominance is next to impossible to achieve. Vitale (2014) is exactly right when he says "Although all truly *is* becoming one, this new connectedness is far from unitary. Rather, it is fractal, multiplying in layers of burgeoning complexity" (p. 2).

The aim of this discussion is to focus less on the theories of cognition and understanding of cyber on an abstract level and to discuss how these ideas could be and are being used in reality. Whether online existence is or is not changing our individual cognitive processes and social cohesion is as yet unknown; as with any new technology, there have been no shortage of works claiming that it does and overwhelmingly for the worse (see, inter alia, Bartlett, 2018; Carr, 2010; Keen, 2015; Lanier, 2010; Loh & Kanai, 2016; Mills, 2016; Storm, Stone & Benjamin, 2016). What cannot be denied is that the growth of the Internet as a global communications medium and the proliferation of devices permitting near-constant, ubiquitous traffic have acted as a force multiplier for many actors (individual, state and nonstate) to spread influence which is clearly deeply harmful to the social fabric, politics and the smooth running of the commonwealth. More than this, the growing use of algorithmically driven news feeds on social media magnifies the 'filter bubble' effect, limiting access to information that may challenge our preconceptions and prejudices (Liao & Fu, 2013; Spohr, 2017). Add to this the deliberate manipulation of the opinions of such groups as these by hostile actors, capitalizing on public resentment of and distrust in mainstream media and political parties, and the potential for serious damage to the body politic is there. I am primarily focussing here on communicative influence deployed in a military context, not just because this offers a clearly defined terrain of investigation but also because 'warfare' in the modern era exemplifies the challenges of operating in an online world. The military use of influence presents a series of baseline operating procedures for dealing with the wide range of cognitive approaches used on those who live in the nonmartial sphere, if such a sphere actually exists. As will be shown in the next section, the idea of 'war' as a clearly defined and distinct sphere of human activity is both outmoded and inaccurate. In 2016, Rosa Brooks published *How Everything Became War and the Military Became Everything*, a brilliant study of the ways in which traditional boundaries between 'war' and 'peace' and civilian and military spheres have blurred. Issues such as trolling, phishing and defacement of websites are no longer solely peacetime issues; they are tools used by forces that see soft power belonging as much to the military arsenal as any more traditional ordnance. Conflict in the Information Age takes many forms and employs strategies and tactics deliberately designed to influence the enemy's cognition. From PSY-OPS to the activities of 4Chan's '/b/tards' or the 'troll army' of the Russian Internet Research Agency is no step at all. This, then, is an introductory exercise in mapping the general contours of the informational landscape in which our interest lies. What follows is an investigation of the ways in which these general trends have manifested in one very specific sphere of human activity, namely warfare. Firstly, because this represents the limit case of human misunderstanding and, secondly, because, as this chapter seeks to emphasize, the boundaries between 'war' and 'not war' have become so porous as to be nonexistent.

## From bullets to bytes: war in the information age

How do you fight in a place you can't see? ***(Sanger (2018), p. 12.)***

The nature of war has never been straightforward; as Van Puyvelde (2015) states, "[w]arfare, whether it be ancient or modern, hybrid or not, is always complex and can hardly be subsumed into a single adjective". All human activity is always interpreted or given 'meaning' within a complex set of interreacting cognitive and intellectual frameworks, both individual and cultural, which have been formed by experience, education and ideology. 'War' is confined and constrained within a tradition of theoretical, moral and legal definitions (inter alia 'just war' theory, the concepts of the *ius in bello* and the *ius ad bellum*, the Geneva Conventions); problems arise when we are confronted by those who do not engage in armed conflict according to these norms. The monolithic concept of 'war' has fragmented into an endlessly proliferating series of subcategories — 'Police Actions', 'Peacekeeping', 'Operations Other Than War', 'Asymmetric Warfare' and, the neologism, 'Hybrid Warfare'. For those of us interested both in the true nature of conflict in the modern era and in the wider issues of the cyber domain, we must add another, vital, term: 'Information Warfare' (IW).

Defining the exact nature of IW is a challenging exercise; Marlatt (2008) presents a wide range of texts grappling with the problem. Hutchinson (2006) offers an admirably clear overview of the evolution of the field, drawing together information from a span of different disciplines, showing it to be a truly hybrid form, blending "psychological operations, military deception, operations security, counterintelligence, public affairs and counter-propaganda" (p. 217). What should be noted is that in recent years, the deployment of IW methods in the cyber realm has become one of the main strategic elements of modern combat. Writing in 1995, Libicki dismissed 'cyberwarfare' as 'a grab bag of futuristic scenarios' (p. x); no military thinker writing today would make such a statement.

IW seeks to apply a blended methodology to impair an enemy's ability to conduct operations through the application of techniques acting on the physical, technical and mental environment (an excellent summary of the aims, approaches and targets of Electronic and Information Warfare is given in Graubert, Bodea, and McQuaid (2018). In the past, Information

Operations have drawn on such traditional methods as propaganda (whether 'black', grey' or 'white') – broadcasts, leaflet drops, the playing of music across the battlefield, etc. – but the introduction of IT and digitally mediated communication (DMC) acted as a true game changer. Not only can information be distributed near instantaneously and ubiquitously (and revised and retransmitted more rapidly), it can also be delivered across a wide range of platforms in a way which best targets the specific weaknesses of the enemy. IW is no longer an adjunct to, but a central tool of, warfare. The military has always appreciated the importance of (even if it has often failed to win) 'hearts and minds'; the history of IW shows a growing awareness of the value and power of what Valley and Aquino (1980) dub 'MindWar', a form of cognitive combat which, in their words, "conducts wars in nonlethal, noninjurious and nondestructive ways (p. 3)".

This vision of IW as "nonlethal, noninjurious and nondestructive" is utopian and does not represent the way in which these tactics have been deployed to date, from black propaganda in the Ukraine to the use of 'doxxing' and trolling by the denizens of 4Chan. However, it does represent a significant shift away from kinetic conflict into the mental sphere and an attempt to engage in what Szafranski (1997) rather grandly terms 'neocortical warfare'. His study begins with a straightforward premise that "[t]he object of war is, quite simply, to force or encourage the enemy to make what you assert is a better choice, or to choose what *you* desire the enemy to choose" (p. 397). Traditional warfare achieves this aim through the exercise of physical force or the threat thereof (consider the Cold War doctrine of Mutually Assured Destruction). For Szafranski, the aim is to overcome the enemy in an entirely nonkinetic manner:

> Neocortical warfare [...] strives to present the adversary's leaders—its collective brain—with perceptions, sensory and cognitive data designed to result in a narrow and controlled (or an overwhelmingly large and disorienting) range of calculations and evaluations. (p. 404)

Szafranski is vague as to the actual means by which his stated goals may be achieved, but it must be remembered that he was writing at a time when online influence as a tool was effectively nonexistent. The Web as an environment open to the general public was barely 6 years old, and the major social networking sites had still to be created (MySpace in 2003, FaceBook in 2004, Twitter in 2006 and WhatsApp in 2009). The single greatest development in IW (and conflict in general) has been the growth of cyber, the so-called 'Fifth Domain' of warfare (after land, sea, air and space).

Warfare today is fundamentally a blended entity, making use of at least three forms of power – hard, soft and smart; those engaged in it at a practical and interpretative level should look to other domains of human activity to operate more effectively. In the general cyber domain, we must look beyond technology to consider the human factors that act on the combatants (anthropological, cultural and ideological). In the realm of Information Warfare (IW), we must reflect that 'information' itself is a complex concept, processed and defined as significant within predefined mental frameworks, which are not of necessity universal. My aim here is to investigate how IW works within the cognitive frameworks of an enemy, hindering their effective operations, to engage in 'perception management', in line with the definition of the term laid down by the American Department of Defense:

> Actions to convey and/or deny selected information and indicators to foreign audiences to influence their emotions, motives, and objective reasoning as well as to intelligence systems and leaders at all to influence official estimates, ultimately resulting in foreign behaviors and official actions favorable to the originator's objectives in Combelles Siegel (2007, p. 28).

Cyber warfare has been defined by the US military as follows:

> The employment of cyberspace capabilities to destroy, deny, degrade, disrupt, deceive, corrupt or usurp the adversaries ability to use the cyberspace domain for his advantage. ***(Department of the Air Force, 2012, p. 2).***

The role played by IW as a central element of this process is all too clear. The modern military must be ready to fight wars on the physical terrain, but the use of DMC-transmitted IW operations requires the development of a set of skills that have previously been seen as the purview of the journalist, the politician and the advertising executive. The challenges faced by these professions in an age where mainstream media and politics appear to be losing influence rapidly mirror the challenges faced by the military. Jamais Cascio has argued that "the mobile phone is, in many respects, the AK-47 of the 21st Century" (CM Films, 2014), and the proliferation of connectivity and tools for information distribution and manipulation, as well as tools for disrupting the smooth flow of information networks (malware, botnets, etc.), has in effect handed every online individual their own informational machine gun:

> Cyberspace has empowered individuals and small groups of non-state actors to do many things, including executing sophisticated computer network operations that were previously only the domain of state intelligence agencies. We have entered the era of *do-it-yourself* (DIY) signals intelligence. ***(SecDev Group & Munk Centre for International Studies, 2009, p. 47).***

In his excellent study of the evolution of IW, *War in 140 Characters*, David Patrikarakos argues that there has been a fundamental shift in the nature of information production and consumption, from the one-to-many model of traditional mass media to the age of the active and reactive producer–consumer, and a similar process has occurred in warfare. The idea of set piece engagements by massed forces of opposing nation states has been replaced by asymmetric conflict across the martial and orthodox political spheres. The rise of what Patrikanos dubs *Homo digitalis* (the 'digital native', existing as much in cyberspace as the nonvirtual world) allows IW to act as an ever-greater tool of influence. Based on his own experiences in Ukraine, where online misinformation was deployed both within and beyond the country's borders (CSS Cyber Defense Project, 2017; Jaitner, 2015), he argues that modern warfare must be seen as an inevitable combination of kinetic and nonkinetic combat, with IW as one of the key weapons in the arsenal. His conclusions are simple, but deeply challenging. Firstly, the war of words (IW) may matter more than traditional conflict; 'the narrative dimensions of war are arguably becoming more important than its physical dimensions' (Introduction, para. 13). Secondly, we (and this refers both to soldiers and citizens, for both are potential victims of IW)

> [...] are in need of a new conceptual framework that takes into account how social media has transformed the way that wars are waged, covered, and consumed. We need to better understand this twenty-first-century war. ***(Introduction, para. 12)***

As with warfare, so with wider issues of human interaction in cyberspace; a central argument here is that the military realm has much to learn from the nonmartial domain, and vice versa (and indeed, that the boundary between the two domains has collapsed), and if we want to understand how the nature of conflict has evolved in recent years, then there is one area that we can and must study. The use of social media as a platform for IW operations in the Ukraine has already been discussed, but this merely reflects the way in which Russian military thinking has a long tradition of engaging in cognitive conflict, based on the sustained use of deception and misinformation. This strategic approach must be examined, as it represents what may well become central to all future conflicts, regardless of the combatants.

Throughout the 20th century, Russian strategic theory has seen *maskirovka* ('masking' or 'camouflage', the term is now taken to cover all forms of deception) as an essential tool of combat; recent operations in the Ukraine and Crimea have seen this elevated to a central position. From simple denial of manifest activity to the use of 'false flag' actions and the highly skilful use of mass postings on social media to engage in perception management, the Russians have shown themselves to be infinitely more adept at IW in the modern era than Western forces (Hickman, 2015; Keating, 1981; Krueger, 1987; Lindley-French, 2015; Moeller, 2014;

Schillinger, 2018). However, in recent years, we have seen a significant evolution in their thinking, marked by the development of what has come to be known as the 'Gerasimov Doctrine'. In February 2012, General Valery Vasilyevich Gerasimov, Russia's Chief of the General Staff, published an article in the Russian *Military-Industrial Kurier* entitled (in translation) 'The Value of Science Is in the Foresight: New Challenges Demand Rethinking the Forms and Methods of Carrying out Combat Operations' (Gerasimov, 2016), in which he argues that the future of warfare lies in a combat which is both kinetic and nonkinetic, fought 'simultaneously in all physical environments and the information space' (Bartles, 2016, p. 36). This leads to "a battlefield war that merges conventional attacks, terror, economic coercion, propaganda, and, most recently, cyber" (Sanger, 2018, p. 156). Of even greater concern is that this model sees 'combat' as not restricted to a physical battlefield or a strictly delineated zone of 'war' as previously conceived; hybrid warfare is continual, omnipresent, insidious, all-pervasive and, in many cases, utterly deniable (as cyberattacks and IW in general are all too often impossible to attribute with absolute accuracy, posing huge problems for a force seeking to retaliate). There are debates as to whether the 'Gerasimov doctrine' actually exists as a clearly defined strategic position (Galeotti, 2018; McDermott, 2016), but the wholesale use of misinformation and online perception management is clearly seen to be a tool of Russian political influence in the Western world, most notably in the activities of the so-called 'troll farm' of the St. Petersburg-based 'Internet Research Agency', which has been shown to be active in seeking to destabilize American and European political activity (Chen, 2015; MacFarquhar, 2018). This does not of course represent a truly new development; what is significant is the way in which online DMC allows a rapid and resource light means of multiplying the power of IW. Russian IW has also introduced the growth of applied confusion as a tool of control, driven by the figure of Vladislav Surkov, a man who (it is suggested) has weaponized the strategies of audience manipulation and influence found in conceptual art and theatre to become what Peter Pomerantsev (2011) calls "Putin's Rasputin".

If we believe even a small amount of what has been written on Surkov (inter alia Milam, 2018; Millard, 2018; Pomerantsev, 2011, 2014a, 2014b, 2014c; Yourgrau, 2018), then he has shown himself to be a preternaturally gifted political operator, who has devised an entirely new model of conflict, war which is not only hybrid but also 'nonlinear' (a term taken from a science fiction story he published pseudonymously in 2014). This form of conflict relies on confusion and uncertainty and the deliberate use of carefully seeded 'information' which seems to come from all points on the political spectrum. Pomerantsev (2014a) describes how this operates in the Russian domestic sphere:

> it climbs inside all ideologies and movements, exploiting and rendering them absurd. [...] The Kremlin's idea is to own all forms of political discourse, to not let any independent movements develop outside of its walls.

Such an approach has two goals; firstly, to 'own' all areas of political discourse and, secondly (and crucially), to provoke confusion and cognitive overload – it becomes impossible for an individual or group bombarded by a multiplicity of rapidly proliferating conflicting messages to determine which, if any, represents a source of untainted 'truth'. In such a situation, the figure of a strong determined leader, embodying a monolithic, uncomplicated message of national renewal and defiance of external threats, becomes all the more attractive. The recent plans to construct a Russia-only national Internet walled off from the rest of the world will also increase the state's ability to flood the information environment with contradiction and uncertainty and reduce any possibility of promulgating a strong counternarrative to combat such misinformation (Ristolainen, 2017).

If we examine the online world beyond Russia's borders, we can see that the Surkovian model of confusing quasi-ludic DMC as a tool of influence is becoming widespread. Social media is being used as a platform for disseminating messages which attack specific political belief systems through the deliberate application of the Trumpian bugbear of 'fake news' (Gu, Kropotov, & Yarochkin, 2017) and also for more general attacks on established pillars of Western thought, which chip away at the fabric of consensus reality. Broniatowski et al. (2018) provide clear examples of a coordinated Russian trolling campaign against vaccination, building on the current trend of disbelief in establishment values (and arguably poses a significant threat to Western public health). Platforms such as Twitter create a discourse space made up of claim and counterclaim, where the use of automated bots and coordinated trolling and inaccuracy leave us unable to determine what, if anything, is the most valid opinion (Chamberlain, 2010). An excellent case study in this process of cognitive disruption can be seen in what happened following a posting on Twitter by the British journalist Carole Cadwalladr.

On 19 July 2018, Cadwalladr posted a retweet from a Russian government feed and commented:

> Unbelievable. Russian ministry of foreign affairs changes its profile photo to **#FreeMariaButina.** This is war. You realise this, right? It's a troll war. But it's still war. It's what war looks like now. ***(Cadwalladr, 2018).***

Maria Butina is a Russian citizen who was arrested in 2018 on suspicion of being a Russian agent seeking to develop channels of influence within the Republican Party and such groups as the National Rifle Organization (Clifton & Folliman, 2018).[1] By choosing to publicize her case, the Ministry of Foreign Affairs is both presenting her as a victim and arguably flagging up the extent to which Russia can intervene in American domestic politics – this tweet is designed to be read very differently within and beyond Russia. Cadwalladr is exactly right to state that this is "what war looks like now"; it is a clear attempt to exert influence and present to a global audience the idea of America imprisoning an 'innocent' Russian citizen. However, Cadwalladr's tweet was picked up on and furiously rebutted by the website offGuardian.org, which posted a string of images of bombed-out buildings and wounded civilians to present what they claim is 'real' war and dismiss her comments as the bleatings of a member of the liberal intelligentsia:

> Words cannot express the smallness of the mind and the gargantuan scale of the ego that shat those words into the world, fully expecting them to be taken seriously. *("No, Caroline Cadwalladr", 2018).*

This cannot be accepted unconditionally for a number of reasons. Firstly, we know that IW exists and has been and is being employed by Russia. Secondly, if we examine the examples OffGuardian presents of 'real war', they are *all* of actions committed by the US, UK, and allied powers. Finally, OffGuardian itself cannot be seen as a neutral source; it is clearly presenting a pro-Russian agenda. However, we cannot at first sight determine whether it is being deliberately used as a front for deliberate pro-Russian influence or if it is simply a 'fellow traveller'.

An observer skimming over the material presented in response to Cadwalladr's comment could easily be led to dismiss her opinion, and there is evidence to suggest that the consumption of online text leads to a reduction in critical thinking skills and analysis (Baron, 2015; Dillon, 1992; Mangen, Robinet, Olivier, & Velay, 2014); such a medium offers a perfect environment for manipulation. Twitter, like all social media platforms, offers a huge range of opinion but offers no effective tools for weighing the veracity and trustworthiness of any of the postings; it is, in short, the perfect environment for the forms of cognitive warfare examined here.

Given this state of affairs, the key question is simple; as Lenin put it, 'What is to be done?' We are faced with the following situation:

1. 'information' (by which is meant 'material seen as meaningful within the interpretative frameworks of the target audience') is open to manipulation and presentation in a way which can influence that target audience.

[1] On 13 December 2018, Butina entered a plea of guilty to the charge of conspiracy to act as an agent of a foreign government; she also agreed to cooperate with prosecustors to reduce her sentence (Smith, 2018).

2. DMC is, as Darczewska (2014) puts it, "cheap, it is a universal weapon, it has unlimited range, it is easily accessible and permeates all state borders without restrictions" (p. 7). It is, in short, a highly effective force multiplier for Information Operations.
3. Modern 'warfare' is a blended entity, operating kinetically and nonkinetically, often outside the traditional zones of war.
4. To respond to such a situation, a blended approach is essential; we should look for other examples beyond warfare of the deliberate manipulation of a target audience's perceptual frameworks to see what can be learnt from them.

In 2013, the NSA released a previously classified history of American cryptography (Burke, 2002) and entitled *It Wasn't All Magic: The Early Struggle to Automate Cryptanalysis, 1930s–1960s*. While the title is a clear reference to the wartime MAGIC codebreaking program (Leonard, 2013), my argument here is that for future cyber conflict, IW operations and life in the online realm in general, we should think less about MAGIC and more about 'magic'. In a world where deception and misdirection are ever-more common tools of perception management, we need to examine how they have been deployed in previous conflicts, not just within the domain of traditional PSY-OPS campaigns. We must also consider learning from the example of those for whom deception is stock in trade or an essential part of their modus operandi. We need, in short, to consider the realm of the professional illusionist.

## 'Pay no attention to the man behind the curtain' – magic, misdirection and 'misinformation warfare'

> The field of magic possesses a rich hoard of esoteric, utilitarian and, to-date, largely untapped knowledge about influence and deception that could make a positive contribution across multiple security domains. ***(Henderson, 2018).***

On 4 June 1903, John Ambrose Fleming and Gugliemo Marconi were presenting a demonstration of wireless telegraphy (Caravan Coop, 2017; Gingerich, 2017). Marconi had previously claimed that his radio transmissions were entirely secure from interception and monitoring, and the British military were becoming interested in the new medium. As Ambrose was ending his demonstration at the Royal Academy of Science, a series of Morse transmissions began to come through on the supposedly secure channel:

> Fleming's assistant translated the Morse Code, as it repeatedly tapped out the word "rats". Eventually "rats" gave way to the message "There was a young fellow of Italy [i.e., Marconi], who diddled the public quite prettily", followed by Shakespeare quotes, and even accusations that Marconi had slept with the sender's wife. ***(Gingerich, 2017).***

The person responsible for this breach of Marconi's (nonexistent) security protocols soon identified himself to the general public; it was Nevil Maskelyne, an employee of the Eastern Telegraphic Company, who stood to lose out from the wholesale adoption of wireless over cable-carried telegraphy. He was also a member of the Maskelyne dynasty of illusionists and as such possessed both a high degree of technical skill and a knowledge of the power of the grand effect. He had previously discussed the lack of security of Marconi's system in a 1902 article in *The Electrician*, but he realised that to really make his point, he needed to impress and create a startling and memorable event.

The greatest challenge of warfare is a continual struggle against the unknown: "three quarters of the factors which action in war is based are wrapped in a fog of greater or lesser uncertainty" (Von Clausewitz, 1989, p. 101). The aim of IW is to use a range of techniques to maximize the 'fog of war' and as such must rest on the key principles of *concealment* and *deception* to ensure that the opponent is left in state of confusion and ignorance as to the true state of play. Proctor and Schiebinger (2008) use the term *agnotology* to describe the study of the ways in which ignorance occurs and (crucially) can be deliberately engineered, arguing that the study of "the historicity and artifactuality of nonknowing and the non-known" (p. 27) is a valuable tool in revealing the ways in which information can be deliberately misrepresented. IW is by its very nature agnotology in action the deliberate cultivation of ignorance as a tool of conflict. We need to consider not just what the enemy knows but what he *thinks* he knows.

Major General J.F.C. Fuller was an early proponent of warfare based on mechanization, mobility and penetration (Heinz Guderian, the German general who pioneered the *blitzkrieg* doctrine, paid to have Fuller's *Provisional Instructions for Tank and Armoured Car Training* translated into German). In *The Foundations of the Science of War*, Fuller outlines the ways in which an enemy's operations may be disrupted, based on the fundamental idea that there is an interpretative gap in an individual" between the objective in his mind and the object which confronts him (Fuller, 1926, p. 221). The issue of the enemy's perception is key, and the way in which altering that perception in effect alters their reality. Human beings, trapped in their cognitive and cultural frames, are all-too ready to forget that "the map is not the territory" (Korzybski, 1931); IW, like all human activity, occurs in informational space, and by altering the nature of the 'information' for a target audience, we effectively rework their reality (as our conception of reality rests on what we perceive). 'Magic' in the occult sense seeks to rework reality through the application of will ("MAGICK is the Science and Art of causing Change to occur in conformity with Will"

(Crowley, 2004, p. xii[2]); IW reworks the perception of reality through the application of misdirection and manipulation of the 'information' the opponent possesses. If we wish to develop our abilities to deceive an opponent (or defend against such deception), then we should turn to those for whom technical skill, psychological knowledge and an ability to create a coherent, convincing and altogether inaccurate picture of reality are essential and turn from 'Magick' to magic and professional illusionists who

> lie by the very nature of what they do ... Magicians lie about their origin, their nationality, their education. They lie about what they are doing onstage when they say they are putting the ball under the cup or in the pocket. ***(Mangan, 2007, p. xix).***

An examination of the history of warfare and intelligence shows a clear thread of cooperation between illusionists and the military and a readiness by the latter to adopt and coopt the methods of the former. In 1856, the French engaged the leading magician of the day, Robert-Houdin, to defuse a rebellion in Algeria led by the Marabout warrior mystics; he used conjuring to demonstrate that the French had supernatural powers (Robert-Houdin, 1860). Through dummy bullets he showed that he could resist gunfire, and an electromagnet in a box appeared to strip a rebel of his strength (and delivered an electric shock for good measure). Closer to the present day, Jasper Maskelyne (the son of the Marconi-confounding Nevil Maskelyne) worked with Dudley Clarke, one of the great figures in the history of military deception (Howard, 1992; Rankin, 2009), during the Western Desert campaign, to construct

> dummy men, dummy steel helmets, dummy guns by the 10000, dummy tanks, dummy shell flashes by the million, dummy aircraft, [ ...] making such a colossal hotchpotch of illusion and trickery as has never been accumulated in the word before. ***(Forbes, 2009, p. 158).***

The Americans made use of similar tactics (and men who had learned their skills as theatrical designers and set painters) when they established the 23rd Special Headquarters Troops (Beyer, 2013). Later, during the Cold War, the CIA engaged the illusionist John Mulholland to train their operatives in the skills of sleight of hand to enable them to conceal and pass on microfilm or slip a pill into someone's drink (Melton & Wallace, 2009).

What might be termed a 'magical mindset' has much to offer the field of IW, and a growing body of academic study has begun to examine magical techniques of deception, misdirection and subverting human

[2] With almost eerie synchronicity, it should be noted that Fuller was a devoted disciple of Crowley and wrote one of the earliest studies of the latter's Magic(k)al practices (Fuller, 1907).

perception. In Performance Studies, Nik Taylor discusses the subgenre of 'Bizarre Magic', which creates disturbing and immersive events playing on all the audience's senses to unsettle them (Minch, 2009; Taylor, 2013, 2014, 2015). Two examples of what might be termed 'Weaponized Bizarre Magic' are the use of the mythic figure of the Filipino *aswang* (equivalent to a vampire) by Edward R Lansdale during his campaign against Huk insurgents in the early 1950s (Lansdale, 1991, pp. 72–3) and the claims that the British Army spread rumours of Satanism in Northern Ireland in the 1970s as part of a sustained PSY-OPS campaign (Jenkins, 2014).

The psychological underpinnings of magic have been examined by a number of cognitive scientists as a means to understanding the limits of human reasoning (Demacheva, Ladouceur, Steinberg, Pogossova, & Raz, 2012; Kuhn, Amlani, & Rensink, 2008; Kuhn et al., 2014; Macknik, King, Randi, Robbins, Teller, Thompson, et al., 2008; Macknik, Martinez-Conde, & Blakeslee, 2011); their researches are a starting point for the consideration of what magic can bring to work on human factors in IW.

Magic is based on effect, method and performance (the way in which the effect and method are presented). Macknik et al. (2008) develop a taxonomy of fundamental magical effects: (Table 4.1 below).

A challenge for future research will be to see how many of these effects can be mapped neatly onto the domain of IW in the cyber realm. Some initial observations are found in Henderson (2018) and Henderson, Hoffmann, Bunch and Bradshaw (2015). These effects are produced through the application of a series of fundamental techniques (AVM, 2015; Lehrer, 2009; Table 4.2 below):

**TABLE 4.1** Types of conjuring effects.

| |
|---|
| Appearance: an object appears 'as if by magic' |
| Vanish: An object disappears 'as if by magic' |
| Transposition: An object changes position in space from position A to position B |
| Restoration: An object is damaged and then restored to its original condition |
| Penetration: Matter seems to magically move through matter transformation: An object changes form (size, colour, shape, weight, etc.) |
| Extraordinary feats: (Including mental and physical feats) |
| Telekinesis: 'Magical' levitation or animation of an object |
| Extrasensory perception (ESP): Including clairvoyance, telepathy, precognition, mental control, etc.) |

*Credit: Adapted from Macknik, S.L., et al., (2008). Attention and awareness in stage magic: Turning tricks into research.* Nature Reviews Neuroscience, *9(11), pp. 874.*

TABLE 4.2 The seven fundamental techniques of magic.

| |
|---|
| Palm: to hold an object in an apparently empty hand. |
| Ditch: To secretly dispose of an unneeded object. |
| Steal: To secretly obtain a needed object. |
| Load: To secretly move a needed object to where it is hidden. |
| Simulation: To give the impression that something that hasn't happened, has. |
| Misdirection: To lead attention away from a secret move. |
| Switch: To secretly exchange one object for another. |

*Credit: Adapted from Lehrer, J. (2009). Magic and the brain: Teller reveals the neuroscience of illusion.* Wired. *https://www.wired.com/2009/04/ff-neuroscienceofmagic/.*

It is easy to see how actions such as the delivery of malware, phishing emails, spoofing and exfiltration of data map neatly onto these, while a more sustained use of deception and cognitive misdirection is seen in the growing use of so-called 'dark patterns', websites which are deliberately designed in such a way as to mislead and confound a user's good intentions (Brignull, 2011; Singer, 2016).

The techniques are tied together through the *performance* of the illusion in such a way that the spectator is misled as to the processes at work, through the deliberate manipulation of psychological factors that actively prevent them from accurately determining what is going on. Misdirection involves issues of framing and priming and the use of attention blindness to focus an audience's perception where the illusionist wishes it to be, secure in the knowledge that this will limit their situational awareness (Quirkology, 2012; Simons & Chabris, 1999). These are merely elements of the full range of techniques of misdirection magic employs as standard and which Kuhn et al. (2014) group into three main types, manipulating

**a.** Perception: Preventing a spectator from accurately observing what is happening.
**b.** Memory: The spectator is actively led to misremember what they observed.
**c.** Reasoning: The spectator is led to a false conclusion regarding how the illusion was performed.

Their study provides a detailed taxonomy of the forms of misdirection employed in magic: (See Fig. 4.1 below)

These principles, and the various techniques outlined above, give us a basic framework for magic as a tool of deception and misinformation; there is, however, one further essential factor. As Nelms (2003) states, "As the object of the effect is to convince the spectators, their interpretation of

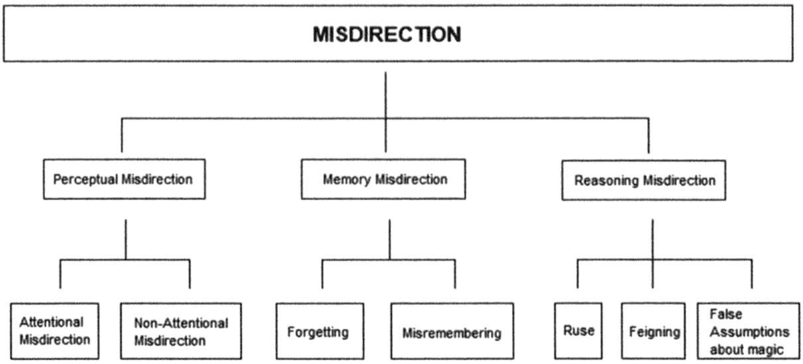


**FIGURE 4.1** A psychologically based taxonomy of misdirection. *Credit: Kuhn, G., et al., (2014). A psychologically-based taxonomy of misdirection.* Frontiers in Psychology, *5(1392), pp. 7.*

the evidence is the only thing that counts" (p. 101). If the techniques and effects used are regarded with suspicion by the target audience, any attempt at influence will fail. For information warfare to be effective, the methods employed must be seen as valid and convincing by the target(s); to maximize the verisimilitude of the intended effects, knowledge of culture and ideology will be vital. Cyber is always a human science. As Lamont and Wiseman (1999) state,

> The performance of magic employs a method (how the trick works) to produce an effect (what the spectator perceives). Success requires that the spectator experience the effect while being unaware of the method (p. 1)

Dariel Fitzkee, an important figure in the development of the theory of magical performance, reinforces this when he writes "Interpretation remains construction in the light of individual interest regardless of the specific reason" (Fitzkee, 2009; Chapter XXXIII, para. 17); it is not so much what the performer says or does that matters, it is what the audience perceives (returning us to the point made previously in a military context by Fuller). This is of vital importance when considering the use of these techniques in IW; as 'information' is meaningful only within a specific context, so we must always be first and foremost concerned with the interpretative frameworks which shape the intended targets of an Information Operation.

In his study of IW, Hutchinson (2006, p. 218) states that "for a successful deception there must be an objective (to measure your success by), a target audience (to choose the applicable means of deception), a story (as a vehicle for the deception), and a means" (see Fig. 4.2 below). Magic, with its emphasis on a convincing immersive performance, offers an ideal framework within which to employ the various techniques he discusses.

It should be noted that I am not outlining how to conduct a 'Magical IW' campaign, as the approach taken will depend entirely on the context in which it is to operate. A number of points have already been made concerning analogues in the cyber realm for the techniques employed in classical magic performance, but it is possible to draw a number of further comparisons. A target-centred, context-driven strategic framework (the starting point for all successful magic) will determine which of Hutchinson's deceptive tactics would be appropriate; a counterradicalization operation would employ the targeted use of misleading social media (Tsikerdekis & Zeadally, 2014), while an operation against hacking might make use of honeypots (Nicholson, 2015) as a means of logging intruders' IP addresses and/or for the delivery of defensive/offensive malware. Similarly, the use of deliberately deceptive 'dark design' (Brignull, 2011; Gawley, 2013) enables the control of a user's interaction with a website through a manipulative interface. As a general tool, the deliberate use of deceptive signals traffic (in terms of volume, direction and apparent sender/receiver) would also seem essential; Riser's (2001) argument that "There are no legal or constructive uses for implementing spoofing of any type" (1) does not apply in combat. Viewed from a magical standpoint, these approaches are IW analogues for such fundamental techniques of illusion as the palm, load, simulation, misdirection and switch (see Table 4.2 above, Fig. 4.2 below).

The aim of IW, and of IW within the framework of magic as discussed here, is to use whatever means are most effective in creating a coherent, apparently genuine scenario within which deception can operate. As Michael Weber puts it in *Our Magic* (Dan & Dave, England, & Wilson, 2014), "magic may be, at its highest and best [...] just another form of storytelling. And a fundamental truth I believe of storytelling, is that whoever tells the best story wins". Casebeer and Russell (2005) argue that narrative is an essential tool of conflict; magic and magicians offer us a wealth of skill and proven expertise in constructing immersive convincing stories for packaging deception, misdirection and misinformation.

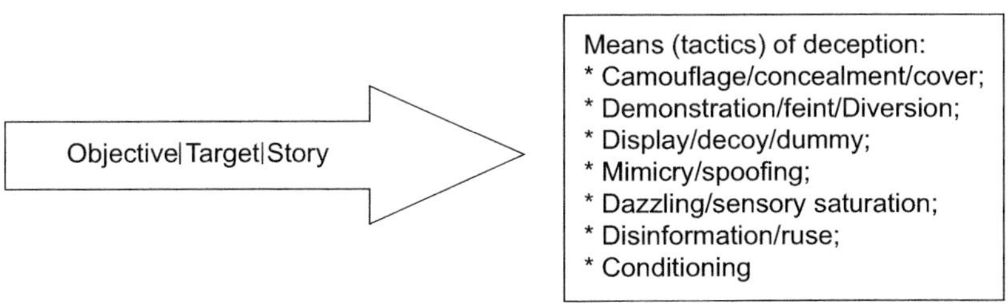


**FIGURE 4.2** The deception planning process. *Credit: Hutchinson, W. (2006). Information warfare and deception.* Informing Science, *9, pp. 218.*

We have now seen how influence operations have become a central element of modern warfare and how 'combat' in this domain involves both military and civilian 'combatants/targets'. The history of military deception has been shown to be closely linked to magic and illusion, and the underlying cognitive factors underlying a successful magic trick have been shown to map onto aspects of cyber. Our challenge for the future will be to learn from the past and prepare for what the future may bring.

## Conclusion: a hogwarts for the cyber domain?

[...] who overcomes/By force, hath overcome but half his foe. ***Milton,* Paradise Lost, *Book I, ll. 648–9.***

The motto of the UK Magic Circle is the Latin phrase *indocilis privata loqui* ('incapable of revealing secrets'). Whatever else he may have done, Edward Snowden has broken the fundamental rules of both intelligence and magic; he has revealed how the tricks are performed. Among his disclosures was a document purporting to be a PowerPoint presentation from the United Kingdom, outlining IW and PSY-OPS strategies (Bell, 2015; Rose, 2014). According to Rose (2014), one of the slides contains the phrase "We want to build Cyber *Magicians*". If this is *not* a key element of the UK and US IW strategy, it *should* be. More than that, it also offers a perfect starting point for any and all future discussions of cybersecurity and the role of cognition within the domain. Magic blends technology, techniques and tactics to manipulate and mislead; it is a hybrid art that has been employed throughout the history of 'conventional' and 'traditional' warfare; as conflict in information space becomes ever more important, we face the challenge of how best to wage war in this sphere. Stupples (2015) claims that "The next war will be an information war, and we're not ready for it"; if we are to be prepared for coming conflicts, we must consider drawing inspiration from as many possible sources as possible. In J.K. Rowling's *Harry Potter* series, the young wizards attend the magical academy at Hogwarts; those engaged in cyber warfare will need to hone their own skills in 'Defence Against the Dark Arts'. Developing a knowledge of the creative, imaginative and deceptive techniques of magic will be an essential aspect of their education by encouraging them to innovate, adopt and adapt ideas and approaches from a field which, as has been argued here, provides the perfect skill set for future combat in the Fifth Domain.

Andy Ozment of the Department of Homeland Security has argued that "cyber attackers come in five types: 'vandals, burglars, thugs, spies and saboteurs' (Sanger, 2018, p. 2). As a taxonomy of cyber threat actors, this is arguably inadequate; it focuses on *who* they are, rather than the issues of *what* they do and *how* they do it. In Lawrence Miles' (2002) words, puts it, "The enemy isn't a single species, or even a distinct political faction. [...] The enemy is a *process*." (p. 55). And that process is grounded in the techniques of perception management and cognitive manipulation that owe their origin to the field of Information Warfare. If we are to operate successfully as combatants or traders in, or citizens of, the cyber domain, we will need to understand how these techniques work and learn from the applied psychologists and anthropologists who employ them, not in the laboratory or the lecture theatre but on the stage. As the more-commonly mute Teller (2012) puts it:

> Magic is an art, as capable of beauty as music, painting or poetry. But the core of every trick is a cold, cognitive experiment in perception: Does the trick fool the audience? A magician's data sample spans centuries, and his experiments have been replicated often enough to constitute near-certainty.

A knowledge of cognitive psychology is essential, but that knowledge must be grounded in the ways in which it can be operationalized; we need to consider not just the theories but also their application, and the magician is one of the best examples of a nonclinical practitioner of applied cognitive psychology. The purpose of this study has been to move from an introductory overview of the current state of affairs as regards the widespread use of IW beyond the traditional realm of military affairs and to argue that to best respond to the widespread use of techniques of perception management in an online world, we should raw on the experience of illusionists as subject matter experts. In an interconnected society, we have need of interdisciplinary approaches.

The number of actors seeking to 'destroy, deny, degrade, disrupt, deceive, corrupt or usurp' our ability to operate effectively in cyberspace is proliferating; if we are to defend ourselves against them, it is time to follow the example of the professional illusionist and begin to wage the Wizard Wars.

## References


AVM. (2015). *Penn and Teller 7 principles of magic.* http://www.youtube.com/watch?v=8S8Peh9XH70.

Baron, N. (2015). *Words onscreen: The fate of reading in a digital world.* Oxford: Oxford University Press.

Bartles, C. K. (2016). Getting Gerasimov right. *Military Review*, 30–38.

Bartlett, J. (2018). *The People vs Tech: How the internet is killing democracy (and how we save it).* London: Ebury Press.

Bell, V. (August 16, 2015). Britain's 'Twitter troops' have ways of making you think.... *The Guardian.* https://www.theguardian.com/science/2015/aug/16/britains-twitter-troops-ways-making-you-think-joint-threat-research-intelligence-group.

Beyer, R. (Producer/Director). *The ghost army* (2013). USA: PBS.

Brignull, H. (November 1, 2011). *Dark patterns: Deception vs. Honesty in UI design. A list apart.* https://alistapart.com/article/dark-patterns-deception-vs.-honesty-in-ui-design.

Broniatowski, D. A., Jamison, A. M., Qi, S., AlKulaib, L., SM, Chen, T., et al. (2018). Weaponized health communication: Twitter bots and Russian trolls amplify the vaccine debate. *American Journal of Public Health, 108*(10), 1378–1384.

Brooks, R. (2016). *How everything became war and the military became everything: Tales from the pentagon.* New York: Simon and Schuster.

Burke, C. B. (2002). *It Wasn't all magic: The early struggle to automate cryptanalysis, 1930s–1960s.* United States Cryptologic History, Special Series, 6. Fort Meade, MD: Center For Cryptologic History, National Security Agency.

Cadwalladr, C., & [@carolecadwalla]. (2018). *Unbelievable. Russian ministry of foreign affairs changes its profile photo to #FreeMariaButina. This is war. [Tweet], July 19.* https://twitter.com/carolecadwalla/status/1020050794937282562.

Caravan Coop. (2017). *The fascinating history of major cyber attacks, hacks and general electronic mischief.* Medium. https://medium.com/caravan-blog/the-fascinating-history-of-major-cyber-attacks-hacks-and-general-electronic-mischief-dd59dc85386e.

Carr, N. (2010). *The shallows: What the internet is doing to our brains.* New York: W. W. Norton and Co.

Casebeer, W. D., & Russell, J. A. (2005). Storytelling and terrorism: Towards a comprehensive counternarrative strategy. *Strategic Insights, 4*(3).

Chamberlain, P. R. (2010). Twitter as a vector for disinformation. *Journal of Information Warfare, 9*(1), 11–17.

Chen, A. (June 2, 2015). The agency. *The New York Times Magazine.* https://www.nytimes.com/2015/06/07/magazine/the-agency.html.

Clifton, D., & Folliman, M. (July 26, 2018). The very strange case of two Russian gun lovers, the NRA, and Donald Trump. *Mother Jones.* https://www.motherjones.com/politics/2018/03/trump-russia-nra-connection-maria-butina-alexander-torshin-guns/.

CM Films. (June 14, 2014). *Everything will be alright episode 5: Jamais Cascio.* https://www.youtube.com/watch?v=3wR_sr0Sys.

Combelles Siegel, P. (2007). Perception management: IO's stepchild. In L. Armistead (Ed.), *Information warfare: Separating hype from reality* (pp. 22–44). Washington: Potomac Books. Washington.

Crowley, A. (2004). *Magick in theory and practice [Book 4 (Liber Aba). Part III].* London: Celephaïs Press.

CSS Cyber Defense Project. (2017). *Hotspot analysis: Cyber and information warfare in the Ukrainian conflict.* Zurich: Center for Security Studies/ETH Zurich.

Dan & Dave, England, J., Wilson, R. P. (Producers/Director). *Our magic* (2014). Tappan, NY: Janson Media.

Darczewska, J. (2014). *The anatomy of Russian information warfare: The crimean operation, a case study. Point of view 42. Center for Eastern Studies.* Warsaw.

Demacheva, I., Ladouceur, M., Steinberg, E., Pogossova, G., & Raz, A. (2012). The applied cognitive psychology of attention: A step closer to understanding magic tricks. *Applied Cognitive Psychology, 26*(4), 541–549.

Department of the Air Force. (2012). *Air force materiel command broad agency announcement (BAA ESC 12-0011).* https://www.fbo.gov/utils/view?id=48a4eeb344432c3c87df0594068dc0ce.

Dillon, A. (1992). Reading from paper versus screens: A critical review of the empirical literature. *Ergonomics, 35*(10), 1297–1326.

Engelhardt, T. (June 19, 2014). Karl Rove unintentionally predicted the current Chaos in Iraq. *Mother Jones.* https://www.motherjones.com/politics/2014/06/us-karl-rove-iraq-crisis/.

Fitzkee, D. (2009). *The trick brain* [Kindle edition]. Provo, Utah: Magic Box Productions.

Forbes, P. (2009). *Dazzled and deceived.* New Haven, CT: Yale University Press.

Fuller, J. F. C. (1907). *The star in the West: A critical essay upon the works of aleister Crowley.* London: Chiswick Press.

Fuller, J. F. C. (1926). *The foundations of the science of war.* London: Hutchinson.

Galeotti, M. (2018). The mythical 'Gerasimov Doctrine' and the language of threat. *Critical Studies on Security, 6*(1). https://doi.org/10.1080/21624887.2018.1441623.

Gawley, K. (2013). *Dark patterns – the art of online deception.* https://www.kylegawley.com/dark-patterns-the-art-of-online-deception/.

Gerasimov, V. (2016). The value of science is in the Foresight: New challenges Demand rethinking the forms and methods of carrying out combat operations. R. Coalson, Trans *Military Review*, 23–29. January/February.

Gingerich, D. (2017). *The first hack. Science non fiction.* https://sciencenonfiction.org/2017/04/06/the-first-hack/.

Graubert, R., Bodeau, D., & McQuaid, R. (2018). *Systems security engineering: Cyber resiliency considerations for the engineering of trustworthy secure systems.* Gaithersburg, MD: National Institute of Standards and Technology.

Gu, L., Kropotov, V., & Yarochkin, F. (2017). *The fake news machine: How propagandists abuse the internet and manipulate the public.* Manila: TrendLabs.

Henderson, S. (June 27, 2018). *The trade of the tricks: How principles of magic can contribute to national security.* CREST. https://crestresearch.ac.uk/comment/henderson-magic-contribute-national-security/.

Henderson, S., Hoffmann, R., Bunch, L., & Bradshaw, J. (2015). Applying the principles of magic and the concepts of macrocognition to counter-deception in cyber operations. In *Paper presented at the 12th international naturalistic decision making conference, McLean, VA, June.* http://www2.mitre.org/public/ndm/papers/HendersonHoffmanBunchBradshaw040215.pdf.

Hickman, K. (Producer) Analysis: Maskirovka: Deception Russian-style. *BBC Radio, 4,* (February 1, 2015). February 4.

Howard, M. (1992). *Strategic deception in the second world war.* Pimlico, London.

Hutchinson, W. (2006). Information warfare and deception. *Informing Science, 9*, 213–223.

Jaitner, M. (2015). Russian information warfare: Lessons from Ukraine. In K. Geers (Ed.), *Cyber war in perspective: Russian aggression against Ukraine* (pp. 87–94). Tallinn: NATO CCD COE Publications.

Jenkins, R. (2014). *Black magic and bogeymen: Fear, rumour and popular belief in the North of Ireland 1972-74.* Sheffield: University of Sheffield Press.

Keating, K. C. (1981). *Maskirovka: The soviet system of camouflage.* Garmisch: US Army Russian Institute. http://www.dtic.mil/dtic/tr/fulltext/u2/a112903.pdf.

Keen, A. (2015). *The internet is not the answer.* London: Atlantic Books.

Korzybski, A. (1931). A non-aristotelian system and its necessity for rigour in mathematics and physics. In *Paper presented to the American mathematical society/American association for the advancement of science, New Orleans, LA, December.*

Krueger, D. W. (1987). *Maskirovka: What's in it for us? School of advanced military studies.* Fort Leavenworth, KS http://www.dtic.mil/dtic/tr/fulltext/u2/a190836.pdf.

Kuhn, G., Amlani, A. A., & Rensink, R. A. (2008). Towards a science of magic. *Trends in Cognitive Sciences, 12*(9), 349–354.

Kuhn, G., et al. (2014). A psychologically-based taxonomy of misdirection. *Frontiers in Psychology, 5*(1392), 1–14.

Lamont, P., & Wiseman, R. (1999). *Magic in theory: An introduction to the theoretical and psychological elements of conjuring.* Hatfield: University of Hertfordshire Press.

Lanier, J. (2010). *You are not a gadget: A manifesto.* New York: A. Knopf.

Lansdale, E. G. (1991). *In the midst of wars: An American's mission to southeast Asia.* New York: Fordham University Press.

Lehrer, J. (April 20, 2009). Magic and the brain: Teller reveals the neuroscience of illusion. *Wired*. https://www.wired.com/2009/04/ff-neuroscienceofmagic/.

Leonard, A. (June 28, 2013). *The NSA's early years: Exposed! Salon*. www.salon.com/2013/06/28/the_nsas_early_years_exposed/.

Liao, Q. V., & Fu, W.-T. (2013). Beyond the filter bubble: Interactive effects of perceived threat and topic involvement on selective exposure to information. In *Proceedings of the SIGCHI conference on human factors in computing systems* (pp. 2359–2368). New York, NY: ACM.

Libicki, M. C. (1995). *What is information warfare?* Washington: National Defense University.

Lindley-French, J. (2015). *NATO: Countering strategic Maskirovka*. Calgary: Canadian Defence & Foreign Affairs Institute.

Loh, K. K., & Kanai, R. (2016). How has the internet reshaped human cognition? *Neuroscientist, 22*(5), 506–520.

MacFarquhar, N. (February 18, 2018). Inside the Russian troll factory: Zombies and a breakneck pace. *New York Times*. https://www.nytimes.com/2018/02/18/world/europe/russia-troll-factory.html.

Macknik, S. L., King, M., Randi, J., Robbins, A., Teller Thompson, J., et al. (2008). Attention and awareness in stage magic: Turning tricks into research. *Nature Reviews Neuroscience, 9*(11), 871–879.

Macknik, S., Martinez-Conde, S., & Blakeslee, S. (2011). *Sleights of mind: What the neuroscience of magic reveals about our everyday deceptions*. London: Profile.

Mangan, M. (2007). *Performing dark arts*. Bristol: Intellect.

Mangen, A., Robinet, P., Olivier, G., & Velay, J-L. (July 2014). *Mystery story reading in pocket print book and on Kindle: Possible impact on chronological events memory.* Turin: In: Paper Presented at IGEL (the International Society for the Empirical Study of Literature and Media).

Marlatt, G. E. (2008). *Information warfare and information operations (IW/IO): A bibliography.* Monterey, CA: Naval Postgraduate School, Dudley Knox Library.

McDermott, R. (2016). Does Russia have a Gerasimov doctrine? *Parameters, 46*(1), 97–106.

McLuhan, M. (2003). Violence as a quest for identity. In *Understanding me: Lectures & interviews* (pp. 264–276). Toronto: McClelland & Stewart.

Melton, H., & Wallace, R. (2009). *The official CIA manual of trickery and deception*. New York: HarperCollins Publishers.

Milam, W. (July 14, 2018). *Who is Vladislav Surkov?* Medium. https://medium.com/@wmilam/the-theater-director-who-is-vladislav-surkov-9dd8a15e0efb.

Miles, L. (2002). *The book of the war*. Metairie, LA: Mad Norwegian Press.

Millard, D. (February 24, 2018). *The Political power of doubt*. The Outline. https://theoutline.com/post/3522/donald-trump-and-vladislav-surkov?zd=1&zi=qx2eehvr.

Mills, K. L. (2016). Possible effects of internet use on cognitive development in adolescence. *Media and Communication, 4*(3), 4–12.

Minch, S. (2009). *The Book of forgotten secrets*. Seattle: Hermetic Press.

Moeller, J. (April 23, 2014). *Maskirovka: Russia's masterful use of deception in Ukraine*. Huffington Post. https://www.huffingtonpost.com/joergen-oerstroem-moeller/maskirovka-russias-master_b_5199545.html?guccounter=1.

Morin, R., & Cohen, D. (August 19, 2018). *Giuliani: 'Truth isn't truth'*. Politico. https://www.politico.com/story/2018/08/19/giuliani-truth-todd-trump-788161.

Nelms, H. (2003). *Magic and showmanship: A handbook for conjurers*. Mineola, WA: Dover Publishing.

Nicholson, A. (2015). *Wide spectrum attribution: Using deception for attribution intelligence in cyber attacks*. PhD thesis. Leicester: De Montfort University.

No, Carole Cadwalladr. (2018). *This is what war looks like....* offGuardian. July 22 https://off-guardian.org/2018/07/22/no-carole-cadwalladr-this-is-what-war-looks-like/.

Patrikarakos, D. (2017). *War in 140 characters [Kindle version]*. New York: Basic Books.

Pomerantsev, P. (October 20, 2011). *Putin's Rasputin. London review of books*. https://www.lrb.co.uk/v33/n20/peter-pomerantsev/putins-rasputin.

Pomerantsev, P. (2014a). The hidden author of putinism: How Vladislav Surkov invented the new Russia. *The Atlantic*. November 7 https://www.theatlantic.com/international/archive/2014/11/hidden-author-putinism-russia-vladislav-surkov/382489/.

Pomerantsev, P. (2014b). How putin is Reinventing warfare. *Foreign Policy.* May 5 https://foreignpolicy.com/2014/05/05/how-putin-is-reinventing-warfare/.

Pomerantsev, P. (March 28, 2014c). *Non-linear war*. LRB Blog. https://www.lrb.co.uk/blog/2014/03/28/peter-pomerantsev/non-linear-war/.

Proctor, R., & Schiebinger, L. (2008). *Agnotology.* Stanford: Stanford University Press.

Quirkology. (November 21, 2012). *Colour changing card trick*. Youtube. https://www.youtube.com/watch?v=v3iPrBrGSJM.

Rankin, N. (2009). *Churchill's wizards*. London: Faber and Faber.

Riser, N. B. (2001). *Spoofing: An overview of some the current spoofing threats*. Swansea: SANS Institute.

Ristolainen, M. (2017). Should 'RuNet 2020' be taken seriously? Contradictory views about cybersecurity between Russia and the West. *Journal of Information Warfare, 16*(4), 113–131.

Robert-Houdin, J.-E. (1860). *Memoirs of Robert-Houdin, ambassador, author, and conjuror*. L. Wraxall, Trans. London: Chapman and Hall

Rose, S. (August 14, 2014). The real men in black, hollywood and the great UFO cover-up. *The Guardian*. http://www.theguardian.com/film/2014/aug/14/men-in-black-ufo-sightings-mirage-makers-movie.

Sanger, D. (2018). *The perfect weapon: War, sabotage, and fear in the cyber age*. London: Scribe.

Schillinger, L. (February 23, 2018). *McMaster gives a belated Russian lesson*. ForeignPolicy.com. https://foreignpolicy.com/2018/02/23/mcmaster-and-maskirovka.

SecDev Group, & Munk Centre for International Studies. (2009). *Tracking GhostNet: Investigating a cyber espionage network*. Toronto: Information Warfare Monitor.

Simons, D. J., & Chabris, C. F. (1999). Gorillas in our midst: Sustained inattentional blindness for dynamic events. *Perception, 28*(9), 1059–1074.

Singer, N. (May 14, 2016). When websites won't take No for an answer. *New York Times*. https://www.nytimes.com/2016/05/15/technology/personaltech/when-websites-wont-take-no-for-an-answer.html?_r=1.

Smith, D. (December 13, 2018). Russian spy Maria Butina pleads guilty to conspiracy against US. *The Guardian*. https://www.theguardian.com/us-news/2018/dec/13/russian-spy-maria-butina-pleads-guilty-conspiracy.

Spohr, D. (2017). Fake news and ideological polarization: Filter bubbles and selective exposure on social media. *Business Information Review, 34*(3), 150–160.

Storm, B. C., Stone, S. M., & Benjamin, A. S. (2016). Using the internet to access information inflates future use of the internet to access other information. *Memory, 25*(6), 717–723.

Stupples, D. (November 26, 2015). *The next war will be an information war, and we're not ready for it*. Theconversation. https://theconversation.com/the-next-war-will-be-an-information-war-and-were-not-ready-for-it-51218.

Suskind, R. (October 17, 2004). Faith, certainty and the presidency of George W. Bush. *The New York Times Magazine*. https://www.nytimes.com/2004/10/17/magazine/faith-certainty-and-the-presidency-of-george-w-bush.html.

Szafranski, R. (1997). Neocortical warfare? The acme of skill. In J. Arquila, & D. Ronfeldt (Eds.), *In Athena's camp: Preparing for conflict in the information age* (pp. 395–416). Santa Monica: RAND Corp.

Taylor, N. (2013). The bizarnival of the strange. *Mystic Menagerie: The Journal of Bizarre Magic, 1*(13), 10–12.

Taylor, N. (2014). Out of tricks. In T. Landman (Ed.), *The magiculum* (pp. 101–111). London: EyeCorner Press.

Taylor, N. (April 2015). The Fairy Goblet of Eden Hall to Hunting Mammoths in the Rain – experiencing the paraxial through performance magic and mystery entertainment. In *Paper presented at tales beyond borders*. The University of Leeds. http://eprints.hud.ac.uk/24343/1/TaylorExperiencing.pdf.
Teller. (March 2012). *Teller reveals his secrets*. Smithsonian.com. https://www.smithsonianmag.com/arts-culture/teller-reveals-his-secrets-100744801/.
Tsikerdekis, M., & Zeadally, S. (2014). Online deception in social media. *Communications of the ACM, 57*(9), 72–80.
Valley, P. E., & Aquino, M. A. (1980). *From PSYOP to MindWar: The psychology of victory*. San Francisco: 7th Psychological Operations Group.
Van Puyvelde, D. (2015). *Hybrid war – does it even exist? NATO review*. https://wwww.nato.int/docu/Review/2015/Also-in-2015/hybrid-modern-future-warfare-russia-ukraine/EN/index.htm.
Vitale, C. (2014). *Networkologies: A philosophy of networks for a hyperconnected age – a manifesto*. Alresford: Zero Books.
Von Clausewitz, C. (1989). *On war*. M. E. Howard, P. Paret, Trans./Eds. Princeton: Princeton University Press
Yourgrau, B. (January 22, 2018). *The literary intrigues of putin's puppet master*. NYRDaily. https://www.nybooks.com/daily/2018/01/22/the-literary-intrigues-of-putins-puppet-master/.

## Further reading

Greenfield, A. (2017). *Radical technologies: The design of everyday life [Kindle version]*. London: Verso.

CHAPTER

# 5

# Digital hoarding behaviours: implications for cybersecurity

*Nick Neave*[1], *Kerry McKellar*[2], *Elizabeth Sillence*[2], *Pam Briggs*[2]

[1] Hoarding Research Group, Department of Psychology, Northumbria University, Newcastle upon Tyne, United Kingdom; [2] Psychology and Communications Technology (PACT) Lab, Department of Psychology, Northumbria University, Newcastle upon Tyne, United Kingdom

OUTLINE



*Cyber Influence and Cognitive Threats*
https://doi.org/10.1016/B978-0-12-819204-7.00005-1

## Physical hoarding

The majority of individuals accumulate personal possessions over their lifetime; these possessions often have great sentimental value over and above their actual worth, and people show great reluctance to part with some of them, these objects coming to embody the 'self' and the personality of their owner. Such accumulating/collecting behaviours are normal and may reflect an evolutionary tendency to acquire items which initially enhance survival (e.g., food, clothing, tools, weapons) but then become less utilitarian and bring meaning and quality to a person's life (Grisham & Barlow, 2005). However, in some individuals, this acquisitive tendency becomes pathological, and they accumulate more and more items such that in the space of a few years (or even less), their personal living spaces have become cluttered to such an extent that normal daily life (e.g., cooking, washing, cleaning) becomes impossible. The most commonly hoarded items are clothing, newspapers/magazines, books, food cartons, packaging and even animals. Studies have estimated that the incidence of hoarding is around 2%–6% of the population, meaning that around the world there are potentially millions of such individuals (Samuels et al., 2008).

These hoarders tend to become more and more socially isolated and refuse to have guests visit the house, and their environment becomes unhygienic and potentially dangerous, with an increased risk of fire and toppling hazards (Frost & Gross, 1993). This leads to significant distress, with anxiety, depression and social phobia being commonly seen in hoarders (Frost, Steketee, & Tolin, 2011). The economic costs of dealing with hoarding behaviours for local authorities, housing associations and emergency services can also be considerable (Neave et al., 2017).

For many years hoarding was viewed as an eccentric lifestyle choice, but after increasing realization of common behavioural and psychological characteristics in hoarders, it was categorized as a mental disorder, initially as a subtype of obsessive-compulsive disorder (OCD). Since then, accumulating evidence has demonstrated that OCD and hoarding form distinct disorders, albeit with some overlap (Mataix-Cols et al., 2010; Pertusa et al., 2010). Hoarding is now regarded as a separate condition in the Diagnostic and Statistical Manual (DSM-V), called 'compulsive hoarding syndrome' or more simply 'hoarding disorder' (American Psychiatric Association, 2013). In June 2018, hoarding was classified as a 'medical disorder' by the World Health Organization (WHO) in its revised International Classification of Diseases (ICD-11). Symptoms of hoarding begin in the middle teens, but recognition that there may be a problem occurs around a decade later when living spaces become obviously cluttered (Grisham, Frost, Steketee, Kim, & Hood, 2006). While we all form emotional attachments to our cherished possessions, hoarders form deep attachments to items which would not normally be associated with such intense connections (i.e., old newspapers, empty food cartons, etc.) (Grisham et al., 2009; Nedelisky & Steele, 2009). Hoarders also tend to 'anthropomorphize', much more so than nonhoarders, i.e., they treat their objects as if they were almost human and possess thoughts and feelings (Burgess, Graves, & Frost, 2018; Neave, Jackson, Saxton, & Hönekopp, 2015; Neave, Tyson, McInnes & Hamilton, 2016) and may display a lack of insight into their hoarding behaviours, strongly resisting attempts to intervene and to help them declutter (Steketee & Frost, 2003).

## Digital possessions

We live in an increasingly digital world, and more and more of our personal possessions (e.g., music, photographs, books) may exist only in digital form. The fact that they are nonphysical does not seem to lessen their emotional significance. Cushing (2012) interviewed 23 people and asked them how they defined their digital possessions and how they related to them. The respondents considered many items to be digital possessions – not only obvious things like digital photographs, text files and e-mails but also social media accounts and computer code they had written. Digital possessions were felt to have three key characteristics. Firstly, they provide unique evidence about the person, perhaps of an activity that the person had engaged in, or something that proves who they are (i.e., a password). Secondly, they represent the individual's identity, storing their memories, experiences, feelings and emotions and enabling the person to share these with the outside world (i.e., via social media). Thirdly, the digital possession has value, and this might be a sentimental value or an economic value. In short, our digital possessions can represent our personality and we become as attached to digital items as we do to physical items, with our digital and personal possessions determining our sense of self (Belk, 1988).

Digital files also extend into the economic realm, with an increasing realization that digital data are a powerful economic resource; in May 2017, a headline in the Economist stated that *'the world's most valuable resource is no longer oil, but data'* (Economist, 2017). On a daily basis, individuals interact with an increasingly large amount of data, creating it, storing it, processing it and sharing it, and understanding the habits and behaviours of data users is becoming important to many large companies. Personal data are especially interesting in this context and individuals are becoming more aware of the serious implications of having their personal data used (and abused) by organizations. The recent scandal concerning Facebook and the voter-profiling company Cambridge Analytica will be fresh in everyone's mind. In this case, Aleksandr Kogan, a researcher for Cambridge Analytica, developed a personality quiz app for Facebook. While only around 270,000 people downloaded the app, due to Facebook's data controls the app could also access the data not only of those who had downloaded it but also data from their friends. The app saved that information into a private database and ended up storing data from around 30 million individuals. Facebook subsequently lost around 12% of its share value and its Chief Executive Mark Zuckerberg was required to answer difficult questions from the US Senate Commerce Committee (Meyer, 2018).

It is no surprise that attempts are being made to strengthen data protection laws. The General Data Protection Regulation (GDPR) is a new European Union regulation which came into force on 25 May 2018. It is designed to harmonize data protection law across Europe and to bring the law up to date with technological advancements, specifically the increasing use of digital data. It aims to promote a more proactive approach to data protection, with an emphasis on transparency, accountability and data protection by default and design. The UK Government has published its Data Protection Bill, which will lead to a new Act replacing the 1998 Data Protection Act. This will implement the provisions of GDPR and will make changes to the rules which organizations must follow, when processing personal data. Personal data refer to any information related to a natural person or 'data subject', which can be used to directly or indirectly identify the person. It can be anything from a name, a photo, an e-mail address, bank details, posts on social networking websites, medical information or a computer IP address. The Regulation places much stronger controls on the processing of 'sensitive' personal data (Information Commissioner's Office, 2017). Where sensitive personal data are processed, it must also satisfy at least 1/10 data processing conditions (e.g., explicit consent, vital interests, substantial public interest, etc.).

Article 5 of the GDPR outlines the *main responsibilities for organizations to ensure that personal data is processed in line with key Principles, essentially personal data can only be used for* 'specified, explicit and legitimate purposes' [article 5, clause 1(b)] and data collected on an individual should be 'adequate, relevant and limited to what is necessary in relation to the purposes for which they are processed' [article 5, clause 1(c)]. In other words, no more than the minimum amount of data should be kept for specific processing. In addition, data must be 'accurate and where necessary kept up to date' [article 5, clause 1(d)], personal data must be 'kept in a form which permits identification of data subjects for no longer than necessary' [article 5, clause 1(e)] and data should only be processed 'in a manner [ensuring] appropriate security of the personal data including protection against unlawful processing or accidental loss, destruction or damage' [article 5, clause 1(f)].

GDPR introduces eight rights that a data subject has over the personal identifiable data which is stored about them. These enable the data subject to request clear information about how their data will be processed; access to all personal data held about them; correct incomplete/inaccurate information and data deletion, data processing to cease, an electronic copy of their data, the right to complain about certain types of data processing and the right not to be subject to a decision made solely on automated processing.

Failure to comply with GDPR could result in fines of up to 4% of annual global turnover or €20 million whichever is the greater. Failure to evidence appropriate controls could lead to a fine of up to €10 million or 4% of global turnover. Compliance with GDPR will involve an organization proving accountability – the ability to demonstrate compliance with all the principles and rights laid out under the GDPR.

## Digital hoarding

If we develop strong attachments to our digital possessions as with our physical possessions, then one would expect that the hoarding of digital items would be as common as the hoarding of physical items and would perhaps share the same kinds of characteristics. Of course, in relation to digital items there are no issues in relation to the cluttering of physical space, but despite the fact that storage is ever expanding and cheap, that does not mean to say that overaccumulation of digital files may not create problems for the individual user and the organization. These problems could include failure to comply with GDPR and other privacy and data protection regulations.

There has been considerable speculation in online forums and blogs about whether or not digital hoarding exists and what might distinguish someone with digital hoarding tendencies from someone without such tendencies, but until fairly recently, scientific evidence relating to digital hoarding was limited. Research interest was sparked by a case study reported by van Bennekom, Blom, Vulink and Denys (2015). They described a 47-year-old man with autistic traits who attended their outpatient clinic asking for help with his digital addiction. He was a physical hoarder who accumulated paperwork and bike components such that his home had become severely cluttered. On obtaining a digital camera, his physical hoarding spread into the digital domain, and he would take around 1000 photographs every day. He would then spend many hours editing, categorizing and copying the pictures onto various external hard drives and found that his normal daily activities and sleep patterns had become compromised. He was also experiencing considerable stress and anxiety as his attempts to classify, store and organize his files had become overwhelming. These authors thus defined digital hoarding as *'the accumulation of digital files to the point of loss of perspective which eventually results in stress and disorganization'*. Interestingly, the authors suggested that digital hoarding was comparative to physical hoarding as it involves the overaccumulation of items, leading to increased clutter and disorganization, difficulties in discarding/deleting because of intense emotional attachments, distress and loss of normal functioning.

## Personal information management

Personal information management (PIM) is the term used to describe how individuals collect, store, organize and retrieve their personal digital information (Lansdale, 1988). Such activities require time, attention and some organizational skills and it is no surprise that it is often described as a 'burden'. For example, Whittaker and Sidner (1996) focused on e-mail, originally intended simply as a communication application but which is now used for many additional functions (e.g., document delivery, archiving, task tracking, appointment scheduling, etc.), with users often reporting 'e-mail overload'. In their sample, 20 office workers from different job roles provided quantitative data about their e-mail (e.g., number of messages in their inbox) and qualitative information relating to how they prioritized e-mails, how they managed their correspondence and how they archived their messages. A key problem was how to read and reply in a timely manner with backlogs being common and difficulties experienced in lost or disorganized information. The mean number of e-mails in an inbox was over 2000, meaning that the system was being used as a task manager, with specific e-mails acting as reminders of tasks to be done, and where relevant information related to these tasks can be readily accessed. Users experienced difficulties in filing e-mails into folders, mainly because creating and organizing such folders takes considerable effort, with the resulting collections being of little use when it comes to retrieving the information if you have forgotten the name you gave to the folder in the first place.

Their respondents fell into three strategic types in relation to PIM. The first group were called 'frequent filers' and typically filed their e-mails on an almost daily basis, resulting in an average inbox of around 43 items. The second type were called 'no filers', as they did not use folders to store e-mails, with a resulting inbox of around 3093 items. The third type were called 'spring cleaners'; they tended to clean up their inboxes periodically and possessed an average inbox of around 1492 e-mails. Each strategy was associated with a loss of efficiency; however, frequent filers spent a larger amount of time in filing activities, with the no filers and spring cleaners spending correspondingly more time in message retrieval and search activities.

Boardman and Sasse (2004) extended Whittaker and Sidner's work to include an analysis of not only e-mails but also files and bookmarks. Semistructured interviews were conducted with 31 users, with a subsample being tracked over a 5-month period. A commonly experienced challenge related to the need to better organize the material, with the buildup of data being a key feature, and typically with little or no time spent on maintenance. Old items were very rarely archived with many inboxes containing a mix of working, archived and ephemeral (spam) information. One participant neatly summed up the problem by stating 'stuff just goes into the computer and doesn't come out – it just buildup'. In a similar vein, Dabbish and Kraut (2006) conducted a nationwide survey exploring the relationship between e-mail use and perceptions of overload. Over 480 participants completed their survey and demonstrated varying degrees of effectiveness in their e-mail management strategies, with larger number of e-mail folders being associated with greater overload. Other studies have revealed that people typically keep half of the e-mails they receive and reply to about one-third of them (Dabbish, Kraut, Fussell, & Kiesler, 2005), with very few people engaging in proactive 'clean-up' of that stored information (Bergman & Beyth-Marom, 2003).

## Implications of digital hoarding

Data clutter is thus highly prevalent, and the case study by van Bennekom et al. (2015) showed that the impact on the individual can be significant, but what of the organization? Gormley and Gormley (2012) discussed the implications of data clutter from an organization's perspective. The first thing they considered was cost, while it is assumed that data storage is cheap; in fact, it has been estimated that in the United States, data servers and centres consume around 2% of national electricity, with this figure likely to expand as data use and storage increases on a year-by-year basis (Sloane, 2011, p. 40). In fact, in an article in the Independent newspaper on 23 January 2016, it was estimated that the world's data centres, processing billions of gigabytes of information, consumed over 400 TW h of electricity per year (https://www.independent.co.uk/environment/global-warming-data-centres-to-consume-three-times-as-much-energy-in-next-decade-experts-warn-a6830086.html). Despite the fact that data centres are becoming more energy efficient, such gains are subsequently negated by rising user demand (Jacob, 2017). Additional costs relate to the amount of time employees spend processing e-mails, searching for data files, etc.

A second implication relates to the life span of the data. It has been estimated that before 1959 a piece of knowledge was profitable for around 21 years, but since 1990, its profitability lasts only around 3 years

(Ishikawa & Naka, 2007). If that is the case then why bother storing the data for many years? As digital hoarding rises, businesses find it more difficult to extract value from the stored information and the risks associated with that information grow significantly (CGOC 2017).

A third implication relates to employee effectiveness and productivity, the hoarding of data while often viewed as a positive aspect (someone will always have access to the data you might need), but as Gormley and Gormley (2012) noted *'information hoarders are not always information sharers'*. Organizations' can often exacerbate this problem as different departments may not share information effectively or indeed even communicate their needs effectively, a problem compounded by lack of internal governance strategies/policies. Related to this, a fourth implication relates to data sharing and the fact that some people are very reluctant to share data and will protect it as if it were their own property, perhaps relishing the feeling of power and control that this gives them.

The information we have provided so far indicates that digital hoarding exists and that such behaviours within organizations can have a range of negative impact at a personal, organizational and environmental level. It is also likely that such behaviours could have cybersecurity implications, as the sheer amount of data (much of it related to personal information or intellectual property) means that hacking (whether for personal, industrial or espionage reasons) is likely to be highly effective. Recent widely reported cases involving Dixons Carphone and Ticketmaster show all too easily that personal financial information can be stolen. The case of Edward Snowden, a computer professional and former CIA employee who copied and then leaked classified information from the National Security Agency in 2013, shows how easily a determined employee can remove large amounts of data. This is not to say that just because an employee has hoarding tendencies means that they are a specific cybersecurity risk, but the fact that large amounts of data may be being stored/copied/transferred without due cause does raise concerns.

However, accurate information relating to digital hoarding behaviours remains sparse, especially in relation to the underlying motivations. Sweeten, Sillence and Neave (2018) conducted a qualitative assessment of digital hoarding behaviours, motivations and consequences in 43 individuals. The volunteers were asked to a series of questions relating to their current e-mail storage and deletion behaviours, file management practises and their attitudes towards personal digital management. Some participants ($n = 18$) answered the questions relating to their personal digital files, while the remainder ($n = 25$) answered in relation to their workplace files. Thematic analysis revealed five barriers to data deletion: 1 – keeping it for the future or just in case; 2 – keeping it as evidence; 3 – too time-consuming or just too lazy to delete it; 4 – emotional attachment and 5 – not being my problem to delete it.

In addition, some of the volunteers felt that the accumulation of digital data was having a negative impact on their psychological well-being and contributing to increased stress and anxiety. This was particularly evident for e-mail, where the sheer volume of e-mails left them feeling 'overwhelmed'. They also clearly recognized the potential cybersecurity implications of their data hoarding – the problem of malicious data acquisition was seen as a key problem in both personal and workplace settings. One quote was as follows *'I think digital clutter is way into your personal life if not monitored properly. Cyber attacks, identify fraud etc ... in case someone was to hack my Gmail. They would find full identity information leading to possible cyber fraud or ID fraud'* (p. 58). Interestingly, the respondents also reflected on their physical hoarding behaviours and there appeared to be clear overlap between physical and digital domains, with digital behaviours also reflecting excessive accumulation, difficulty discarding (deleting) and emotional distress. These authors noted that the ability to properly identify and quantify digital hoarding behaviours was currently lacking, and so our research team set out to develop a reliable and valid measure of digital hoarding behaviours and to explore digital hoarding in the workplace in more detail.

## Our research

We obtained funding from the Centre for Research and Evidence on Security Threats (CREST) to achieve our research aims and objectives. These were as follows:

**a)** To devise and validate a new empirical questionnaire to measure the extent of digital hoarding behaviours within organizations.
**b)** To explore the potential similarities between digital hoarding and physical hoarding behaviours.
**c)** To explore the potential cybersecurity implications of digital hoarding behaviours.

In an initial sample we recruited over 400 participants, all of whom were working and regularly used computers as part of their employment. We created a Digital Hoarding Questionnaire (DHQ), comprising 12 statements adapted from established physical hoarding questionnaires which addressed the core aspects of physical hoarding, namely clutter, difficulty discarding and emotional distress (Frost & Gross, 1993; Steketee & Frost, 2003). In addition, we created the Digital Behaviours at Work Questionnaire (DBWQ) as a way to quantify the extent of digital hoarding by employees. This questionnaire asked for relevant demographic and employment information and then asked specifically about the number of digital files stored, deletion behaviours and beliefs about the negative consequences of digital hoarding in relation to oneself and one's employer. Both questionnaires were combined to form a Digital Behaviours Questionnaire (DBQ).

In this initial survey we established the psychometric properties of the questionnaires and confirmed their reliability and validity. After some minor revisions, the questionnaires were circulated to a new sample of over 200 employees. As in the initial study, the DHQ was found to comprise two factors which we called 'accumulating' and 'difficulty discarding' and both of these factors related strongly to digital hoarding behaviours. Digital hoarding was common, with some individuals reporting, for example, that they kept many thousands of e-mails in inboxes and archived folders – while we asked about the different types of files routinely encountered in the workplace, e-mails were found to be the most popular type of hoarded file. Deleting activity was also problematic, with some individuals reporting that they never deleted e-mails. We provided a list of reasons why people may not delete e-mails, and the rank ordering of the key reasons is presented in Table 5.1.

The reasons for not deleting e-mails will make sensible reading to those employees who are acting in a completely professional and responsible manner, as essentially they relate to high conscientiousness and efficiency. Employees are concerned that by deleting e-mails they may lose information that may come in use in the future, that are important for their job and that might provide evidence that something has been done. Data might also act as a 'reminder' of outstanding tasks or simply be kept 'just in case'. Interestingly, the lowest endorsed reason related to laziness.

In some follow-up questions we then asked the participants their perceptions in relation to the potential negative consequences if their digital files were released (either inadvertently or maliciously). Using a scale of 1–7 (where 1 = no consequences and 7 = very severe consequences), the respondents were clearly aware of the risks with the mean rating for e-mails, for example, being 3.4/7 in relation to themselves and 3.7 in relation to their company. Thus, while individuals are clearly aware of the negative consequences should their digital files be made widely available, they still show great reluctance to delete.

Our findings echo those from a recent study by Vitale, Janzen and McGrenere (2018). The focus of their research was how people decide what data to keep and what to discard. They conducted interviews with 23 individuals from diverse employment backgrounds and asked them to consider their past and current digital behaviours. They asked participants what kinds of information they had stored over the years, why and how they had used it, what they considered to be important and how they stored it. Their sample appeared to be mostly divided into two extremes – 'hoarders' who accumulated a wealth of data (much of it of little value) and 'minimalists' who avoided storing much data and regularly engaged

**TABLE 5.1** Reasons why employees keep e-mails, the questions are ranked in order of importance, based on a seven-point Likert-type scale data (1 = not at all, 7 = very much so). The mean score is presented with standard deviations in parentheses.

| Reasons for non-deletion (in rank order) | Mean rating/7 |
|---|---|
| 1. I don't delete them because they may come in useful in the future | 4.9 (1.87) |
| 2. I don't delete them because they may contain information vital for my job | 4.8 (1.82) |
| 3. I don't delete them in case I need to have 'evidence' that something has been done | 4.1 (2.04) |
| 4. I don't delete them because I am worried that I might accidently delete something important | 3.8 (2.01) |
| 5. I don't delete them because I feel a sense of professional responsibility about them | 3.5 (2.00) |
| 6. I don't delete them because I keep an example from everyone so that it is easier to reply in future | 3.4 (1.95) |
| 7. I don't delete them because they 'belong' to my company and are not mine to do with as I wish | 3.0 (1.92) |
| 8. It is my company policy never to delete information so I don't have a choice | 2.9 (1.95) |
| 9. I don't delete them because storing them is not my problem, if they take up too much space then my company can delete them | 2.9 (1.90) |
| 10. I Simply don't have the time to delete them all | 2.8 (1.82) |
| 11. I don't delete them because I feel a sense of attachment to them | 2.7 (1.89) |
| 12. I am too lazy to delete them | 2.4 (1.81) |

in data clean-ups. However, some people showed elements of both types and some appeared more difficult to classify. The 'hoarders' displayed elements of what we had uncovered, the hoarding had an emotional component in that people were anxious about forgetting things and had a sentimental need to retain certain data from their past. There was also a practical element related to the professional aspect of their data – information kept for their employment or to other external requirements was retained in case it was needed in future. The large amount of data provided unique challenges for the individual; they became frustrated at trying to 'keep up' with their data, in knowing exactly what they had got and trying to remember where it was all stored.

As part of the same study funded by CREST, we were able to conduct further research using our newly validated hoarding questionnaires (unpublished data). We circulated the DBQ around two large organizations, one a University and the other to a large private organization. We then contacted those individuals who had scored at the top end of our digital hoarding scale and who had also scored highly on a standard questionnaire of physical hoarding – the Savings Inventory-Revised (Frost, Steketee, & Grisham, 2004). We then asked some of those high scorers to come along to be interviewed about their digital hoarding behaviours and have potentially identified four types of digital hoarders. These are the 'Collector' (organized, systematic, in control of their data); the 'Accidental Hoarder' (disorganized, do not know what they have, do not have control over it); the 'Hoarder by Instruction' (keeping data for their company) and the 'Anxious Hoarder' (worried about deleting data, strong emotional ties to their data). These findings point to the complexity of digital hoarding behaviours and provide a starting point from which to develop a range of alternative strategies for digital decluttering within organizations. We are currently exploring associations between these different types and other personality characteristics; we are also exploring the links already noted between digital and physical hoarding (Vitale et al., 2018; Neave et al., 2019; Oravec, 2015; Sweeten et al., 2018; van Bennekom et al., 2015).

## Implications of digital hoarding behaviours

Physical hoarders and hoarding itself are often presented in a negative light in the media and popular culture (Lepselter, 2011); however, the societal stigma surrounding physical hoarders does not appear to apply to digital hoarding in the same way. Sweeten et al. (2018) noted that despite their attempts to avoid the term, their participants raised the issue of digital hoarding themselves, and our recent (as yet unpublished) qualitative work has also shown that not everyone scoring highly on the

DBQ is concerned by the term 'digital hoarder'. In fact, for some of our interviewees, it was seen as a badge of honour.

At first glance, digital hoarding may not appear to be much of a problem, especially for a large organization, storage is now limitless and cheap, and does not now require additional external storage devices, being typically stored in 'the cloud'. Major technology companies have a vested interest in encouraging users to move their digital data onto cloud platforms; this may seem generous but there is clearly a strong business motive in having access to huge amounts of data that can be mined and analyzed. The very fact that there is now unlimited and cheap data storage may in fact encourage more and more people to move from a 'minimalist' approach to a 'hoarding' approach.

We suggest that digital hoarding may have key negative consequences for an organization. Firstly, efficiency may be compromised; if individuals are storing thousands of files or retaining many thousands of e-mails, then simply finding the right file in good time may be problematic, leading to significant wasted time and loss of productivity. Certain kinds of organizations may be more prone to digital hoarding than others; for example, Peyton (2015) observed that law firms are especially notorious for hoarding digital data, often without any legitimate justification. Strasser and Edwards (2017) also note that scientists are notorious data hoarders, and despite the fact that the sharing of data is widely encouraged to improve the quality of science and reduce fraud and error, the vast majority of data is only used once (i.e., for a publication).

Secondly, there are obvious cybersecurity concerns associated with the retention of large amounts of data, especially if it relates to high-security information or intellectual property. We hear all the time about the effects of malicious hacking and the considerable reputational and financial loss experienced by organizations.

Related to this is the new GDPR legislation brought in to better control personal data. The types of data people accumulate, especially in relation to e-mails which typically contain personal information, have clear implications for GDPR compliance and how an organization can enhance its communication with its employees to achieve compliance. Individuals within organizations necessarily hold data, some of it being personal identifiable data. Organizations may be unsure as to the extent of that data particularly in situations where individuals are accumulating (either deliberately or inadvertently) e-mails and other files that may contain personal data, for example, CV attachments. They may also adopt strategies such as forced bulk e-mail deletion in an attempt to prevent over-accumulation. How employees may try and circumvent such policies, or the long-term effectiveness of such policies, is unknown. Some recent cases of personal data breaches experienced by Ticketmaster and Dixons Carphone are currently under legal review, with hefty fines sure to follow.

The final consequence is an environmental one; the hoarding of huge amounts of data has a significant impact on the environment; the data has to be stored somewhere and so increasingly larger servers are being developed, which use considerable amounts of energy to cool and maintain them. In fact, it is estimated that about 40% of the total energy used by data centres is associated with cooling the equipment (Song, Zhang, & Eriksson, 2015).

## Strategies for digital decluttering

There is an interesting distinction between personal and work-related digital data. In our personal lives, we tend to seek out digital files (e.g., music files, apps, photos, etc.) and accumulate them; with digital information this can be very easy to do with no obvious problems in relation to 'space'. This is similar to physical hoarding where people tend to over-accumulate and quite quickly find themselves overwhelmed, but here it becomes quickly obvious if your personal living space is being eroded. Research has shown that physical hoarders can develop strategies to reduce their accumulation behaviours, but helping people to discard physical possessions is much more difficult (Frost & Steketee, 2010; Tolin, Frost, & Steketee, 2014). It will be interesting to see whether digital hoarding shows the same kinds of characteristics, but as yet we know very little about the characteristics of digital hoarding. We have found though that asking people how many files they think they have often surprises and alarms them and makes them reflect on their digital accumulation and storing behaviours.

In comparison, in our working lives, the accumulation of digital data is rather more passive – we are typically sent information (normally in the form of e-mails) over which we have little control. We then have to decide what to do with that information, some people read and then delete their messages, giving them no more thought, but those with hoarding tendencies find that very difficult to do. They keep the data 'just in case' and experience great emotional conflict when thinking about whether or not to delete it.

Organizations could make this dilemma much easier by considering their e-mail policies and instead of sending out mass e-mails to all of their employees, consider more carefully who exactly needs to see that information. Some companies though have taken even stronger steps by bringing in 'deletion' policies, whereby e-mails are routinely deleted after a certain period of time. How such policies may influence digital hoarding behaviours remains to be examined, but anecdotally such policies are not liked by employees and may be associated with lower job satisfaction. An extreme solution described by Oravec (2018) sees organizations updating, altering or even deleting data on users' devices without their explicit consent.

Other potential solutions often focus on ways of enabling individuals to prioritize relevant or useful data making it more accessible. Rather than encouraging users to part with data that is no longer needed, these solutions often promoted in relation to the problem of 'digital hoarding', see accumulation as inevitable and deletion difficult and time consuming. Given that storage is cheap, this approach aims to help the user to visualize the data that is currently relevant or important to them.

A different approach is to give individuals a greater awareness of their data. Large tech companies such as Apple and Google have both released tools that enable users to see how and where they are storing data. These tools provide information on features such as the largest files stored, when they were last accessed and also suggestions to the user as to how to free up storage space on devices. Such features and applications may be useful in providing hoarders with greater self-awareness although as yet there are no data on how these tools are really being used. Whether or not this approach will be acceptable or even useful to different kinds of hoarders also remains to be seen.

In recent years, a range of bestselling books have been published relating to 'decluttering' in the physical world (e.g., Kondo, M., 2011; Hasson, 2018). While such books may differ in their background philosophy (the principles are often derived from Danish or Japanese principles), they all provide similar sensible advice relating to changing the way we view our possessions and decluttering our homes and offices. Interestingly, they discuss the reasons why people tend to accumulate so much 'stuff' and the reasons they provide show close parallels with the reasons we have discovered why people hoard digital files. For example, people keep physical things 'for the future', 'or just in case', as 'mementos and souvenirs' or because we 'think we need it' (Hassan, 2018, p. 15). The books then typically provide practical advice to help us to declutter – usually cognitive strategies for enabling us to make better decisions about what to keep and what to discard, and practical steps to enable us to begin to take the first steps in clearing stuff out. While such texts may help the ordinary person to declutter their life, the extent to which they would help a diagnosed hoarder or would indeed apply to the digital realm is difficult to assess.

Treatment for hoarding disorder has historically been less than effective with high rates of recidivism. For example Tolin, Frost, Steketee and Muroff (2015) conducted a metaanalysis of studies which had used cognitive-behavioural therapies (CBT) to address the key symptoms of acquisition and difficulty discarding. While a significant reduction in overall hoarding severity was noted posttreatment and a stronger effect was noted for difficulty discarding, hoarding scores usually remained within the clinical range; only 35% of the patients showed clinically significant reductions in their hoarding severity. In a review of CBT and other forms of treatments, Thompson, Fernández de la Cruz, Mataix-Cols and Onwumere (2017) note that while most studies report some improvements in hoarding severity, the reductions were generally modest; the authors noted though that long-term evaluations are lacking, and the current evidence base comprised many low-quality studies.

## Directions for future work

Research into digital hoarding is still in its infancy. We are interested in expanding our work on different types of digital hoarders. Exploring in more detail the differences in the way different types of digital hoarder relate to their personal digital data in comparison to their workplace data will be an important starting point. Moreover, a more systematic examination will need to consider a wider range of organizational settings to establish whether certain types of digital hoarder are more prevalent in particular workplace environments. Understanding this relationship may well help to explain whether different digital types of digital hoarder pose different levels of cybersecurity threat to their organizations. Examining the potential impact of strategies to support digital decluttering will need to examine different digital hoarder types across a range of organizational settings. Different tools may be effective within certain workplace cultures and providing people with an awareness of their current hoarding behaviour or indications as to how to start decluttering may be important. Understanding how and why different users would engage with such tools warrants further exploration.

It will also be interesting to explore the potential relationships between physical and digital hoarding behaviours. In the case study of the digital hoarder reported by van Bennekom et al. (2015), the individual was clearly a physical hoarder. In our research we have also found that those individuals scoring high on those behaviours most commonly associated with physical hoarding (accumulation and difficulty discarding) also show more digital hoarding behaviours. As Oravec notes, *'The hoarding of virtual items has not yet been shown to be a direct substitute in psychological terms for the hoarding of physical items'* and *'Researchers have provided few clues as to whether the individuals who collect massive quantities of physical goods will have tendencies to collect large amounts of virtual goods as well'* (Oravec, 2018, p. 31). We are currently pursuing such questions but do suspect that physical and digital hoarding and the personality characteristics underlying them might show some interesting commonalities.

Going forward, we are keen to explore the ways in which digital hoarding behaviours develop and alter over time. We will seek to identify the ways in which younger adults (see, for example, the work of Finneran, 2010) and indeed children engage with and manage their digital data. For younger adults, the increasing reliance on digital services and storage allows habitual patterns to develop around digital data – ones that may have potentially risky consequences for cybersecurity. On the other hand, younger adults are also increasingly concerned about their privacy and are choosing to engage in practises that demonstrate an awareness of the data they have, how it's stored and the extent of its public exposure (Dhir, Kaur, Lonka, & Nieminen, 2016).

For even younger children, it would be worthwhile to explore their perceptions of digital data, ownership and security alongside their current behaviours in respect of PIM. Children and teenagers may already have a sense of the complexity of digital data, its longevity and the risks associated with storing and more specifically sharing potentially sensitive personal data. The relationship that children and young people have with the accumulation and deletion of digital data may be more complex as they engage with apps such as Snapchat and others that play with the sense of permanency and ownership (Piwek & Joinson. 2016).

## References


American Psychiatric Association. (2013). *Diagnostic and statistical manual of mental disorders* (5th ed.).

Belk, R. W. (1988). Possessions and the extended self. *Journal of Consumer Research, 15*, 139–168.

van Bennekom, M. J., Blom, R. M., Vulink, N., & Denys, D. (2015). A case of digital hoarding. *British Medical Journal Case Report*. https://doi.org/10.1136/bcr-2015-210814.

Bergman, O., & Beyth-Marom, R. (2003). The user-subjective approach to personal information management systems. *Journal of the American Society for Information Science and Technology, 54*, 872–878.

Boardman, R., & Sasse, M. A. (2004). Stuff goes into the computer and doesn't come out. A cross-tool study of personal information management. In *Proceedings of the SIGCHI conference, Vienna, 24–29 April*. Vol. 6 number 1.

Burgess, A. M., Graves, L. M., & Frost, R. O. (2018). My possessions need me: Anthropomorphism and hoarding. *Scandinavian Journal of Psychology, 59*, 340–348.

*CGOC information governance process maturity model*.(January, 2017). Retrieved from http://www.cgoc.com/.

Cushing, A. L. (2012). "It's stuff that speaks to me": Exploring the characteristics of digital possessions. *Journal of the American Society for Information Science and Technology, 64*, 1723–1734.

Dabbish, L. A., & Kraut, R. E. (2006). Email overload at work: An analysis of factors associated with email strain. In *Proceedings of CSCW, november 4-8, Banff, Canada* (pp. 431–440).

Dabbish, L. A., Kraut, R. E., Fussell, S., & Kiesler, S. (2005). Understanding email use: Predicting action on a message. In *Proceedings of the SIGCHI conference on human factors in computing systems* (pp. 691–700).

Dhir, A., Kaur, P., Lonka, K., & Nieminen, M. (2016). Why do adolescents untag photos on Facebook? *Computers in Human Behavior, 55*, 1106–1115.

Economist, 2017 downloaded on August 6th 2018 Retrieved from https://www.economist.com/news/leaders/21721656-data-economy-demands-new-approach-antitrust-rules-worlds-most-valuable-resource.

Finneran, C. M. (2010). *Factors that influence users to keep and leave information items: A case study of college students' personal information management behavior*. Syracuse University. Retrieved from https://surface.syr.edu/it_etd/63/.

Frost, R. O., & Gross, R. C. (1993). The hoarding of possessions. *Behaviour Research and Therapy, 31*, 367–381.

Frost, R. O., & Steketee, G. (2010). *Stuff: Compulsive hoarding and the meaning of things*. New York: Houghton-Miflin-Harcourt.

Frost, R. O., Steketee, G., & Grisham, J. (2004). Measurement of compulsive hoarding: Saving inventory-revised. *Behaviour Research and Therapy, 42*, 1163–1182.

Frost, R. O., Steketee, G., & Tolin, D. F. (2011). Comorbidity in hoarding disorder. *Depression and Anxiety, 28*, 876–884.

Gormley, C. J., & Gormley, S. J. (2012). Data hoarding and information clutter: the impact of cost, life span of data, effectiveness, sharing, productivity and knowledge management culture. *Issues in Information Systems, 13*, 90–95.

Grisham, J. R., & Barlow, D. H. (2005). Compulsive hoarding: Current research and theory. *Journal of Psychopathology and Behavioral Assessment, 27*, 45–52.

Grisham, J. R., Frost, R. O., Steketee, G., Kim, H.-J., & Hood, S. (2006). Age of onset of compulsive hoarding. *Journal of Anxiety Disorders, 20*, 675–686.

Grisham, J. R., Frost, R. O., Steketee, G., Kim, H.-J., Tarkoff, A., & Hood, S. (2009). Formation of attachment to possessions in compulsive hoarding. *Journal of Anxiety Disorders, 23*, 357–361.

Hassan, G. (2018). *Declutter your life: How outer order leads to inner calm*. Chichester: Capstone.

Information Commissioner's Office. (2017). *Overview of the general data protection regulation (GDPR)*. Retrieved from https://ico.org.uk/media/for-organizations/data-protection-reform/overview-of-the-gdpr-1-13.pdf.

Ishikawa, A., & Naka, I. (2007). *Knowledge management and risk strategies*. Hackensack, NJ: World Scientific.

Jacob, J. (2017). *Date centers: A latent environmental threat*. Retrieved from https://sites.duke.edu/lit290s-1_02_s2017/2017/03/08/data-centers-a-latent-environmental-threat/.

Kondo, M. (2011). *The life-changing magic of tidying: A simple effective way to banish clutter forever*. London: Vermilion.

Lansdale, M. (1988). The psychology of personal information management. *Applied Ergonomics, 19*, 55–66.

Lepselter, S. (2011). The disorder of things: Hoarding narratives in popular media. *Anthropological Quarterly, 84*, 919–947.

Mataix-Cols, D., Frost, R. O., Pertusa, A., Clark, L. A., Saxena, S., Leckman, J. F., et al. (2010). Hoarding disorder: A new diagnosis for DSM-V? *Depression and Anxiety, 27*, 556–572.

Meyer, R. (2018). *The Atlantic*. Retrieved from https://www.theatlantic.com/technology/archive/2018/03/the-cambridge-analytica-scandal-in-three-paragraphs/556046/.

Neave, N., McKellar, K., Sillence, E., & Briggs, P. (2019). Digital hoarding behaviours: measurement and evaluation. *Computers in Human Behavior, 96*, 72–77.

Neave, N., Caiazza, R., Hamilton, C., McInnes, L., Saxton, T. K., Deary, V., et al. (2017). The economic costs of hoarding behaviours in local authority/housing association tenants and private home owners in the North-east of England. *Public Health, 148*, 137–139.

Neave, N., Jackson, R., Saxton, T., & Hönekopp, J. (2015). The influence of anthropomorphic tendencies on human hoarding behaviours. *Personality and Individual Differences, 72*, 214–219.

Neave, N., Tyson, H., McInnes, L., & Hamilton, C. (2016). The role of attachment style and anthropomorphism in predicting hoarding behaviours in a non-clinical sample. *Personality and Individual Differences, 99*, 33–37.

Nedelisky, A., & Steele, M. (2009). Attachment to people and to objects in obsessive-compulsive disorder: An exploratory comparison of hoarders and non-hoarders. *Attachment & Human Development, 11*, 365–383.

Oravec, J. A. (2015). Depraved, distracted, disabled or just "pack rats"? Workplace hoarding personas in physical and virtual realms. *Persona Studies, 1.2*, 75–87.

Oravec, J. A. (2018). Digital (or virtual) hoarding: Emerging implications of digital hoarding for computing, psychology, and organization science. *International Journal of Computers in Clinical Practice, 3*, 27–39.

Pertusa, A., Frost, R. O., Fullana, M. A., Samuels, J., Steketee, G., Tolin, D., et al. (2010). Refining the diagnostic boundaries of compulsive hoarding: A critical review. *Clinical Psychology Review, 30*, 371–386.

Peyton, A. (2015). Kill the dinosaurs, and other tips for achieving technical competence in your law practice. *Richmond Journal of Law and Technology, 21*, 1–27.

Piwek, L., & Joinson, A. (2016). "What do they snapchat about?" Patterns of use in time-limited instant messaging service. *Computers in Human Behavior, 54*, 358–367.

Samuels, J. F., Bienvenu, O. J., Grados, M. A., Cullen, B., Riddle, M. A., Liang, K.-Y., et al. (2008). Prevalence and correlates of hoarding behaviour in a community-based sample. *Behaviour Research and Therapy, 46*, 836–844.

Sloane, S. (2011). *The problem with packrats: The high costs of digital hoarding. Forbes, 25th march.*

Song, Z., Zhang, X., & Eriksson, C. (2015). Data center energy and cost saving evaluation. *Energy Procedia, 75*, 1255–1260.

Steketee, G., & Frost, R. (2003). Compulsive hoarding: Current status of the research. *Clinical Psychology Review, 23*, 905–927.

Strasser, B. J., & Edwards, P. N. (2017). Big data is the answer...but what is the question? *Osiris, 32*, 328–345.

Sweeten, G., Sillence, E., & Neave, N. (2018). Digital hoarding behaviours: Underlying motivations and potential negative consequences. *Computers in Human Behavior, 85*, 54–60.

Thompson, C., Fernández de la Cruz, L., Mataix-Cols, D., & Onwumere, J. (2017). A systematic review and quality assessment of psychological, pharmacological, and family-based interventions for hoarding disorder. *Asian Journal of Social Psychology, 27*, 53–66.

Tolin, D. F., Frost, R. O., & Steketee, G. (2014). *Buried in treasures: Help for compulsive acquiring, saving, and hoarding* (2nd ed.). Oxford: Oxford University Press.

Tolin, D. F., Frost, R. O., Steketee, G., & Muroff. (2015). Cognitive behavioral therapy for hoarding disorder: A meta-analysis. *Depression and Anxiety, 32*, 158–166.

Vitale, F., Janzen, I., & McGrenere, J. (2018). Hoarding and minimalism: Tendencies in digital data preservation. *Proceedings of CHI, 18*. https://doi.org/10.1145/3173574.3174161.

Whittaker, S., & Sidner, C. (1996). Email overload: Exploring personal information management of email. *Proceedings of CHI, 96*, 276–283.

CHAPTER

# 6

# A review of security awareness approaches: towards achieving communal awareness

*Azma Alina Ali Zani, Azah Anir Norman, Norjihan Abdul Ghani*

**Department of Information Systems, Faculty of Computer Science and Information Technology, University of Malaya, Kuala Lumpur, Malaysia**

OUTLINE




https://doi.org/10.1016/B978-0-12-819204-7.00006-3

## Introduction

Employees' security awareness is an important factor in an organization's security management (Rantos, Fysarakis, & Manifavas, 2012). It helps employees to better understand how to use information security techniques and procedures (Siponen, 2000) and the organization's security measures as specified in the information security policies (Puhakainen, 2006). Security awareness can be interpreted through one's understanding of the importance of information security, the actions and reactions that occur and the effort of protecting the organization's network and data (Shaw, Chen, Harris, & Huang, 2009). One of the most effective ways to promote security awareness is by educating employees of the recent and relevant security issues and by modifying their behaviour towards the intended security culture (Thomson & Solms, 1998), thereby fostering security-aware users (Wolf, Haworth, & Pietron, 2011) and increasing the understanding of the organization's security policy (Soomro, Shah, & Ahmed, 2016).

As an organization's information security awareness is a result of its employees' collective security awareness (Tariq, Brynielsson, & Artman, 2014), it is important that organizations not only provide training and education for awareness raising but also these trainings must be effective enough in changing behaviour both individually and collectively. Thus, in ensuring effective security awareness aimed at changing an organization's security behaviour, there must be organizational learning (Guynes, Windsor, & Wu, 2012), which is possible through exchange of experience (Caldwell, 2016) and knowledge (Hagen & Johnsen, 2010) between members of an organization. Although one can gain experience individually, organizational learning only takes place when the experience, idea and knowledge are shared between the other members of the organization.

However, each organization has different areas of risk (Abawajy, 2014) making a one-size-fits-all approach to security awareness impossible (Rizza & Pereira, 2013). This consequently contributes in the varying studies on security awareness approach which discusses the different content, delivery methods, underlying theories and assessment methods used. Content, such as laws and regulations (Wilson et al., 1998), existing and emerging security threats (McCrohan, Engel, & Harvey, 2010), the organization's security policy (Tsohou, Karyda, & Kokolakis, 2015) and procedure and best practises (Cindy, 2009) were among what was discussed. Delivery methods like instructor-led, computer-based (Hansche, 2001) and web-based or distance learning-based (Chen, Shaw, & Yang, 2006) were some of the methods studied. The variation in the study of security awareness approaches would help practitioners design a more suitable approach that would suit their organization's security goal.

Nevertheless, as approaches to security awareness is more than just a tool for checking compliance (Caldwell, 2016), academic studies on security awareness approach should go beyond awareness raising but rather facilitating in communal learning. Abundance of studies focuses on varying approaches for instilling security awareness but the many lack in having an underlying theory, practical proficiency (Puhakainen, 2006) and empirical evidence of their efficacy (Ding, Meso, & Xu, 2014; Flores, Antonsen, & Ekstedt, 2014; Puhakainen & Siponen, 2010). While there are studies of approaches that are based on underlying theories, further investigation on whether it supports communal learning is called for.

The objective of this review is to present an overview of the research on security awareness approaches. The specific aims of this review are (1) to present the underlying theories used; (2) to identify the delivery methods selected; (3) to provide information on commonly discussed topics or program content and (4) to find out if this research provides empirical evidence of communal learning in the security awareness approach design and consequently to help readers associate the suitable delivery methods, program content or underlying theory for their own security awareness program designs, thus adding to the body of knowledge in the field of IS security literature.

## Designing an effective approach to increasing security awareness

In nurturing a security-aware culture (Rantos et al., 2012) employees should have basic security awareness knowledge and understand the organization's security measures (Spears & Barki, 2010) as specified in the information security policies and instructions (Puhakainen, 2006) and the possible outcomes of their actions (Ahlan & Lubis, 2011). Karjalainen and Siponen (2011) in their study suggest that, fundamentally, security awareness training should be persuasive and noncognitive in nature; consist of an explanation of the need for the training by including security-sensitive organizational assets, threats towards them and protection of the organization's assets from different technical, social and organizational mechanisms; and that the practise of IS security training at organizations promotes communal transformation. This altogether defines what should be included as the program content for a security awareness approach.

Karjalainen and Siponen (2011) also state that there are four pedagogical contexts which a security awareness training approach should fulfil. The four pedagogical requirements are the explicit psychological context based on a group-oriented theoretical approach of teaching and learning; the training content based on collective learners' experience; teaching methods that concentrate on collaborative learning for revealing and producing collective knowledge and, lastly, evaluation of the learning emphasized experiential and communication-based methods from the perspective of the learning community. Thus, as knowledge creation is a collaborative process (McNiff, Whitehead, & Education, 2006), sharing collective experience and enabling collaborative learning should form the basis of an effective approach to increasing security awareness, which is subsequently reflected in the selection of the underlying theory, contents, delivery methods and overall evaluation.

Additionally, studies on approaches to increasing security awareness that propose an empirically proven approach will considerably help practitioners in making an informed decision when selecting a suitable approach for their organization.

## Program content and delivery method

The content of an approach varies according to an organization's aims as detailed by its security policy, tools and procedures (Peltier, 2005). Content should be customizable and easy to update (Ghazvini & Shukur, 2016). It is important the content facet of a security awareness program to include the learners' collective experience (Karjalainen & Siponen, 2011), as employees learn how to behave according to what was outlined in the policies and standard procedures, how their coworkers behave and their experience accumulated by the decisions they previously made (Leach, 2003; Stephanou & Dagada, 2008). This is in hope that with the appropriate design, a security awareness program can inspire employees to tune their experience, knowledge and expertise collectively and to convert it into corporate memory where the individuals will then be able to retrieve these memories and improvise their actions accordingly (Guynes et al., 2012).

When the content has been decided on, it is time to choose an appropriate delivery approach. This mostly depends on the availability of the expertise and resources (Furnell, Gennatou, & Dowland, 2002), the complexity of the intended message (Wilson & Hash, 2003), the security needs (Johnson, 2006), the budget (Tsohou, Kokolakis, Karyda, Kiountouzis, & Systems, 2008) and the target audience (Aloul, 2012). Therefore, customization is required to suit organizational needs because one size does not fit all (Rizza & Pereira, 2013). While choosing between the wide variety of delivery methods, such as using paper-based, online-based, computer-based, instructor-led or game-based (Ghazvini & Shukur, 2016), one must bear in mind the importance of selecting one that will promote collaborative learning (Karjalainen & Siponen, 2011), which will produce collective knowledge (Khan et al., 2011a, 2011b). Although some studies found that using a mixture of approaches is more effective than using a single approach (Abawajy, 2014; Puhakainen, 2006; Tsohou, Karyda, Kokolakis, & Kiountouzis, 2012), some organizations prefer using only one approach because of limited resources.

## Underlying theory

Even with abundant discussions on the significance of having an underlying theory (Al-Omari, El-Gayar, & Deokar, 2012; Dinev & Hu, 2007; Pfleeger & Caputo, 2012; Sohrabi et al., 2015), some studies still do not present an underlying theory (Heikka, 2008; Puhakainen, 2006), lack empirical support of the practicality of the proposed approach (Puhakainen, 2006) or focus on methods and techniques (Stephanou & Dagada, 2008), which results in practitioners' contemplation on the usefulness of the selected approach in enhancing employees' policy compliance (Puhakainen, 2006), consequently changing employees' security behaviour. Security awareness research should be able to provide significance (Lebek, Uffen, Breitner, Neumann, & Hohler, 2013) and recommendations for the design, selection and evaluation of the pedagogical ability of the varying approaches (Karjalainen, 2011). It is also vital that the development and validation of the proposed approach for raising awareness and changing behaviour be based on existing theoretical knowledge (Lebek et al., 2013). Therefore, as proposed by Karjalainen and Siponen (2011), for an approach to be communally effective, it should not only have a sound underlying theory, but it should specifically use a group-oriented theoretical approach.

Thus, we focused our study on whether the approach proposed in prior studies embedded collaborative learning and experience sharing when selecting underlying theories, program content and delivery methods.

## Methodology

This review studies research on different approaches to increasing security awareness, with the main focus on the application of the underlying theory in each one's design, and investigates the delivery methods and content used. With the aim of contributing to the existing body of knowledge, the review was conducted in accordance with the approach suggested by Webster and Watson (2002). Appropriate literature was selected by performing a structured literature search; then, the selected literature was examined by focussing on the approach to increasing security awareness. To ensure that only valid literature was selected, we performed a thorough literature search that is replicable using the same database, keywords and publications. Additionally, a forward and backward search was executed.

Thus, this paper aims to provide a comprehensive review of current IS approaches to increasing security awareness by examining the application of the underlying theories, program content and delivery methods, by answering the following research questions:

**RQ1:** What theories are applied when designing the current approaches to increasing security awareness?
**RQ2:** What program contents and delivery methods are used in the designs of the approaches to increasing security awareness?
**RQ3:** Do the theory, content and delivery method chosen promote communal learning in an organization?

## Search process

We chose to include both high-ranking and non–high-ranking conferences and journals. White papers and book chapters were excluded. We searched the following databases: IEEEXplorer, Science Direct, Springer Link, ProQuest, Emerald, WOS and Scopus. The search process is depicted in Fig. 6.1.

The overlapping databases ensure wider coverage. Only articles written in English were considered, and publications that do not predominantly deal with the development of information security awareness training were excluded. The search was performed manually by filtering the articles according to their title and abstract and, if required, by skimming through the full text.

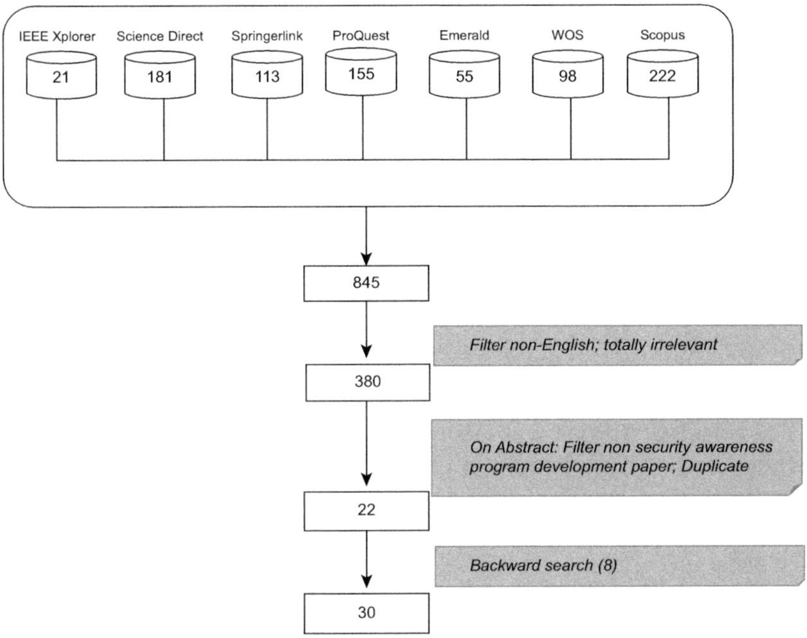


FIGURE 6.1 The search process.

## Search terms

The search terms used revealed the articles tabulated in Table 6.1. The databases were set to find the search terms in the title, abstract or keywords unless unable to do so. We then performed a full-text search. We conducted the search using the following search string:

(("information security awareness" OR "cyber security awareness") AND (program OR Training) AND (Development OR Design))

Stephanou and Dagada (2008) stated that information security awareness research is focused on four main branches: the importance and

TABLE 6.1 Search terms.

| (1) Information security awareness | (2) Program | (3) Development |
|---|---|---|
| Information security awareness | Program* (programs, programme, programmes) | Development |
| Cyber security awareness | Training | Design |

techniques of security awareness; computer abuse; insider threat and behavioural information security. For the purpose of this study, we only included research that falls under the importance and techniques of security awareness branch. Through the literature search, we identified twenty-two articles that were specifically related to the development of cybersecurity awareness training. We also performed a manual backward search on the articles and found an additional eight articles (marked *) related to the topic. In total, thirty articles were found to be relevant for this review (Table 6.2).

## Findings and discussions

The selected studies were examined to find the content and delivery method, if the study provided empirical support and if it had any underlying theory. We then asked if this study supported the sharing of experience and collaborative learning. The findings are summarized in Table 6.3.

We found that 50% of the studies used conceptual research, while the other 50% provided empirical support for their research, and that 14 did not discuss the use of any underlying theory. However, these studies mentioned the use of existing standards or guidelines, such as NIST Special Publication 800-16, NIST Special Publication 800-50, NIST800-55 and NIST800-100.

## Overview of theories used

### RQ1: What theories are applied when designing the current approaches to increasing security awareness?

Of the 30 studies, 17 are theory-based. We categorized the theories used into Behavioural Theory, Cognitive Theory, Cognitive Development Theory, Information Security Theory, Learning Theory, Organizational Learning Theory, Psychological Theory and Sociological Learning Theory. Learning theories, behavioural theories and organizational learning theories are the three categories of the most applied theories among the selected studies. The distribution of the applied theories is depicted in Fig. 6.2.

Learning Theory used in the studies are Brain-Based Learning and teaching, Brain-Compatible Learning, Constructionist Learning Theory, Constructivism, Game-Based Learning, Instructional Design, Theory of Instruction and Theory of Learning. While the Behavioural Theory and Organizational Learning Theory include Information-Motivation-

TABLE 6.2 Selected studies.

| Author, year | | | |
|---|---|---|---|
| Label | | Label | |
| 1 | Awawdeh and Tubaishat (2014) | 16 | Eminağaoğlu, Uçar and Eren (2009) |
| 2 | Reid and van Niekerk (2014) | 17 | Hagen and Albrechtsen (2009) |
| 3 | SanNicolas-Rocca, Schooley, and Spears (2014) | 18 | Shaw et al. (2009) |
| 4 | Ding et al. (2014) | 19 | Tolnai and von Solms (2009) |
| 5 | Faisal, Nisa', and Ibrahim (2013) | 20 | Fung, Khera, Depickere, Tantatsanawong, and Boonbrahm (2008) |
| 6 | Gundu and Flowerday (2012) | 21 | *Heikka (2008) |
| 7 | Mangold (2012) | 22 | Cone, Irvine, Thompson, and Nguyen (2007) |
| 8 | *Nagarajan, Allbeck, Sood, and Janssen (2012) | 23 | *Forget, Chiasson, and Biddle (2007) |
| 9 | Jordan, Knapp, Mitchell, Claypool, and Fisler (2011) | 24 | *Greitzer, Kuchar, and Huston (2007) |
| 10 | (Khan et al., 2011a) | 25 | Maeyer (2007) |
| 11 | Labuschagne, Burke, Veerasamy, and Eloff (2011) | 26 | Endicott-popovsky, Orton, Bailey, and Frincke (2005) |
| 12 | Reid, Van Niekerk, and Von Solms (2011) | 27 | *Biros (2004) |
| 13 | Albrechtsen and Hovden (2010) | 28 | *McCoy and Fowler (2004) |
| 14 | Boujettif and Wang (2010) | 29 | *S. Furnell et al. (2002) |
| 15 | Chan (2009) | 30 | *Cox, Connolly, and Currall (2001) |

TABLE 6.3 Summary of findings.

| | | | | Research Approach | | |
|---|---|---|---|---|---|---|
| | | | | Empirical | | Conceptual |
| Study | Applied theory/Mode l | Program Content | Delivery Method | QN (n) | QL (n) | Proposed Program |
| 1 | Not mentioned | Designated Topic | Not mentioned | | | Proposed a designated SAP for IT unit |
| 2 | Brain-Based Learning and Teaching (Jensen, 1995)<br>Brain-Compatible Learning (McGeehan, 2001) | Not mentioned | Web-Based | 83 | | |
| 3 | Theory of Knowledge Transfer<br>A Dynamic Theory of Organizational Knowledge Creation (Nonaka, 1994)<br>User Participation and Motivation (Mitchell, 1973) | Not mentioned | Discussion | 128 | | |
| 4 | PMT – Protection Motivation Theory (Rogers, 1983) | Basic Computer Skill | Hands-On | 120 | | |
| 5 | Not mentioned | Social Engineering | Not mentioned | | | Proposed Islamic perspectives into SAP |
| 6 | TRA – Theory of Reasoned Action (Ajzen and Fishbein, 1974)<br>PMT – Protection Motivation Theory (Rogers, 1983)<br>Organizational Learning Models (Van Niekerk and Von Solms, 2004) | Basic Computer Skills | Web-Based | 28 | | |

| | | | | | | |
|---|---|---|---|---|---|---|
| **7** | Not mentioned | Designated Topic | Instructor-Led | | | Proposed an adaptive SAP |
| **8** | Not mentioned | Basic Computer Skills<br>Social Engineering<br>Access Management | Game-Based | | | Proposed interactive training using a gaming environment |
| **9** | Not mentioned | Basic Computer Skills | Game-Based | 20 | | |
| **10** | Knowledge-Deficit Model of Behaviour Change (Schultz, 1999)<br>Information-Motivation-Behavioural Skills Model of Diabetes Self-Care (Osborne et al., 2010)<br>Information-Motivation-Behavioural Skills Model —HIV Risk Behaviour Intervention (Fisher et al., 2002) | Basic Computer Skills<br>Access Management | Discussions | | | Proposed a SAP integrated with the best practises of health awareness and environmental awareness models |
| **11** | TAM – Technology Acceptance Model (Davis, 1986)<br>Extended TAM (Moon and Kim, 2001) | Basic Computer Skills<br>Social Engineering | Game-Based | | | Developed a conceptual prototype of an interactive game that runs on social networking sites |
| **12** | Brain-Compatible Learning (McGeehan, 2001) | Basic Computer Skills<br>Social Engineering<br>Ethics<br>Rules and Regulations | Web-Based | | | Proposed an approach based on the five brain-compatible education principles |

*Continued*

TABLE 6.3 Summary of findings.—cont'd

| Study | Applied theory/Mode l | Program Content | Delivery Method | Research Approach | | |
|---|---|---|---|---|---|---|
| | | | | Empirical | | Conceptual |
| | | | | QN (n) | QL (n) | Proposed Program |
| 13 | Worker Participation (Greenberg, 1975)<br>Collective Reflection | Basic Computer Skills<br>Designated Topic | Discussions | 196 | | |
| 14 | Constructivism (Psychological Theory of Learning) (1996)<br>Theory of Learning by Doing (1979) | Not mentioned | Hands-On | 116 | | |
| 15 | Piaget's Genetic Epistemology (1970)<br>Kuhn's paradigm shift and incommensurability (1970)<br>Theory of Conceptual Change (Posner et al., 1982) | Basic Computer Skills | Instructor-Led | 102 | | |
| 16 | Not mentioned | Basic Computer Skills<br>Designated Topic<br>Rules and Regulations | Instructor-Led | 2900 | | |
| 17 | Not mentioned | Basic Computer Skills<br>Social Engineering<br>Access Management | Computer-Based | 1897 | | |
| 18 | Theory of Instruction (Bruner, 1966)<br>Theory of Situation Awareness in Dynamic Systems (Endsley, | Basic Computer Skills<br>Social Engineering | Web-Based | 153 | | |

| | | | | | | |
|---|---|---|---|---|---|---|
| | 1995)<br>Concept Maps and Vee Diagram (Novak, 1990)<br>Instructional Design (Sweller, 1999) | | | | | |
| **19** | Not mentioned | Basic Computer Skills | Web-Based | | | Proposed a portal with comprehensive knowledge |
| **20** | Not mentioned | Basic Computer Skills<br>Social Engineering<br>Ethics | Game-Based | 16 | | |
| **21** | Constructivism (Psychological Theory of Learning) (Piaget 1972) | Basic Computer Skills<br>Rules and Regulations | Discussion | | 29 | |
| **22** | Game-Based Learning (Prensky, 2001) | Basic Computer Skills<br>Social Engineering<br>Access Management | Game-Based | | | Proposed using gaming environment CyberCIEGE to be used as interactive training |
| **23** | Persuasive Technology | Not mentioned | Computer-Based | | | Proposed a persuasive authentication framework |
| **24** | Theories of Motivation<br>Cognitive Theory (Miller, 1956)<br>Constructionist Learning Theory (Bruckman, 1998) | Basic Computer Skills<br>Social Engineering<br>Access Management | Game-Based | | | Proposed using an interactive gaming environment: CyberCIEGE |

*Continued*

TABLE 6.3 Summary of findings.—cont'd

| Study | Applied theory/Mode l | Program Content | Delivery Method | Research Approach | | |
|---|---|---|---|---|---|---|
| | | | | Empirical | | Conceptual |
| | | | | QN (n) | QL (n) | Proposed Program |
| 25 | Not mentioned | Basic Computer Skills<br>Social Engineering | Computer-Based | N not stated | | |
| 26 | Not mentioned | Basic Computer Skills | Simulation | | | Proposed using simulation of Google Hacking for awareness |
| 27 | Signal Detection Theory (SDT)<br>Theory of Task Performance (Campbell et al., 1993)<br>Constructivism (Psychological Theory of Learning) (1996) | Social Engineering | Instructor-Led<br>Computer-Based<br>Simulation | 205 | | |
| 28 | Not mentioned | Basic Computer Skills<br>Social Engineering | Instructor-Led | | | Proposed a flexible security awareness program |
| 29 | Not mentioned | Not mentioned | Computer-Based | | | Proposed the use of a self-paced software tool |
| 30 | Not mentioned | Basic Computer Skills<br>Social Engineering<br>Ethics | Discussions | | | Proposed a multiple method for security awareness |

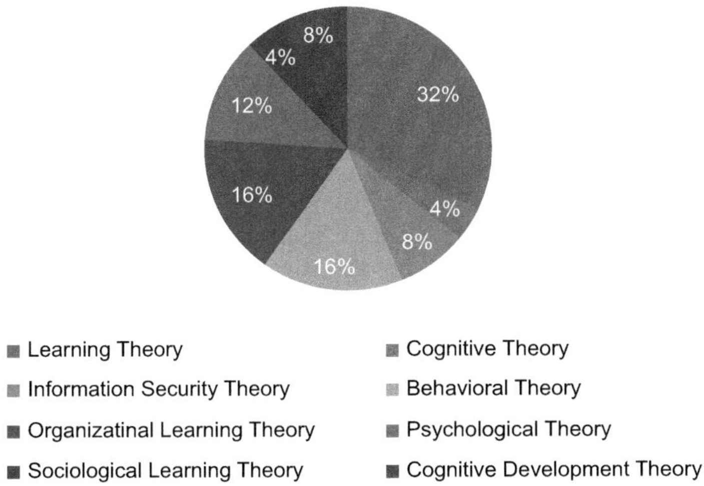


FIGURE 6.2 Percentage of applied theories in the studies.

Behavioural Skills Model-HIV Risk Behaviour Intervention, Information-Motivation-Behavioural Skills Model of Diabetes Self-Care, Knowledge-Deficit Model of Behaviour Change, Protection Motivation Theory, Organizational Learning Models, Theory of Task performance, Theory of Worker Participation and Theory of Knowledge Transfer.

The most used theories are the Constructivism Theory of Learning, Protection Motivation Theory and Brain-Compatible Learning Methods (see Fig. 6.3).

Constructivism Theory is a psychological theory of learning where it promotes active learning and commitment by the participants based on their experience. Heikka (2008) implemented Constructivism Theory in the delivery methods whereby the discussions between the middle managers reflect on their previous action, consequently cascading the training outcome and experience to their subordinates. Biros (2004) also applied both Constructivism and security awareness approach where the participants need to relate to their past experience and a prior instructor-led training course to solve the deceptive scenario quiz given using a computer-based approach.

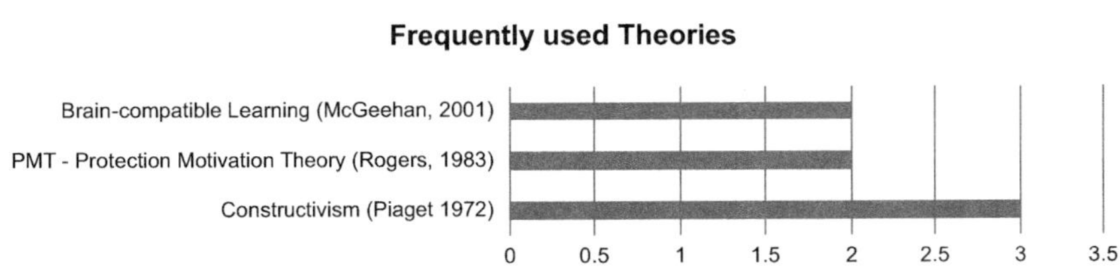


FIGURE 6.3 Frequently used theories.

Protection Motivation Theory suggests that there are four elements that contribute to self-protection which are perceived severity of a threat, perceived possibility of the threat occurring, the efficiency of the proposed preventive behaviour and perceived self-usefulness. Ding et al. (2014) discussed the application of Protection Motivation Theory in both their delivery approach and program content where they embedded their hands-on delivery approach with perception altering content. Participants' existing knowledge on an information security topic is altered by providing new information on possible threat concerning the said topic.

While these studies mentioned the application of individual experience when executing the security awareness approach, group-oriented experience sharing was not applied. Although more than half of the studies were theory-based, only one study emphasizes an approach that is based on a group-oriented theoretical approach. The selection of theory is important as it influences the type of delivery methods and/or the program content chosen later.

Study by Albrechtsen and Hovden (2010) applied Worker Participation Theory and collective reflection, which focus on worker participation, collective reflections, group work and experience transfer as an approach to shape the intended security behaviour as the intended output of their security awareness approach. Their security awareness approach supported the exchange and sharing of experience within group.

## Program contents and delivery methods

### RQ2: What program contents and delivery methods are used in the designs of the approaches to increasing security awareness?

We categorized the content discussed in the studies into seven topics: Basic Computer Skills (BCS), Social Engineering (SE), Access (A), Rules and Regulations (R), Designated Topics (DT), Ethics (E) and Information Assurance (IA). The categorization of these topics is listed in Table 6.4. It was found that the most discussed topic was BCS.

We found that twenty-five out of thirty studies mentioned BCS and SE. Five studies did not mention the discussed topics while three studies only discussed only one topic category for their security awareness content. We found that twenty-two studies used multiple topics. Findings are tabulated in Table 6.5.

We found that there were studies which pointed out the importance of linking prior individual experience with the newly gained knowledge (Biros, 2004; Chan, 2009; Nagarajan et al., 2012; Reid et al., 2011) without integrating the sharing of communal experience with the program content and delivery methods. While the content of the security awareness

**TABLE 6.4** Categories of topics.

| Label | Topic | Label | Topic | Label | Topic |
|---|---|---|---|---|---|
| Basic Computer skills (BCS) | | Social Engineering (SE) | | Access (A) | |
| B1 | Password management | S1 | Data safeguarding | A1 | Remote access |
| B2 | Password hacking | S2 | Social engineering | A2 | Access control |
| B3 | Information security | S3 | Social media | | |
| B4 | Virus | S4 | Physical security | Rules and Regulations (R) | |
| B5 | Internet security | S5 | Information deception | R1 | Policy |
| B6 | Firewall | | | | |
| B7 | E-mail | Designated Topics (DT) | | Ethics (E) | |
| B8 | Malicious software | D1 | Task-related | E1 | Ethics |
| B9 | Basic computing | D2 | IT department designated | E2 | Security behaviour |
| B10 | Hacking | | | E3 | Insider threat |
| B11 | Backup | Information Assurance (IA) | | | |
| B12 | Patch management | I1 | Information assurance | | |
| B13 | Network security | | | | |

approaches varies according to the needs of the organization, any of the topics should be able to be linked with the personal experience of the user and then shared to the user community to promote communal learning. The users may then be able to associate these shared experience with the existentialistic facets of the need of the security awareness training (existence of security-sensitive organizational assets; threats towards them and protection for the organization's assets from different technical, social and organizational mechanisms and that the practise of IS security training at organizations promotes the communal transformation).

When examining the delivery methods, we found that twenty-eight studies mentioned the type of delivery method used. Two of the studies

TABLE 6.5 Distribution of topics.

| Study | Topics | | | | | | | |
|---|---|---|---|---|---|---|---|---|
| | Basic Computer Skills (BCS) | Social Engineering (SE) | Ethics (E) | Access (A) | Information Assurance (IA) | Designated Topics (DT) | Rules and Regulations (R) | Not Mentioned |
| 1 | | | | | | D2 | | |
| 2 | | | | | | | | / |
| 3 | | | | | | | | / |
| 4 | B1,B2,B3 | | | | | | | |
| 5 | | S1 | | | | | | |
| 6 | B1,B4,B5,B6 | | | | | | | |
| 7 | | | | | | D1 | | |
| 8 | B1,B7,B8,B12 | S2 | | | | | | |
| 9 | B1,B3,B10 | | | | | | | |
| 10 | B3,B12 | | | | | | | |
| 11 | B1,B7, | S3 | | | | | | |
| 12 | B1,B3,B4,B11 | S1,S2,S3,S4 | E1 | | | | R1 | |
| 13 | B3 | | | | | D1 | | |
| 14 | | | | | | | | / |
| 15 | B5 | | | | | | | |

| | | | | | | | | |
|---|---|---|---|---|---|---|---|---|
| 16 | B1,B3 | | | | | D1 | R1 | |
| 17 | B3 | S4 | | A1 | | | | |
| 18 | B1,B7,B3,B4 | S2 | | | | | | |
| 19 | B5 | | | | | | | |
| 20 | B3,B13,B6 | S1,S2,S4 | E2 | | | | | |
| 21 | B3 | | | | | | R1 | |
| 22 | B1,B9,B3,B8 | S1,S2,S4 | | A2 | I1 | | | |
| 23 | | | | | | | | / |
| 24 | B1,B4,B6,B7,B9,B11,B13, | S4 | | A1,A2 | | | | |
| 25 | B1,B3,B5 | S2 | | | | | | |
| 26 | B1,B13 | | | | | | | |
| 27 | | S5 | | | | | | |
| 28 | B1,B4,B7, | S2,S4 | | | | | | |
| 29 | | | | | | | | / |
| 30 | B1,B3,B4,B5,B11 | S1,S4 | E3 | | I1 | | | |

(Awawdeh & Tubaishat, 2014; Faisal et al. 2013) did not. After assessing the studies, we categorized the delivery methods into seven categories: Instructor-Led, Computer-Based, Game-Based, Web-Based, Hands-On, Discussions and Simulation (see Table 6.6).

We found that the most frequently used were Instructor-Led, Game-Based, Web-Based and Computer-Based delivery methods. The frequency percentage of the applied delivery methods is summarized in Fig. 6.4.

Twenty-eight studies applied only a single type of delivery method except one (Biros, 2004) that applied Instructor-Led, Computer-Based and Simulation as the main delivery methods. The findings are summarized in Table 6.7.

Caldwell (2016) shared from the interviews with executives involved with information security training, some of the reasons why security awareness failed to change employees' behaviour, which includes failure to manage follow-up on training efficacy, providing only a one-off training, having targeted training instead of involving all employees and providing standard training that is out of context.

Although a security awareness approach should be carried out as regular and incessant effort (Tsohou et al., 2012) instead of a one-time thing (Gardner and Thomas, 2014) to ensure continuous learning from past information security occurrences (Webb et al., 2014), most studies discussed having only the main delivery methods without any supporting security awareness delivery methods and were carried out either only once or over a short time span. Hence we also looked if the studies provide supporting delivery methods.

We found twenty studies applied a main delivery method, while the other eight had supporting delivery methods. We categorized the supporting delivery methods into six categories: Flyer, Web Portal, Intranet, Media Coverage, E-mail and Instructor-Led (see Tables 6.8 and 6.9).

Among the eight studies that used supporting delivery methods, four had multiple supporting delivery methods.

## Attaining communal learning

### RQ3: Do the theory, content and delivery method chosen promote communal learning in an organization?

It is known that the content of the approach varies according to the needs of the organization. The main aim of an organization's approach is to communally change security behaviour; thus, it is crucial that the content is linked to the personal experience of the employee (Caldwell, 2016) and then shared to other employees to promote communal learning. The employees may then be able to associate these shared experiences

TABLE 6.6 Main delivery methods categories.

| Instructor Led | Label | | Computer-Based | Game-Based | Label | | Web-Based |
|---|---|---|---|---|---|---|---|
| Instructor-led learning-assisted via ontology tools for adaptive e-learning | I1 | C1 | E-learning | CyberNEXS | G1 | W1 | E-learning Moodle 2.0 |
| Lecture | I2 | C2 | Built-in persuasive technology | Countermeasures mission completion | G2 | W2 | E-learning |
| Training | I3 | C3 | Training courses | Gaming via social networking sites | G3 | W3 | E-learning embedded hypermedia, multimedia and hypertext |
| Lecture and presentation slides | I4 | C4 | Agent 99 | Gaming environment CyberCIEGE | G4 | W4 | Information security awareness portal |
| In-person training | I5 | C5 | Security training tool | | | W5 | Web-based training |
| ***Hands-On*** | ***Label*** | | ***Discussions*** | | ***Label*** | | ***Simulation*** |
| User participated in simulation of password cracking | H1 | D1 | Two-way discussion participation in program development | | | S1 | Google Hacking |
| User participated in security awareness training development | H2 | D2 | Group discussion as informal meeting | | | S2 | Scenario-based test |
| | | D3 | Forum for discussion | | | | |
| | | D4 | Interactive lecture with social interaction (cascade training) | | | | |
| | | D5 | Lunch series lecture | | | | |

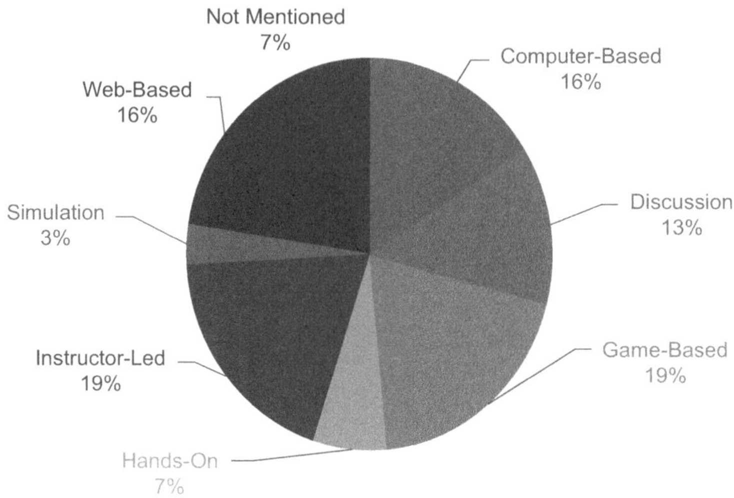


**FIGURE 6.4** Percentage of the delivery methods used in the studies.

with the need for security awareness training (existence of security-sensitive organizational assets; threats towards them; protection for the organization's assets from different technical, social and organizational mechanisms; and that the practise of IS security training at organizations promotes communal transformation).

We found that a few studies applied a delivery method and/or content which support communal learning. Only one study (Albrechtsen & Hovden, 2010) focused on ensuring experience sharing and collaborative learning, thus enabling communal learning in the selection of theory, content and delivery methods while providing empirical support. Other studies focused on a security awareness approach that was directed towards modifying individual security behaviour instead of aiming at attaining communal change.

The aforementioned studies which pointed out the importance of linking prior individual experience with newly gained knowledge were Khan et al., 2011a, 2011b, Albrechtsen and Hovden (2010), Boujettif and Wang (2010) and Tolnai and von Solms (2009, pp. 1–5). Only four studies (SanNicolas-Rocca et al., 2014; Khan et al., 2011a, 2011b; Albrechtsen & Hovden, 2010; Boujettif & Wang, 2010; Tolnai & von Solms, 2009, pp. 1–5) emphasized the significance of using a delivery method that supports the exchanging of communal experience in moulding the intended security behaviour through discussion and forum.

These findings suggests that academic literature on security awareness approaches are still largely focused on methods and techniques of

TABLE 6.7 Distribution of main delivery methods applied.

| Studies | Instructor Led | Computer-Based | Game-Based | Web-Based | Hands-on | Discussion | Simulation | Not Mentioned |
|---|---|---|---|---|---|---|---|---|
| 1 | | | | | | | | / |
| 2 | | | | W1 | | | | |
| 3 | | | | | | D1 | | |
| 4 | | | | | H1 | | | |
| 5 | | | | | | | | / |
| 6 | | | | W2 | | | | |
| 7 | I1 | | | | | | | |
| 8 | | | G1 | | | | | |
| 9 | | | G2 | | | | | |
| 10 | | | | | H2 | | | |
| 11 | | | G3 | | | | | |
| 12 | | | | W1 | | | | |
| 13 | | | | | | D3 | | |
| 14 | | | | | H2 | | | |
| 15 | I2 | | | | | | | |
| 16 | I3 | | | | | | | |
| 17 | | C1 | | | | | | |

*Continued*

TABLE 6.7 Distribution of main delivery methods applied.—cont'd

| Studies | Instructor Led | Computer-Based | Game-Based | Web-Based | Hands-on | Discussion | Simulation | Not Mentioned |
|---|---|---|---|---|---|---|---|---|
| 18 | | | | W3 | | | | |
| 19 | | | | W4 | | | | |
| 20 | | | G4 | | | | | |
| 21 | | | | | | D4 | | |
| 22 | | | G4 | | | | | |
| 23 | | C2 | | | | | | |
| 24 | | | G4 | | | | | |
| 25 | | C3 | | | | | | |
| 26 | | | | | | | S1 | |
| 27 | I4 | C4 | | | | | S2 | |
| 28 | I5 | | | W5 | | | | |
| 29 | | C5 | | | | | | |
| 30 | | | | | | D5 | | |

TABLE 6.8 Categories of supporting delivery methods.

| Flyers Brochure | Label | | Intranet | Media coverage | Label |
|---|---|---|---|---|---|
| Printed leaflets | F1 | I1 | Messages animation | News coverage on | M1 |
| ISA brochures | F2 | I2 | Newsletter | Students newspaper ads | M2 |
| Poster of slogan and graphic | | I3 | Topical article e-learning with topical interview videos | Campaign posters | M3 |
| Topical posters | | I4 | Newsletters payroll stuffers | | |
| Campaign posters | | I5 | Checklist | | |
| ***Web Portal*** | ***Label*** | | ***E-mail*** | ***Instructor-Led*** | |
| Presentation videos caricatures Puzzles and quizzes | W1 | E1 | Targeted mass e-mail | PowerPoint Presentation | L1 |
| Online tutorial | W2 | | | | |

disseminating awareness at individual level rather than ensuring the approaches' contribution towards facilitating communal learning. This can be seen by types of theoretical base, delivery methods and content chosen. Although individual learning is connected to organizational learning (Stelmaszczyk, 2016), organizational culture cannot be built with just individual employee but it must include exchange of knowledge and experience with other employees and other stakeholders. Additionally, by involving employees in their personal security risks experience exchange would help them become more engaged thus resulting in a more holistic approach to security awareness raising.

## Limitations

Some related publications might be missing from this literature review because of the selection of search terms and/or databases. The limitation on the search terms and identified literature might exist as we only selected literature in English, and non—peer-reviewed papers were not included. It is also possible that communal learning is the unspoken aim of every security awareness approach mentioned in the selected studies; thus, we only analyzed the information that was known to us.

TABLE 6.9 Distribution of supporting delivery methods.

| Studies | Flyers Brochure | Intranet | Posters | Instructor-Led | E-mail | Web Portal | Media Coverage |
|---|---|---|---|---|---|---|---|
| 3 | | | | L1 | | | |
| 10 | F1 | | | | | | |
| 16 | | I1 | P1 | | | W1 | |
| 17 | | I2 | | | | | |
| 25 | F2 | I3 | P2 | | | | |
| 26 | | | | | | | M1 |
| 28 | | I4 | P3 | | E1 | | M2 |
| 30 | | I5 | | | | W2 | |

## Conclusion and future work

An organization's information security awareness is a result of its employees' collective security awareness (Tariq et al., 2014). Thus, organizations adopting a security awareness approach that is aimed to effectively change behaviour communally should opt for theories, content and delivery methods that promote experience sharing and collaborative learning. It was found that the wide varieties of approaches, although generally meant to change behaviour communally, mostly used an underlying theory, delivery methods and content that focused on altering individual security behaviour and not promoting the sharing of communal experiences and collaborative learning.

Additionally, research in approaches to increasing security awareness still lacks empirical support to prove its effectiveness, as most studies were conducted conceptually. Practitioners may benefit greatly from a study that proposes an empirically proven approach. Although it is understood that the selection of an ideal approach may differ from one organization to another, if more research was done empirically and aimed at instilling change communally, it would provide wider options to practitioners.

Rosemann and Vessey (2008) stated that to avoid academic research becoming obsolete, it has to offer some significance to the practitioner. Thus, studies on approaches should move towards embedding experience in theories, content, delivery methods and feedback. By moving towards enabling collaborative approaches, future studies could also utilize and investigate potential tools that would support this effort, such as using current tools like Twitter that have already been used for real-time collaborations and experience sharing.

## Acknowledgements

The authors would like to express their gratitude for and acknowledge the support provided by the BKP Special Programme 2017 at the University of Malaya under research grant number BKS080-2017.

## References

Abawajy, J. (2014). User preference of cyber security awareness delivery methods. *Behaviour and Information Technology, 33*, 236–247.

Ahlan, A. R., & Lubis, M. (2011). Information security awareness in university: Maintaining learnability, performance and adaptability through roles of responsibility. In *Proc. 2011 7th int. Conf. Inf. Assur. Secur. IAS 2011* (pp. 246–250).

Ajzen, I., & Fishbein, M. (1974). Factors influencing intentions and the intention-behavior relation. *Human Relations, 27*(1), 1–15.

Al-Omari, A., El-Gayar, O., & Deokar, A. (2012). Security policy compliance: User acceptance perspective. In *2012 45th Hawaii int. Conf. Syst. Sci* (pp. 3317–3326).

Albrechtsen, E., & Hovden, J. (2010). Improving information security awareness and behaviour through dialogue, participation and collective reflection. An intervention study. *Computers and Security, 29*, 432–445.

Aloul, F. a. (2012). The need for effective information security awareness. *Journal of Advances in Information Technology, 3*, 176–183.

Al Awawdeh, S., & Tubaishat, A. (2014). An information security awareness program to address common security concerns in IT unit. In *2014 11th int. Conf. Inf. Technol. New gener* (pp. 273–278).

Biros, D. P. (2004). Scenario-based training for deception detection. In *Proc. 1st annu. Conf. Inf. Secur. Curric. Dev* (pp. 32–36).

Bruckman, A. (1998). Community support for constructionist learning. *Computer Supported Cooperative Work (CSCW), 7*(1-2), 47–86.

Bruner, J. S. (1966). *Toward a theory of instruction* (Vol. 59). Harvard University Press.

Boujettif, M., & Wang, Y. (2010). Constructivist approach to information security awareness in the middle east. In *2010 int. Conf. Broadband, wirel. Comput. Commun. Appl.* (pp. 192–199).

Caldwell, T. (2016). Making security awareness training work. *Computer Fraud and Security, 2016*, 8–14.

Campbell, J. P., McCloy, R. A., Oppler, S. H., & Sager, C. E. (1993). A theory of performance. *Personnel selection in organizations, 3570*, 35–70.

Chan, Y.-Y. (2009). Using anomalous data to foster conceptual change in security awareness. In *2009 int. Symp. Intell. Signal process. Commun. Syst* (pp. 638–642).

Chen, C., Shaw, R., & Yang, S. (2006). Mitigating information security risks by increasing user security awareness: A case study of an information security awareness system. *Information Technology and Learning, 24*, 1–14.

Cindy, B. (2009). NS Ins titu Au tho r r eta ins l rig. *Sans Inst, 27*.

Cone, B. D., Irvine, C. E., Thompson, M. F., & Nguyen, T. D. (2007). A video game for cyber security training and awareness. *Computers and Security, 26*, 63–72.

Cox, A., Connolly, S., & Currall, J. (2001). *Raising information security awareness in the academic setting raising information security awareness in the academic setting* (pp. 11–16).

Davis, F. D. (1986). *A technology acceptance model for empirically testing new end-user information systems*. Cambridge, MA.

Dinev, T., & Hu, Q. (2007). The centrality of awareness in the formation of user behavioral intention toward protective information technologies. *Journal of the Association for Information Systems, 8*, 386–408.

Ding, Y., Meso, P., & Xu, S. (2014). Protection motivation driven security learning. In *20th Am. Conf. Inf. Syst.* (pp. 1–6).

Eminağaoğlu, M., Uçar, E., & Eren, Ş. (2009). The positive outcomes of information security awareness training in companies – a case study. *Information Security Technical Report, 14*, 223–229.

Endicott-popovsky, B., Orton, I., Bailey, K., & Frincke, D. (2005). Community security awareness training. In *Proc. from sixth annu. IEEE SMC inf. assur. work* (pp. 373–379).

Endsley, M. R. (1995). Measurement of situation awareness in dynamic systems. *Human factors, 37*(1), 65–84.

Faisal, A. A., Nisa, B. S., & Ibrahim, J. (2013). Mitigating privacy issues on Facebook by implementing information security awareness with Islamic perspectives. In *2013 5th int. conf. inf. commun. technol. Muslim world, ICT4M 2013*.

Fisher, J. D., Fisher, W. A., Bryan, A. D., & Misovich, S. J. (2002). Information-motivation-behavioral skills model-based HIV risk behavior change intervention for inner-city high school youth. *Health Psychology, 21*(2), 177.

Flores, W. R., Antonsen, E., & Ekstedt, M. (2014). Information security knowledge sharing in organizations: Investigating the effect of behavioral information security governance and national culture. *Computers and Security, 43*, 90–110.

Forget, A., Chiasson, S., & Biddle, R. (2007). Persuasion as education for computer security. In *Proc. E-Learn world conf. E-Learning corp. gov. heal. high. educ.* (pp. 822–829).

Fung, C. C., Khera, V., Depickere, A., Tantatsanawong, P., & Boonbrahm, P. (2008). Raising information security awareness in digital ecosystem with games-a pilot study in Thailand. In *IEEE int. conf. digit. ecosyst. technol.* (pp. 375–380).

Furnell, S., Gennatou, M., & Dowland, P. S. (2002). A prototype tool for information security awareness and training. *Logistics Information Management, 15*, 352–357.

Gardner, B., & Thomas, V. (2014). *Building an information security awareness program: Defending against social engineering and technical threats*. Elsevier.

Ghazvini, A., & Shukur, Z. (2016). Awareness training transfer and information security content development for healthcare industry. *International Journal of Advanced Computer Science and Applications, 7*, 361–370.

Greitzer, F. L., Kuchar, O. A., & Huston, K. (2007). Cognitive science implications for enhancing training effectiveness in a serious gaming context. *ACM Journal of Educational Resources in Computing, 7*, 2–11.

Greenberg, E. S. (1975). The consequences of worker participation: A clarification of the theoretical literature. *Social Science Quarterly*, 191–209.

Gundu, T., & Flowerday, S. V. (2012). *The enemy Within : Enemy within a behav. Intent. Model an inf. Secur. Aware. Process P1-8.*

Guynes, C. S., Windsor, J., & Wu, Y.'A. (2012). *Security Awareness Programs, 16*, 165–169.

Hagen, J. M., & Albrechtsen, E. (2009). Effects on employees' information security abilities by e-learning. *Information Management and Computer Security, 17*, 388–407.

Hagen, J., & Johnsen, S. O. (2010). *The long-term effects of information security e-learning on organizational learning* (pp. 140–154).

Hansche, S. (2001). Designing a security awareness program: Part I. *Information Systems Security, 9*, 14.

Heikka, J. (2008). A constructive approach to information systems security training: An action research experience. In *14th am. conf. inf. syst. AMCIS 2008 paper 319* (pp. 15–22).

Jensen, E. (1995). *Brain-based learning & teaching*. Brain Store Incorporated.

Johnson, E.C. Security awareness: Switch to a better programme. Netw. Secur., 15-18.

Jordan, C., Knapp, M., Mitchell, D., Claypool, M., & Fisler, K. (2011). *CounterMeasures: A game for teaching computer security* (pp. 1–6).

Karjalainen, M. (2011). *Improving Employees' Information Systems (IS) Security Behavior-Toward a Meta-Theory of IS Security Training and a New Framework for Understanding Employees' IS Security Behavior. PhD. University of Oulu.*

Karjalainen, M., & Siponen, M. (2011). Toward a new meta-theory for designing information systems ( IS ) security training approaches. *Journal of the Association for Information Systems, 12*, 518–555.

Khan, B., Alghathbar, K. S., & Khan, M. K. (2011). Information security awareness campaign: An alternate approach. *Information Security and Assurance, 200*, 1–10.

Khan, B., Alghathbar, K. S., Nabi, S. I., & Khan, M. K. (2011). Effectiveness of information security awareness methods based on psychological theories. *African Journal of Business Management, 5*, 10862–10868.

Labuschagne, W. a., Burke, I., Veerasamy, N., & Eloff, M. M. (2011). Design of cyber security awareness game utilizing a social media framework. In *2011 inf. Secur. South Africa 1–9.*

Leach, J. (2003). Improving user security behaviour. *Computers and Security, 22*, 685–692.

Lebek, B., Uffen, J., Breitner, M. H., Neumann, M., & Hohler, B. (2013). Employees' information security awareness and behavior: A literature review. In *2013 46th Hawaii Int. Conf. Syst. Sci.* (pp. 2978–2987).

Maeyer, D. De (2007). *Setting up an effective information security awareness Programme* (pp. 49–58).

Mangold, L. V. (2012). Using ontologies for adaptive information security training. In *Seventh int. conf. availability, reliab. secur.* (pp. 522–524).

McCoy, C., & Fowler, R. (2004). "You are the key to security": Establishing a successful security awareness program. In *Proc. 32nd annu. ACM SIGUCCS fall conf. SE – SIGUCCS '04* (pp. 346–349).

McCrohan, K. F., Engel, K., & Harvey, J. W. (2010). Influence of awareness and training on cyber security. *Journal of Internet Commerce, 9*, 23–41.

McGeehan, J. (2001). Brain-compatible learning. *Green Teacher, 64*(7), 7–12.

McNiff, J., Whitehead, J., & Education, L. (2006). *Action research.*

Miller, G. (1956). Human memory and the storage of information. *IRE Transactions on Information Theory, 2*(3), 129–137.

Mitchell, T. R. (1973). Motivation and Participation: An Integration. *Academy of Management Journal, 16*, 670–679.

Moon, J. W., & Kim, Y. G. (2001). Extending the TAM for a World-Wide-Web context. *Information & Management, 38*(4), 217–230.

Nagarajan, A., Allbeck, J. M., Sood, A., & Janssen, T. L. (2012). Exploring game design for cybersecurity training. In *2012 IEEE int. Conf. Cyber technol. Autom. Control. Intell. Syst* (pp. 256–262).

Nonaka, I. (1994). A dynamic theory of organizational knowledge creation. *Organization Science, 5*(1), 14–37.

Novak, J. D. (1990). Concept maps and Vee diagrams: Two metacognitive tools to facilitate meaningful learning. *Instructional Science, 19*(1), 29–52.

Osborne, C. Y., Bains, S. S., & Egede, L. E. (2010). Health literacy, diabetes self-care, and glycemic control in adults with type 2 diabetes. *Diabetes technology & therapeutics, 12*(11), 913–919.

Peltier, T. R. (2005). Implementing an information security awareness program. *Information Systems Security, 14*, 37–49.

Pfleeger, S. L., & Caputo, D. D. (2012). Leveraging behavioral science to mitigate cyber security risk. *Computers and Security, 31*, 597–611.

Piaget, J. (1972). Development and learning. *Readings on the development of children*, 25–33.

Posner, G. J., Strike, K. A., Hewson, P. W., & Gertzog, W. A. (1982). Accommodation of a scientific conception: Toward a theory of conceptual change. *Science education, 66*(2), 211–227.

Prensky, M. (2001). *Types of learning and possible game styles*. Digital Game-Based Learning.

Puhakainen, P. (2006). *A design theory for information security awareness*. Processing.

Puhakainen, P., & Siponen, M. (2010). Improving employees' compliance through information systems security training: An action research study. *Management Information System, 34.*

Rantos, K., Fysarakis, K., & Manifavas, C. (2012). How effective is your security awareness program? An evaluation methodology. *Information Security Journal A Global Perspective, 21*, 328–345.

Reid, R., & van Niekerk, J. (2014). Brain-compatible, web-based information security education: A statistical study. *Information Management and Computer Security, 22*, 371–381.

Reid, R., Van Niekerk, J., & Von Solms, R. (2011). Guidelines for the creation of brain-compatible cyber security educational material in Moodle 2.0. In *2011 information security for South Africa* (pp. 1–8). IEEE.

Rizza, C., & Pereira, Â. G. (2013). *Social networks and cyber-bullying among teenagers.*

Rogers, R. W. (1983). Cognitive and psychological processes in fear appeals and attitude change: A revised theory of protection motivation. *Social psychophysiology: A sourcebook*, 153–176.

Rosemann, M., & Vessey, I. (2008). Toward improving the relevance of information systems research to practice: The role of applicability checks. *MIS Quarterly, 32*, 1–22.

SanNicolas-Rocca, T., Schooley, B., & Spears, J. L. (2014). Designing effective knowledge transfer practices to improve is security awareness and compliance. In *, Vol. 1. Proc. annu. Hawaii int. conf. syst. sci.* (pp. 3432–3441).

Shaw, R. S. S., Chen, C. C., Harris, A. L., & Huang, H.-J. (2009). The impact of information richness on information security awareness training effectiveness. *Computers and Education, 52*, 92–100.

Schultz, P. W. (1999). Changing behavior with normative feedback interventions: A field experiment on curbside recycling. *Basic and applied social psychology, 21*(1), 25–36.

Siponen, M. T. (2000). A conceptual foundation for organizational information security awareness. *Information Management and Computer Security, 8*, 31–41.

Sohrabi, N., Sookhak, M., Von Solms, R., Furnell, S., Abdul, N., Herawan, T., et al. (2015). Information security conscious care behaviour formation in organizations. *Computers and Security, 53.*

Soomro, Z. A., Shah, M. H., & Ahmed, J. (2016). information security management needs more holistic approach : A literature review. *International Journal of Information Management, 36*, 215–225.

Spears, J., & Barki, H. (2010). User participation in information systems security risk management. *MIS Quarterly, 34*, 503–522.

Stelmaszczyk, M. (2016). Relationship between individual and organizational learning: Mediating role of team learning. *Journal of Economics Management, 26*, 107–127.

Stephanou, T., & Dagada, R. (2008). *The impact of information security awareness training on information security behaviour : The case for. Inf. Secur* (pp. 309–330).

Sweller, J. (1999). Instructional design. In *Australian educational review.*

Tariq, M. A., Brynielsson, J., & Artman, H. (2014). The security awareness paradox: A case study. In *2014 IEEE/ACM int. conf. adv. soc. networks anal. min. (ASONAM 2014)* (pp. 704–711).

Thomson, M. E., & Solms, R. von (1998). Information security awareness: Educating your users effectively. *Information Management and Computer Security, 6*, 167–173.

Tolnai, A., & von Solms, S. (2009). *Solving security issues using information security awareness portal* (pp. 1–5).

Tsohou, A., Karyda, M., & Kokolakis, S. (2015). Analyzing the role of cognitive and cultural biases in the internalization of information security policies: Recommendations for information security awareness programs. *Computers and Security, 52*, 128–141.

Tsohou, A., Karyda, M., Kokolakis, S., & Kiountouzis, E. (2012). Analyzing trajectories of information security awareness. *Information Technology and People, 25*, 327–352.

Tsohou, A., Kokolakis, S., Karyda, M., Kiountouzis, E., & Systems, C. (2008). Investigating information security awareness: Research and practice gaps. *Inforamtion Security Journal A Global Perspective, 17*, 207–227.

Van Niekerk, J., & von Solms, R. (2004). Organisational learning models for information security. In *The ISSA 2004 Enabling Tomorrow Conference, 30.*

Webb, J., Ahmad, A., Maynard, S. B., & Shanks, G. (2014). A situation awareness model for information security risk management. *Computers & Security, 44*, 1–15.

Webster, J., & Watson, R. T. (2002). Analyzing the past to prepare for the future: Writing a literature review. *MIS Quarterly, 26*, xiii–xxiii.

Wilson, M., & Hash, J. (2003). *Building an information Technology security awareness and training program.* Nist Spec. Publ. 800-50 1–38.

Wilson, M., Zafra, D., Dorothea, E., de Pitcher, S. I., Tressler, J. D., Ippolito, J. B., et al. (1998). *Information Technology security training requirements: A role- and performance-based Model.* NIST Special Publication 800-16.

Wolf, M., Haworth, D., & Pietron, L. (2011). Measuring An Information Security Awareness Program. *Review of Business Information Systems (RBIS), 15*(3), 9–22.

CHAPTER

# 7

# Understanding users' information security awareness and intentions: a full nomology of protection motivation theory[1]

*Farkhondeh Hassandoust, Angsana A. Techatassanasoontorn*

Auckland University of Technology, Auckland, New Zealand

OUTLINE



[1] The previous version of this paper was published in the Proceedings of the 22nd Pacific Asia Conference on Information Systems, 26–30 June 2018, Yokohama, Japan.


https://doi.org/10.1016/B978-0-12-819204-7.00007-5

## Introduction

Owing to the pervasive usage of the Internet worldwide and the presence of information security violations on the Internet, users' information security awareness is a critical first step to achieve the safe and secure environment globally. Recent studies have attempted to identify effective approaches to motivate users to protect their information assets with a particular emphasis on information security behaviours of individuals within an organizational context (Boss et al., 2015; Johnston & Warkentin, 2010). Despite the importance of appropriate information security behaviours in organizations, users' personal information security practice still remains a significant concern, and the current literature on information security does not pay enough attention to how users deal with information security threats in their personal lives.

According to Hanus and Wu (2016), more than 40% of computer users globally were victims to cybercrimes such as phishing, worm or malware attacks, and it is estimated that more than half of these users were not completely sure whether their computers were free of any kind of viruses. In addition, almost one-third of users do not recognize the potential risks associated with not properly protecting themselves and their information on the Internet. This evidence suggests that, regardless of all technological developments in the information security domain, providing information security training to improve users' awareness and their security protection regarding potential threats remains a priority to achieve safe and secure environments. Although previous research examined the role of security education, training and awareness (SETA) (D'Arcy, Hovav, & Galletta, 2009), the focus was largely on deterring individuals from fear of organizational sanctions rather than motivating them to engage in security behaviours based on their own calculations of consequences of information security threats. Drawing on protection motivation theory (PMT), this study aims to extend the current body of knowledge by investigating the role of SETA programmes on users' awareness and subsequent coping and threat appraisals. This study offers an explanation that links information security awareness with intentions to practise information security behaviours.

Our study is in line with the recent shift from general deterrence theories to PMT as an explanatory mechanism of information security behaviour. General deterrence theories emphasize the concept of command and control, whilst PMT mostly focuses on using persuasive messages to warn individuals of a threat and explain countervailing measures and protective behaviours. PMT is applicable to information security contexts, where users require additional motivation to protect their information assets (Boss et al. 2015; Floyd, Prentice-Dunn, & Rogers, 2000). Several information security studies (e.g., Dang-Pham & Pittayachawan, 2015; Dinev & Hu, 2007; Hanus & Wu, 2016; Ifinedo, 2012) have adopted PMT in their investigations, but most of them have not fully leveraged PMT. In particular, they do not offer an explanation on how fear appeal and maladaptive rewards shape information security behaviours (Boss et al., 2015). Although PMT has been used to examine different aspects of information security, researchers have mostly paid attention to information security issues in organizational contexts. In addition, previous studies that applied PMT to investigate individuals' information security protective behaviours reported conflicting results on the significance of users' protection motivation mechanism (e.g., Hanus & Wu, 2016; Liang & Xue, 2010). The review of information security literature reported a gap in an investigation of antecedents of users' threat and coping appraisals (Hanus & Wu, 2016; Milne, Sheeran, & Orbell, 2000). Therefore, the present study aims to apply all PMT core constructs by investigating security awareness as an antecedent of threat and coping appraisals and their influence on information security protection intention among computer and Internet users.

In general, SETA programmes provide users with knowledge on information security threats and solutions to avoid or mitigate the impact of security attacks. This study classifies awareness into threat awareness and countermeasure awareness to precisely examine how different types of awareness shape users' information security protection intention. According to previous information security studies, providing effective information security awareness is considered the most cost-effective solution to encourage users to adopt a stronger protective and proactive approach rather than a reactive approach (Hanus & Wu, 2016). Although the need for research on security awareness among users has been suggested, most of previous studies focused on organizational security policies to deter information security threats. although the literature on PMT presents the importance of the sources of information that users apply to assess the importance of threats and their abilities to address such threats (Milne et al., 2000), the antecedents of threat and coping appraisals are frequently neglected in the information security literature. This study aims to fill this gap and answer the question of 'what is the influence of SETA and user's coping and threat appraisals on their information security protection intention?' Therefore, the objective of this study is to investigate the antecedents of threat and coping appraisals in relation to information security protection intention among students in higher education institutions.

The rest of this chapter is organized as follows. First, the relevant information security literature and a full nomology of PMT are presented.

Then, the research model and hypotheses are proposed, followed by the discussion of research methodology and measurement scales. Finally, the results from a pilot study are reported, along with the discussion of the expected theoretical and practical contributions and possible limitations of this research.

## Literature review

Information security protection is recognized as a systematic effort to protect users from negative effects of cyberattacks. Users are vulnerable to security threats and the lack of awareness contributes to their vulnerability. Previous research investigated information security education and awareness programme in relation to information security protection and prevention strategies and reported a positive significant influence of information security awareness on information security protection intentions (Dinev & Hu, 2007). SETA programmes include a variety of designs and approaches of institutional information SETA-raising activities (Haeussinger & Kranz, 2017). SETA programmes promote information security awareness by equipping users with general information security knowledge about threats along with skills to perform necessary information security protection methods. SETA programmes apply ongoing attempts (e.g., training, workshops, posters) that emphasize acceptable usage guidelines and highlight potential consequences of information security risks, threats and vulnerabilities (D'Arcy et al., 2009), as well as how to protect information and computer from them. Previous studies argued that SETA programmes increase the information security awareness levels of users (Haeussinger & Kranz, 2013, 2017). In addition, general information security trainings in organizations significantly improve information security awareness of users both on the cognitive and the behavioural level (Wipawayangkool, 2009). Although previous studies looked at the benefits of SETA programmes and their positive influence on users' security protective intentions (D'Arcy et al., 2009), there is a lack of empirical studies that explain the underlying cognitive processes connecting the relationship between SETA programmes and information security protection intentions.

Recently, information security researchers have relied on PMT to investigate users' information security–related processes. Originally, PMT is developed based on the anticipation of a negative outcome in individuals' health and their willingness to minimize it to protect themselves. By extending this logic to information security protection behaviours, one can argue that a user is motivated to practise information security protection to avoid consequences of information security threats. In particular, PMT uses the concept of protection motivation to predict users' protective intention after receiving fear-arousing recommendations known as fear appeals (Floyd et al., 2000). Fear appeals are persuasive messages to cause fear by explaining harmful consequences that will happen to individuals if they do not follow the recommendations in the messages. Findings from previous studies indicated that fear appeals explain a user's protective intentions (Boss et al., 2015; Johnston & Warkentin, 2010).

PMT explains the relationship between fear appeals and protective intentions through two mechanisms – coping appraisal and threat appraisal. A fear appeal raises information security threat and efficacy by providing users with a recommendation to address the threat (Boss et al., 2015). Threat appraisal refers to the procedure of noticing the severity and vulnerability to a threat against the maladaptive rewards and maladaptive intentions or practises. Threat severity demonstrates users' belief on how serious a threat would be to themselves. Threat vulnerability presents how susceptible users feel in relation to a potential threat (Milne et al., 2000). Maladaptive rewards refer to the intrinsic and extrinsic rewards of not protecting oneself against the fear appeal, such as saving time, money and pleasure of being sabotaged (Rogers & Prentice-Dunn, 1997). For example, maladaptive rewards can be related to users' perception to save time or money by not following suggested safe information security recommendations (Boss et al., 2015; Rogers & Prentice-Dunn, 1997). If these wrongly perceived maladaptive rewards outweigh the perceived threat severity and vulnerability, users may choose the maladaptive practices by intending not to follow the recommended protective mechanisms. Conversely, perceived threat must be greater than the perceived maladaptive rewards for an adaptive response to occur (Boss et al., 2015).

Coping appraisal refers to the procedure of considering user's response efficacy, self-efficacy and the costs of performing the adaptive response in relation to the fear appeal (Floyd et al., 2000; Rogers & Prentice-Dunn, 1997). Response efficacy is a user's belief that an adaptive response will be effective in protecting the self or others (Floyd et al., 2000). Self-efficacy refers to a user's perception about self-ability and skill to accomplish the coping response (Floyd et al., 2000). Response cost refers to any cost (e.g., time, monetary cost) associated with the coping response (Floyd et al., 2000). Response and self-efficacy must be greater than the response cost for an adaptive response to happen (Boss et al., 2015). Adaptive response refers to an intentional response to fear appeal that protects self or others against the threat raised in the fear appeal (Floyd et al., 2000; Rogers & Prentice-Dunn, 1997). Protection intentions are users' intention to protect themselves against the threat raised in the fear appeal (Boss et al., 2015).

Despite the relevance of PMT in explaining information security intention and behaviour, most information security studies investigated only the core elements of PMT (partial nomologies). In particular, fear and maladaptive rewards have been excluded from the PMT model (e.g., Dang-Pham & Pittayachawan, 2015; Hanus & Wu, 2016; Johnston & Warkentin, 2010; Liang & Xue, 2010). To address this gap, the present study will develop a full nomology of PMT to explain information security protection intentions.

## Research model and hypotheses

This study proposes the research model that applies the full nomology of PMT to investigate the impact of users' information security awareness on their security protection intention through threat appraisal and coping appraisal mechanisms (see Fig. 7.1). This research model introduced SETA programme as an influencing factor on multidimensional awareness factors, users' threat awareness and countermeasure awareness. The model links the awareness constructs and two appraisal mechanisms: the threat appraisal mechanism that involves threat vulnerability, threat severity and maladaptive rewards and the coping appraisal that involves response efficacy, self-efficacy and response cost. The threat appraisal and coping mechanism together shape security protection intention and behaviour. It should be noted that fear and maladaptive reward

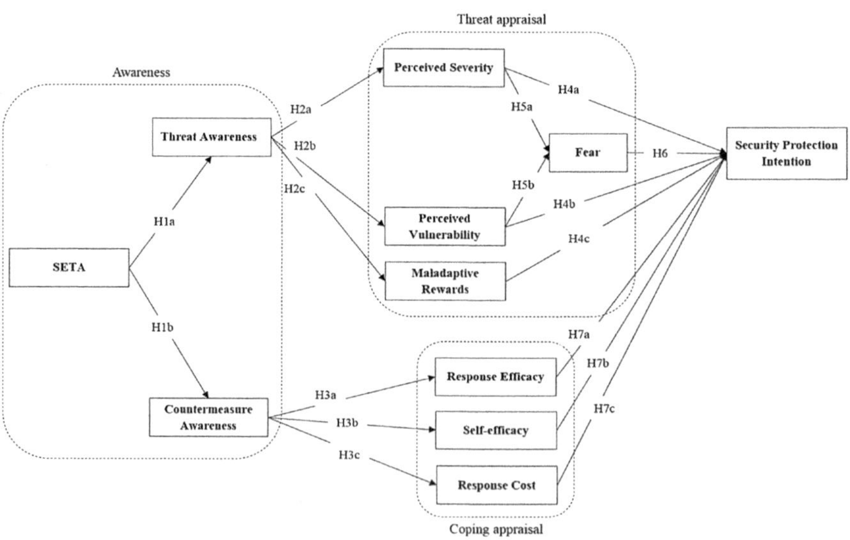


FIGURE 7.1 The proposed research model.

constructs are included as additional elements in the full PMT model (Floyd et al., 2000; Rogers & Prentice-Dunn, 1997), which have been mostly ignored in previous studies.

This study considers users' information security awareness as a multidimensional variable that includes threat awareness and countermeasure awareness. SETA programmes are not only about providing different information security contents for target audiences but also about providing general information about information security environment, potential threats and practices against information security violations to promote information security knowledge and skills as well as raise users' awareness of accountability for their actions (D'Arcy et al., 2009), such as threat identifications and countermeasure actions (Hanus & Wu, 2016). SETA workshops will be ineffective if users only learn about different types of countermeasures against potential threats but do not learn how to recognize and identify these threats in the first place. Similarly, objectives of SETA programmes will not be successfully met, if users are only able to identify threats and risks but do not know how to avoid them. Both threat and countermeasure awareness are likely to materialize if target audiences are provided with proper information security training programmes such as customized workshops, courses, posters, regular emails and brochures. In addition, previous research showed that training users in security measures increases their information security awareness (Haeussinger & Kranz, 2013; Mani, Mubarak, & Choo, 2014). Thus, we hypothesize the following:

> H1a: SETA programme will positively influence users' threat awareness.
> H1b: SETA programme will positively influence users' countermeasure awareness.

Threat awareness and countermeasure awareness constructs are conceptualized based on the concept of technology awareness used in previous studies (Dinev & Hu, 2007; Hanus & Wu, 2016). Threat awareness refers to users' awareness of threats that may negatively influence their computer security, and countermeasure awareness refers to users' awareness of related countermeasures that can be adopted to minimize the risks associated with threats. Users' awareness is about their problem solving techniques through identifying the problem (threat awareness), speaking out, raising consciousness and seeking solutions to solve the problem (countermeasure awareness) (Dinev & Hu, 2007).

Users' knowledge about information security threats results in more accurate anticipation about vulnerability and risks associated with threats. A better understanding about the intensity of negative impact of threats and the likelihood of being impacted by those threats would enable users to better estimate the associated risks and to avoid them. A similar concept of threat probability and its impact had been applied in risk assessment processes of threat avoidance study (Sumner, 2009). In addition, previous research reported the positive association of users' threat awareness and perceived severity and vulnerability of threat (Hanus & Wu, 2016). The other element of threat appraisal that has been missing from previous research is maladaptive rewards that have an impact on the threat appraisal process (Boss et al., 2015). Maladaptive rewards are any type of rewards for the response of not protecting oneself, such as mistaken perception about cost or time savings, pleasure or sabotage (Boss et al., 2015; Floyd et al., 2000; Rogers & Prentice-Dunn, 1997). Users' knowledge and awareness about information security threats and their negative impact would diminish their perception of earning pseudo-benefits from denying information security guidelines associated with maladaptive rewards. On the other hand, users would be able to estimate the likelihood of implementing solutions against information security threat, if they are aware of these possible solutions (Hanus & Wu, 2016). If users know about available countermeasures against information security threats, they are likely to recognize the benefit of recommended information security responses to protect themselves. Similarly, if users obtain knowledge about potential solutions against threats, they would have higher confidence in their competencies to take these protective responses. Therefore, threat awareness will positively influence threat appraisal process through perceived severity and perceived vulnerability. Moreover, threat awareness will negatively influence maladaptive rewards. In contrast, countermeasure awareness positively influences coping appraisal through response efficacy and self-efficacy. Reversely, countermeasure awareness negatively influences response cost. Thus, we hypothesize the following:

H2a: Users' threat awareness will positively influence their perceived severity of threat.
H2b: Users' threat awareness will positively influence their perceived vulnerability of threat.
H2c: Users' threat awareness will negatively influence their maladaptive rewards perception.
H3a: Users' countermeasure awareness will positively influence their response efficacy.
H3b: Users' countermeasure awareness will positively influence their self-efficacy.
H3c: Users' countermeasure awareness will negatively influence their response cost perception.

PMT explains how users cognitively appraise positive or negative responses and their motivation to perform certain behaviours (Dang-Pham & Pittayachawan, 2015). According to the extended model of PMT, threat appraisal involves three cognitive factors, namely perceived vulnerability, perceived threat and maladaptive rewards (Boss et al., 2015). Drawing on the original PMT model, vulnerability is the probability that an undesired incident will happen if no actions are taken to avoid it. When users feel vulnerable against a threat, they would be more inclined to accomplish the recommended processes to counter such threat (Rogers, 1975). It is also reported that users' intention to perform information security protection behaviours would increase if they perceive themselves to be vulnerable against threats (Dang-Pham & Pittayachawan, 2015). Similarly, users intend to be more protective if they perceive the severity of threat (Rogers, 1975). Perceived threat severity is the users' perception about the level of the potential impact of the threat (i.e., how severe the damage that a threat can cause) (Vance, Siponen, & Pahnila, 2012). Hence, users' perception of being vulnerable against a threat and the information security threat severity could motivate their intention to perform security protection behaviour. On the other hand, users' realized benefits of performing risky unsecure actions (maladaptive rewards) such as saving time, money or psychological pleasure, or peer approval would weaken their intention to perform adaptive protective responses (Dang-Pham & Pittayachawan, 2015). If these mistakenly perceived rewards outweigh the perceived threat (severity and vulnerability), users may choose the maladaptive option of not intending to follow the recommended protective behaviours. If a user perceives that the reward for not adopting the appropriate protective response is greater than adopting it, then the user will be less likely to adopt the coping response. Then, an increase in users' perception about maladaptive rewards would decrease users' protection intention to perform protective behaviours (Boss et al., 2015; Vance et al., 2012). Therefore, we hypothesize the following:

H4a: Users' perceived severity will positively influence their intention to perform information security protective behaviours.
H4b: Users' perceived vulnerability will positively influence their intention to perform information security protective behaviours.
H4c: Users' maladaptive rewards will negatively influence their intention to perform information security protective behaviours.

Users engage in cognitive appraisal when they are confronted with a stressful or negative emotional situation, making this an appraisal of threat vulnerability. The motivation to consider the threat further depends on users' perception of existing vulnerability. According to PMT model, a given threat is considered as fear generator that functions as a motivator because of the complementary positive coping response (Burns et al., 2017). If users perceive a relevant and severe threat, then fear, which is a negative emotional response, is generated as an outcome. Previous studies found that threat vulnerability and threat severity predict fear (Floyd et al., 2000; Rogers & Prentice-Dunn, 1997). Therefore, we posit that

H5a: Users' perceived severity will positively influence their perceived fear.
H5b: Users' perceived vulnerability will positively influence their perceived fear.

According to PMT and relevant empirical studies, invoking fear leads users to take protective instructions more seriously (Boss et al., 2015; Rogers, 1975). Ideally, a strong fear appeal should be introduced to measure fear and explore the role of fear in mediating the relationship between perceived severity, perceived vulnerability and security protection intention (Boss et al., 2015). Fear appeal studies predicated that a conditioned fear response can evoke a positively adaptive intention and behaviour (Boss et al., 2015; Burns et al., 2017; Johnston & Warkentin, 2010; Milne et al., 2000). Therefore, if a sense of information security fear is emerged, a user is more likely to intend to perform security protection responses. Thus, we hypothesize the following:

H6: Users' perceived fear will positively influence their intention to perform information security protective behaviours.

PMT theorizes that, parallel with threat appraisal, users perform coping appraisal that subsequently shapes their intention to perform protective behaviours. Users intend to engage in adaptive responses if they perceive that those behaviours are effective and they believe in their abilities to perform those behaviours (Boss et al., 2015; Rogers, 1975). Users' self-efficacy has an impact on their ability to perform protective tasks. Previous research found that users with a high level of self-efficacy performed information security tasks in their workplace more than those with a low level of self-efficacy (Ifinedo, 2012). In contrast, the costs of performing behaviours such as time required or inconvenience would diminish the intention to engage in protective behaviours (Rogers, 1975). Thus, users are reluctant to adopt the recommended information security responses if they perceive that a considerable amount of resource (time, effort and money) will be expended towards that effort (Ifinedo, 2012; Milne et al., 2000). Therefore, users who believe that their protection responses against information security threat are effective would more likely to intend to perform information security protection responses. Similarly, if users believe in their abilities, skills, competencies and experiences to take information security responses, they would more likely intend to perform information security protection behaviours. In contrast, users who feel that information security protection responses are time/cost-consuming and inconvenient would be less likely to intend to engage in information security protection behaviours. As a result, we hypothesize the following:

H7a: Users' response efficacy will positively influence their intention to perform information security protective behaviours.
H7b: Users' self-efficacy will positively influence their intention to perform information security protective behaviours.
H7c: Users' response cost will negatively influence their intention to perform information security protective behaviours.

## Research methodology and pilot data analysis

We plan to conduct a cross-sectional field experiment and use a fear appeal message to study user security protection intentions. Samples of tertiary students from two institutions in New Zealand have been selected. There are two groups of participants; one group of participants will not receive a fear appeal message while the other group of participants will receive a fear appeal message that reports the actual statistics of cybercrimes in New Zealand, such as different types of cyberattacks, frequency of data losses and financial and nonfinancial harm of data loss. Then, an online survey will be administered to all participants. All measurement items in the survey are adapted from previous studies (Boss et al., 2015; D'Arcy et al., 2009; Hanus & Wu, 2016) and measured on a seven-point Likert scale.

To fine-tune the survey, the questionnaire was evaluated and refined in two steps: pretest and pilot study. The questionnaire was pretested with five knowledgeable experts. Modifications were made based on their comments. Then, a pilot study was conducted with the purpose of collecting a small set of data to refine the questionnaire and assess the reliability and validity of the measurement model. The pilot study was conducted with a sample of higher education students at a college in Auckland, New Zealand, in February 2018. A comment box was provided for participants to give comments on the questionnaire at the end of the survey. Findings of the pilot study from 47 participants indicate that there are no major difficulties in understanding the instructions and questionnaire items. In the measurement model, all items exhibit high loadings (>0.65), except some items (TA3, TA4, TA8, TA9, FEAR1, MALR5, MALR6, RCOS1, RCOS2 and RCOS4) from threat awareness, fear, maladaptive rewards and response cost constructs. Besides these low loading values, the rest range from 0.66 to 0.96 on their respective constructs. The items with <0.65 loadings will be removed for the main study. The composite reliability of all constructs is 0.85 or higher, which indicates that the constructs are within accepted limits and therefore reliable. All items except the treat awareness construct had average variance extracted values ranging from 0.55 to 0.89, which is considered adequate (>0.5), suggesting that convergent validity is sufficient. Reliability of all the indicators is acceptable except for a few indicators of treat awareness and fear (TA4, TA9 and FEAR1), which are removed from the questionnaire for the main study.

The planned procedural remedies for controlling common method bias are the following: providing clear and concise questions in the questionnaire and assuring respondents' anonymity. In addition, the Harmon single factor test will be used to evaluate if such bias is indeed a problem in this study.

## Expected contributions

Drawing on PMT, this research aims to investigate the antecedents of threat and coping appraisals in relation to the individuals' information security protection intention. Therefore, this study contributes to a better understanding of individuals' information security awareness through an examination of the impact of SETA programme on information security threat and countermeasures awareness and the role of information security awareness as an antecedent to the cognitive processes associated with coping and threat appraisals. This research extends the current body of knowledge by investigating both threat awareness and countermeasure awareness associated with SETA programme as predictors of coping and threat appraisal processes and subsequent security protection intentions. It offers an insight into the intricate relationship between information security threat and countermeasure awareness and the cognitive processes involved in explaining users' information security protection intentions. This study highlights the role of fear appeal manipulations in information security studies. This suggestion is in line with the report from Boss et al. (2015) that fear appeal manipulation is a core component of the underlying protective behaviours, according to PMT. In particular, omitting a fear appeal manipulation is likely to violate the PMT model and cause false and misleading results that diminish the established PMT nomology. This is because a fear manipulation generates a fear of threat that subsequently shapes information security protection intention and behaviour. In addition, most previous studies (e.g., Marett, McNab & Harris, 2011) that applied fear appeal manipulation used one sample for the model that may convolute the results by failing to identify the main differences among effective and ineffective threat and coping appraisals. In contrast, this study will use two samples, one with fear appeal manipulation and the other without fear appeal manipulation, to test the differences of the underlying cognitive processes associated with information security protection behaviours.

The findings of this study will have implications for practice. The findings help practitioners to identify important factors that influence users' information security protection intention. In particular, the results may highlight the importance of the severity of threats, vulnerability of threats or fear appeal in SETA programmes.

This study would be able to suggest effective information security awareness, educating and training programmes that reflect the concept of multidimensionality of awareness. In particular, these programmes should focus on both threats and their respective countermeasures. Information security awareness is not just about designing various contents for different audiences but more about assuring that information security awareness activities address each aspect of awareness in a comprehensive way.

The findings can also be used to guide the design of effective information security training programmes that balance the differences between users' perception about their information security knowledge and protection actions and how they are intended to engage in information security protection behaviours. Furthermore, these findings will be especially useful for higher education institutions that are considering or currently adopting bring-your-own-device practices in classrooms to deliver appropriate information security campaigns and courses to their students.

By investigating different aspects of cognitive processes of the PMT model, this study will reveal additional insights about users' information security intentions. For example, the self-efficacy factor will reveal users' perception and reliance on their own information security–related skills and abilities. Then, this may alert management about the willingness or reluctance of users in relation to their information security skills and difficulties that they have when making information security decisions. More important, it would emphasize that information security training and educating programmes should not be a one-off attempt. In addition, organizations may develop a community of practice to promote information security matters to encourage ongoing assistance among users to develop security culture and climate in long term.

## Limitations

The cross-sectional design of this study may limit the interpretation of the results. Hence, future studies may want to observe any changes in users' information security protection intention and behaviours through fear appeal conditions over time or asking participants to recall their perceptions of maladaptive responses or fear. Because data will be collected from students in higher educational institutions, the generalisability to other populations should be done with caution. Students may have different levels of computer literacy than others (e.g., employees in a workplace). As the sample of this study are students who have little to no professional experience, we will not be able to evaluate the impact of different sources of information in performing information security protection. Future research may investigate the impact of users' protective intentions on their actual protective behaviours and explore the possibility of information security knowledge transfer between work and home settings.

## Conclusion

Because of the prevalent role of digital technology and the Internet in people's lives, users' information security awareness is important for the safe and secure global community. Drawing on the full explanation of PMT, this study offers in-depth insights into how users' information security awareness shapes and motivates their information security protection intentions. This research extends the current body of knowledge by introducing SETA programmes as an antecedent of threat and countermeasure information security awareness, which are antecedents of information security protection intentions mediated by coping and threat appraisals.

## References

Boss, S. R., Galletta, D. F., Lowry, P. B., Moody, G. D., & Polak, P. (2015). What do users have to fear? Using fear appeals to engender threats and fear that motivate protective security behaviors. *MIS Quarterly, 39*(4), 837–864.

Burns, A. J., Posey, C., Roberts, T. L., & Lowry, P. B. (2017). Examining the relationship of organizational insiders' psychological capital with information security threat and coping appraisals. *Computers in Human Behavior, 68*, 190–209.

D'Arcy, J., Hovav, A., & Galletta, D. (2009). User awareness of security countermeasures and its impact on information systems misuse: A deterrence approach. *Information Systems Research, 20*(1), 79–98.

Dang-Pham, D., & Pittayachawan, S. (2015). Comparing intention to avoid malware across contexts in a BYOD-enabled Australian university: A protection motivation theory approach. *Computers and Security*, (48), 281–297.

Dinev, T., & Hu, Q. (2007). The centrality of awareness in the formation of user behavioral intention toward protective information technologies. *Journal of the Association for Information Systems, 8*(7), 386–408.

Floyd, D. L., Prentice-Dunn, S., & Rogers, R. W. (2000). A meta-analysis of research on protection motivation theory. *Journal of Applied Social Psychology, 30*(2), 407–429.

Haeussinger, F., & Kranz, J. (2013). Information security awareness: Its antecedents and mediating effects on security compliant behavior. In *Proceedings of the 15th international conference on information Systems (ICIS), Italy, Milan, Paper 1149.*

Haeussinger, F., & Kranz, J. (2017). Antecedents of employees' information security awareness-review, synthesis, and directions for future research. In *Proceeding of the 25th European conference on information Systems (ECIS), Portugal, Guimarães.*

Hanus, B., & Wu, Y. A. (2016). Impact of users' security awareness on desktop security behavior: A protection motivation theory perspective. *Information Systems Management, 33*(1), 2–16.

Ifinedo, P. (2012). Understanding information systems security policy compliance: An integration of the theory of planned behavior and the protection motivation theory. *Computers and Security, 31*(1), 83–95.

Johnston, A. C., & Warkentin, M. (2010). Fear appeals and information security behaviors: An empirical study. *MIS Quarterly, 34*(3), 549–566.

Liang, H., & Xue, Y. (2010). Understanding security behaviors in personal computer usage: A threat avoidance perspective. *Journal of the Association for Information Systems, 11*(7), 394–413.

Mani, D., Mubarak, S., & Choo, K. R. (2014). Understanding the information security awareness process in real estate organizations using the SECI model. In *Proceedings of the 20th Americas conference on information Systems* (pp. 1–11). USA, Georgia, Savannah: AMCIS).

Marett, K., McNab, A. L., & Harris, R. B. (2011). Social networking websites and posting personal information: An evaluation of protection motivation theory. *AIS Transactions on Human-Computer Interaction, 3*(3), 170–188.

Milne, S., Sheeran, P., & Orbell, S. (2000). Prediction and intervention in health-related behavior: A meta-analytic review of protection motivation theory. *Journal of Applied Social Psychology, 30*(1), 106–143.

Rogers, R. W. (1975). A protection motivation theory of fear appeals and attitude change. *Journal of Psychology, 91*(1), 93–114.

Rogers, R. W., & Prentice-Dunn, S. (1997). Protection motivation theory. In D. S. Gochman (Ed.), *Handbook of health behavior research I: Personal and social determinants* (pp. 113–132). New York, NY: Plenum Press.

Vance, A., Siponen, M., & Pahnila, S. (2012). Motivating IS security compliance: Insights from habit and protection motivation theory. *Information and Management, 49*(3), 190–198.

Wipawayangkool, K. (2009). Security awareness and security training: An attitudinal perspective. In *Proceedings of the 40th southwest decision sciences annual conference* (pp. 266–273). USA, Oklahoma, Oklahoma City: SWDSI).

CHAPTER

# 8

# Social big data and its integrity: the effect of trust and personality traits on organic reach of facebook content

*Vladlena Benson*[1], *Tom Buchanan*[2]

[1]Professor of Information Systems, Aston Business School, Aston University, Birmingham, United Kingdom; [2]School of Social Sciences, University of Westminster, London, United Kingdom

OUTLINE



*Cyber Influence and Cognitive Threats*
https://doi.org/10.1016/B978-0-12-819204-7.00008-7

## Introduction

A new set of business models and revenue opportunities emerge oriented towards easing individual work and enhancing well-being, based on smart applications. Extant literature reports on the advantages offered by the crowd intelligence embedded in social networking sites (SNS) (see, e.g., Benson, Saridakis, & Tennakoon, 2015; Dumas, 2013; Watson-Manheim & Belanger, 2007). Big data insights into user behaviour offer potential opportunities to smart applications which can match individual needs based on the anticipation of users' wants. Despite the lucrative advantages, the nature of social intelligence and SNS-generated big data creates fundamental challenges with respect to the techniques and applications relying on the objectivity and accuracy of social big data (Liu, Li, Ji, North, & Yang, 2017). In addition to the assurance of algorithm effectiveness, computation speed, energy performance, individual information privacy, data security, system compatibility and scalability, the threat of malicious manipulation of social big data has manifested itself on social networks in recent months (Söllner, Benbasat, Gefen, Leimeister, & Pavlou, 2016). This chapter aims to address the risks associated with social content propagation. It reveals strategies that malicious entities, such as hostile governments, could employ to manipulate individual social networking users' behaviour, thereby influencing the integrity of social big data.

Identification of the human needs is driven by emergent computing paradigms. With the proliferation of ubiquitous technologies supported by scalable cloud and hypermobility, social computing has the promise to extend the boundaries of interactivity. We are on the cutting edge of when humans start looking for more with the development of applications, such as in the case of robotic technologies expanding into the realm of human social interactions and social networks. Scenarios have been created dealing with how robots are expected to maintain close relationship with human social contacts to alleviate the pressures of busy lives and distance constraints. In other words, making the human life easier and anticipating human needs are based on their behaviour analysis. This interaction is executed based on mimicking human thinking pattern, behaviour and contextual big data with the view to anticipate every human move, in this case termed *anticipatory computing*. For these possibilities to come to fruition, the integrity of the underpinning behavioural and contextual data is critical.

The effects of social networking content integrity are of particular relevance to current settings as cybercriminals are increasingly targeting SNS perceived risks associated with SNS activity (Coopamootoo & Ashenden, 2011; Dumas, 2013). In this chapter, we explore factors affecting 'fake' content propagation on SNS, namely personality, risk propensity and interpersonal trust. In the next sections, we present a review of literature on risk and trust behaviours on social platforms and fake content propagation and then develop the research hypotheses of organic reach on social platforms. We then outline an experiment conducted to test these hypotheses (Buchanan & Benson, 2019). The chapter concludes with a discussion of findings and their implications for theory and practise.

## Conceptual background

*Fake news* is essentially disinformation spread through the media and then propagated through peer-to-peer communication (Albright, 2017). Considerable attention has recently been paid to disinformation aimed at influencing political processes. There have been claims that organizations acting on behalf of political parties have targeted such information at specific sectors of the population through a process of data-driven microtargeting. A key issue is that once seeded, the disinformation snowball keeps on rolling through a phenomenon dubbed *organic reach*.

Organic reach is the mechanism whereby material on Facebook spreads to a wider audience through user actions, rather than paid advertising. Liu et al. (2017) describe the Facebook actions of 'like', 'share' and 'comment' as being aspects of 'electronic word of mouth'. Kim and Yang (2017) describe these three as distinct behaviours people use to communicate via Facebook and found that different message characteristics were associated with different user behaviours. The 'reaction' tool, introduced in 2016, is an extension of the original Facebook 'like' button. It allows users to respond to content in other ways – for example, by posting an emoji. The way a user responds to a post through these behaviours influences the likelihood of Facebook's algorithms promoting the post to a wider audience. Such user behaviours therefore contribute to the organic reach of an item.

Thus, while the number of individuals receiving an initial piece of disinformation may be relatively low, through their interactions with the content (sharing it, liking it and responding to it with comments on their timeline), they make other people within their wider networks aware of it. This can lead to an exponential spread of the material. Timberg (2017) reports research by Albright suggesting that disinformation seeded to a few thousand social media users may have been propagated to hundreds of millions of people before the 2016 US presidential election, greatly amplifying its scope for influence.

Alongside claims that people have been targeted to receive political content based on their demographic characteristics, there is evidence that it is possible, through analysis of social media data footprints, to identify segments of the user population that possess particular attributes. For example, the kinds of items individuals have 'liked' on Facebook are associated with personality traits such as Extraversion or Openness to Experience. This makes it possible to target tailored persuasive communications at individuals with particular profiles, and Matz, Kosinski, Nave, and Stilwell (2017) have shown that such efforts can impact on user behaviour at a large scale. If there are particular individual characteristics that make a person more or less likely to interact with fake news items, then it should be possible to target communications at those types of individual to increase the organic reach of the material. The controversies about microtargeting of persuasive communication on social media and the role it may have played in recent elections and referenda such as those held in the United States and United Kingdom make it relevant and timely to look at factors influencing the likelihood that a user will spread a 'fake news' item through the organic reach phenomenon.

In anticipatory computing, trust, security and privacy take the central stage as determinants of future applications' success and their commercial viability. If human behaviour, interactions and social data generated through activity on SNS have in some way been manipulated by external actors, then there may be profound implications for the integrity of social big data and threat mitigation. One way in which the loss of social data integrity can be orchestrated is by 'fake' content. Governments are concerned about individuals being influenced by 'fake news' and consider propaganda through social platforms a form of cybercrime (YouGov, 2017). Do risk factors influencing vulnerability to other forms of cybercrime also apply to individuals who are influenced to propagate 'fake news'?

Extant research indicates that risk propensity and trust impact cyber victimization of individuals. Saridakis, Benson, Ezingeard, and Tennakoon (2015) show that on social platforms users with high levels of risk propensity are more likely to become victims of cybercrime. In evaluating the ways in which users are being influenced to share fake news, we conceptualize them as victims of a cybercrime and consider whether they might be affected in the same way as victims of other crimes such as fraud or phishing. We start with the consideration of trust and risk in the social networking context.

## Trust

This study follows a broad definition of trust based on Gefen, Karahanna, and Straub (2003) expressed as a willingness of one party (the trustor) to rely on another party (the trustee) in cases that involve risk and potential loss to the trustor. The preparedness to rely is driven by the judgement of the trustee's characteristics. The level of trust is based on the assessment of competence, benevolence and integrity of the trustee (Cases, 2002).

The user system trust cluster concentrates on trust relationships between people and technology, in this context between SNS users and social technology. Of particular interest to this study are the works investigating the decision-making process based on user-generated content or third-party social data. Trust into social data has been addressed by a number of studies, such as those exploring user trust into recommendation systems or decision support systems (Gregor & Benbasat, 1999; Han, Serkan, Sharman, & Raoet, 2015; Komiak & Benbasat, 2006; Xiao & Benbasat, 2007). The role of trust in connection to systems use, and relying on information gathered from them, has been highlighted in Han et al. (2015) and Komiak and Benbasat (2006). Social networking sites draw from the systems design principles in order for their users to perceive them as trustworthy (Gregor & Benbasat, 1999). The increased sense of trust is drawn from the principles of highly personalized content based on Komiak and Benbasat (2006) to drive user trust. Furthermore, Xiao and Benbasat (2011) highlight that the lost integrity of information or deception on social and e-commerce platforms is perceived differently depending on whether this information came from a trusted SNS or not. Therefore trust is context-contingent and is influenced by the system's characteristics and user beliefs.

## Risk propensity

In light of the cybersecurity threats increasingly targeting SNS and the rise of perceived risks associated with personal data sharing by users, it is important to consider how risk propensity of users impacts social networking behaviour (Dumas, 2013). According to Dhillon and Backhouse (2001), the concept of risk has been fundamental in rationalizing user behaviour and the individual predisposition towards risk taking helps explain the decision-making process. Risk propensity is defined as an action state that determines how much risk an individual is inclined to take (Cases, 2002) and has been shown to depend on sources of risk. Risk propensity relies on the willingness to assume risk (Mayer, Davis, & Schoorman, 1995; Sheppard & Sherman, 1998). According to Sitkin and Pablo (1995), user's tendency to take or avoid risks determines user behaviour. In this chapter, we follow the definition of risk propensity as representative of 'the action stage that follows the decision to take or avoid risk' and it is seen as the result of attitudes and perceptions influencing individual behaviour (Liu, Marchewka, Lu, & Yu, 2005, p. 291).

Through SNS usage individuals engage in risk-taking behaviour which involves communicating with unknown entities, exchanging personal content and media, as well as providing and propagating sensitive information (Whittle et al., 2013). Thus, one might propose that SNS users with a higher level of risk propensity might be more likely to interact with 'fake news' items and extend their organic reach. On the other hand, those who are more risk averse might be more likely to simply ignore such messages and not contribute to their propagation.

## Personality traits

In addition to risk propensity, it is likely that other individual characteristics influence likelihood of interacting with fake news items. The personality profiles of Facebook users, for example, may influence their behaviour and interactions with disinformation. Within personality psychology, the current dominant paradigm is the Five-Factor Model (Costa & McCrae, 1992), which claims there are five main dimensions of individual differences in personality. Extraversion is a tendency towards engaging in social processes with others. Openness to Experience is a preference for abstract rather than concrete ideas and experiences. Neuroticism is a tendency towards emotional distress, in contrast to emotional stability. Agreeableness is a tendency towards positive, prosocial and interpersonal behaviour. Conscientiousness is a tendency towards reliability, attention to detail and self-control. There is evidence that individuals' social media footprints can be used to infer their status on all these dimensions (Azucar, Marengo & Settani, 2018).

Personality variables have been shown to influence behaviour in social media (which is of course why they can be inferred from social media footprints). For example, Hollenbaugh and Ferris (2014) reported that Openness to Experience was positively associated, and Neuroticism negatively associated, with users' self-reports of the breadth of their self-disclosure on Facebook. Extraversion was positively associated with depth of self-disclosure. These findings have implications for information sharing behaviour and therefore imply some personality characteristics may well have scope to influence our likelihood of interacting with fake news items and thus their organic reach.

## Case study: Buchanan and Benson (2019)

We set out to examine these research questions in an online study examining the likelihood that a user would propagate fake content to their wider social networks (Buchanan & Benson, 2019). In line with our conceptualization of social network users as potential cybercrime victims, we hypothesized that users who trust the source of a message would be more likely to interact with it and thereby extend its organic reach. Thus, 'fake news' items coming from trusted sources would be more likely to be propagated by the message recipients.

Given the known relationship between risk propensity and cybercrime victimization, we further hypothesized that people higher in risk propensity would be more likely to extend the organic reach of such messages. We did not specify any hypotheses about whether recipients' personality traits influence their likelihood of extending the organic reach of a message, choosing instead to evaluate those relationships through exploratory analyses. The framework of hypothesized predictors of organic reach of a message is shown in Fig. 8.1.

The measurement of trust has been shown as problematic, context-contingent and subjective (Basheer & Ibrahim, 2010; Benson et al., 2015) as we need to define who and what the user is placing their trust in. We therefore chose to manipulate trust experimentally. In one condition of the experiment, the source of a message was described as a trusted source (a close friend). In the second condition, the source was a relative stranger who the participant had no real reason to trust.

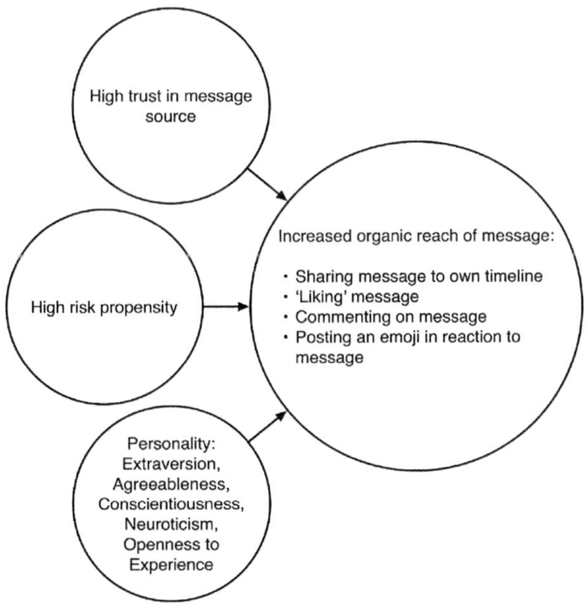


**FIGURE 8.1** Proposed relationships between trust in message source, recipient individual differences and organic reach of message.

The study was conducted online, with participants recruited through a personality testing website. Three hundred and fifty seven Facebook users completed measures of the five main dimensions of personality: Extraversion, Neuroticism, Openness to Experience, Agreeableness and Conscientiousness (Buchanan, Johnson, & Goldberg, 2005). To measure their generalized tendencies to take risks in everyday life, they also completed risk propensity scale by Meertens and Lion (2008). Participants were then shown a scenario about being asked to share a message about political corruption on their Facebook timeline. They were randomized to one of the two conditions, in which the trustworthiness of the message source was manipulated. In one condition, the request came from a trusted individual and in the other condition it came from someone they had no reason to trust. Samples of the materials from each condition are shown in Figs 8.2 and 8.3.

Participants then rated their likelihood of interaction with the message; users can respond to postings in each of the main ways – 'reactions' (including 'likes'), 'comments' and 'shares'. All of these contribute to the organic reach of a message (sharing it on one's own timeline broadcasts it to one's friends network for example, and the other interactions influence the likelihood of it being shared further by Facebook's algorithms). Their ratings were combined to create an overall 'organic reach' score.

Multiple regression analysis was used to evaluate the effects of level of trust in the message originator and individual differences in the recipient on organic reach. The five personality variables, along with risk propensity and trust condition, were used as predictors. The analysis indicated there was a statistically significant effect of trust on organic reach. Participants gave ratings consistent with a higher level of reach for posts in the higher trust condition. Level of risk propensity was not significantly associated with the index of organic reach, as well as with most of the personality variables. Only Agreeableness was statistically significantly associated with organic reach. Less agreeable people were more likely to increase the message's reach.

As expected, therefore, messages coming from a more trustworthy source appeared likely to have greater organic reach. The implication is thus that fake news is more likely to be propagated on Facebook if it appears to come from a trusted, rather than untrusted, source. The fact that risk propensity did not significantly influence organic reach of fake news implies that the propagation of fake news is unlike other types of cybercrime. This raises the question of whether social media users who propagate such material online are really best thought of as cybercrime victims. It may be that other perspectives on their behaviour will be more informative.

In the run-up to an important national election, stories are circulating on Facebook about allegations of corruption against one of the candidates. A close friend, who you know very well, has made a post about it on their Facebook timeline and asked all their friends to share it.

Thinking about the Facebook posting described above:

| | Not at all likely | | | | Very likely |
|---|---|---|---|---|---|
| How likely would you be to **trust** information posted by someone like that? | ○ | ○ | ○ | ○ | ○ |
| How likely would you be to **share** it to your own public timeline? | ○ | ○ | ○ | ○ | ○ |
| How likely would you be to **'like'** it? | ○ | ○ | ○ | ○ | ○ |
| How likely would you be to **comment** on it (whether positively or negatively)? | ○ | ○ | ○ | ○ | ○ |
| How likely would you be to **react** to it by posting an emoji? | ○ | ○ | ○ | ○ | ○ |

**FIGURE 8.2** High-trust condition.

The only personality variable Buchanan and Benson (2019) found to affect organic reach of a Facebook posting was Agreeableness, with more agreeable people rating themselves as less likely to contribute to the propagation of a fake news item. The reasons for that finding are not clear – it is possible that less agreeable people were more likely to interact with the post because it was negative/critical in nature; more agreeable people might have been concerned to avoid offending people by liking or forwarding it. Current data give no clues as to whether the effect is generalizable or specific to the item described in the scenario used. However, if

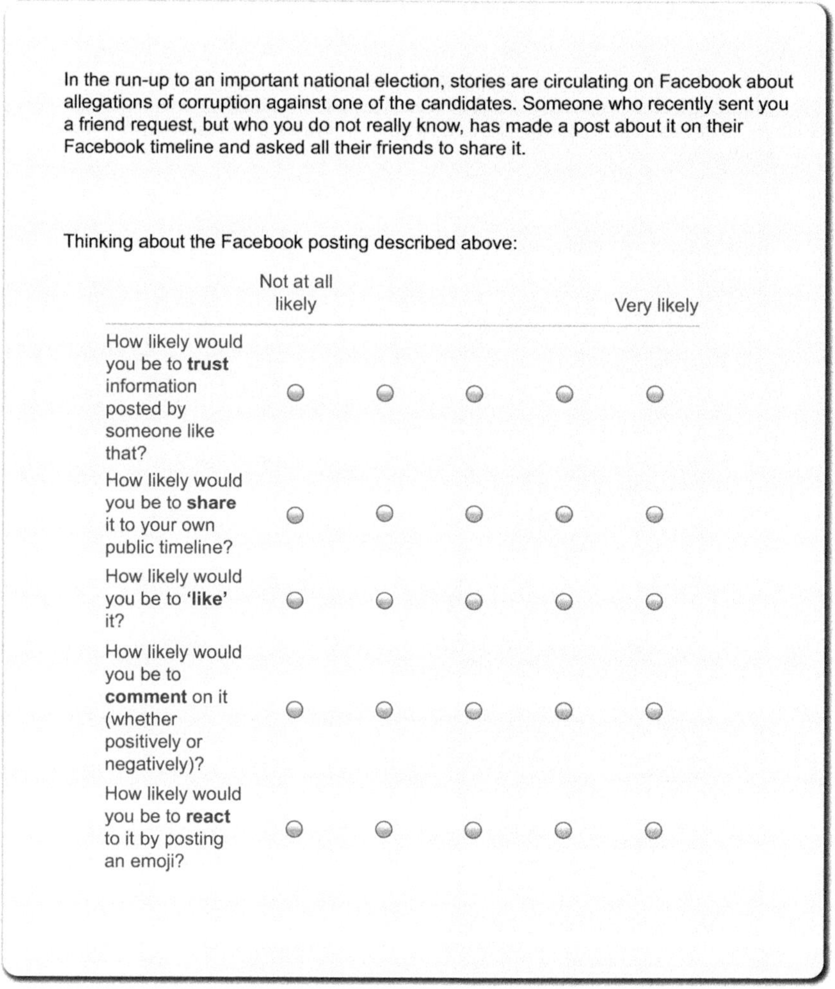
In the run-up to an important national election, stories are circulating on Facebook about allegations of corruption against one of the candidates. Someone who recently sent you a friend request, but who you do not really know, has made a post about it on their Facebook timeline and asked all their friends to share it.

Thinking about the Facebook posting described above:

| | Not at all likely | | | | Very likely |
|---|---|---|---|---|---|
| How likely would you be to **trust** information posted by someone like that? | ○ | ○ | ○ | ○ | ○ |
| How likely would you be to **share** it to your own public timeline? | ○ | ○ | ○ | ○ | ○ |
| How likely would you be to **'like'** it? | ○ | ○ | ○ | ○ | ○ |
| How likely would you be to **comment** on it (whether positively or negatively)? | ○ | ○ | ○ | ○ | ○ |
| How likely would you be to **react** to it by posting an emoji? | ○ | ○ | ○ | ○ | ○ |

**FIGURE 8.3** Low-trust condition.

the effect is generalizable, then one could hypothesize that individuals low on Agreeableness might be susceptible to targeting by individuals or organizations wishing to propagate fake news on Facebook. The fact that Agreeableness, along with other personality characteristics, is thought to be detectible from social media big data footprints (Azucar, Marengo, & Settani, 2018) suggests that this might well be feasible.

The study by Buchanan and Benson (2019) is not without limitations. It used a single example of a potential fake news item, concerned with corruption of an electoral candidate. It is possible that different scenarios, with different trust manipulations, might produce different results. Conceptual replications varying such parameters are required before the findings can be accepted as being broadly generalizable. However, the findings are consistent with other work around the role of trust (e.g., Williams, Beardmore, & Joinson, 2017). They also suggest individual differences (in this case in Agreeableness) can have an influence on the likelihood of spreading disinformation through the mechanisms of organic reach.

## Practical implications

Governments are concerned about individuals being influenced by 'fake news' and consider propaganda through social platforms a form of cybercrime (YouGov, 2017). We addressed the extent to which message originator and recipient characteristics influence the organic reach of fake news articles.

The recent allegations of personal data manipulation without user consent for achieving political agendas highlight the prominence of understanding of user personality traits in influencing their decisions (The Guardian, 2018). When the social data incident harvesting over 50 million personal Facebook records by a third-party data analytics firm is used to inform political choices of countries, it is conceivable that in the near future any developer will be able to have access to personality information on SNS. Hence, it is possible to predict a situation when hostile governments or cybercriminals may be interested in using personality traits harvested from social big data to identify individuals who are more likely to enable the organic reach of 'fake' content, thereby affecting the social content integrity. One such attack scenario would comprise identifying individuals with disagreeable traits and targeting them with false information. As they are likely to propagate the 'fake' content further, users with high disagreeable characteristics can be identified through social data harvesting such as reported by The Guardian (2018). They in turn unknowingly can serve as bots propagating the false content further through the social network. In the realm of the anticipatory computing paradigm, the decision-making process relies on the 'truthful' state of social big data. In case its integrity is compromised, the 'serve before you ask' approach may be circumvented by cybercriminals, and propaganda is one such crime. We therefore highlight further need for research into the social big data 'consensus' to distinguish between 'fake' and 'truthful' state of information driving the adoption of anticipatory applications.

## Conclusion

It is conceivable that a day will come when in this instance the artificial intelligence will gain full control over predictions based on social networking interactions. The actions grounded on the anticipatory analysis of social networking content and activity will drive the phenomenon of 'serve before you ask'. However, this phenomenon will become an opportunity for technology disruption; it also raises challenging issues in the field of social big data integrity, 'fake' information and propaganda. This chapter highlighted some of the personal user traits which may be exploited in attacks on social data integrity with some far reaching consequences for the future of anticipatory computing. The extensive research on trust, personality traits and the broad range of methodological approaches applied to studying the organic reach shows the centrality and complexity of social big data in contexts of interest to the research community. It is our intent that this chapter will contribute to the continued interest and development of the study of social data integrity in its variety of applications, including the anticipatory computing settings.

## References


Albright, J. (2017). Welcome to the era of fake news. *Media and Communication, 5*(2), 87–89. https://doi.org/10.17645/mac.v5i2.977.

Azucar, D., Marengo, D., & Settanni, M. (2018). Predicting the big 5 personality traits from digital footprints on social media: A meta-analysis. *Personality and Individual Differences, 124*, 150–159. https://doi.org/10.1016/j.paid.2017.12.018.

Basheer, A. M. A.-A., & Ibrahim, A. M. A. (2010). Mobile marketing: Examining the impact of trust, privacy concern and consumers' attitudes on intention to purchase. *International Journal of Business, 5*(3), 28–41.

Benson, V., Saridakis, G., & Tennakoon, H. (2015). Individual information security, user behaviour and cyber victimisation: An empirical study of social networking users. *Information Technology and People, 28*(3), 426–441.

Buchanan, T., & Benson, V. (2019). *Spreading disinformation on facebook: Do trust in message source, risk propensity or personality affect the organic reach of 'fake news'?*. Manuscript submitted for publication.

Buchanan, T., Johnson, J. A., & Goldberg, L. R. (2005). Implementing a five-factor personality inventory for use on the internet. *European Journal of Psychological Assessment, 21*(2), 115–127. https://doi.org/10.1027/1015-5759.21.2.115.

Cases, A. S. (2002). Perceived risk and risk-reduction strategies in internet shopping. *International Review of Retail, Distribution and Consumer Research, 12*, 375–394.

Coopamootoo, P. L., & Ashenden, D. (2011). Designing useable online privacy mechanisms: What can we learn from real world behaviour? In A. J. Turner (Ed.), *Privacy and identity management for life* (pp. 311–324). Heidelberg: Springer.

Costa, P. T., & McCrae, R. R. (1992). *Revised NEO personality inventory (NEO PI-R) and NEO five-factor inventory (NEO FFI): Professional manual*. Odessa, FL: Psychological Assessment Resources.

Dhillon, G., & Backhouse, J. (2001). Current directions in IS security research: Towards socio-organizational perspectives. *Information Systems Journal, 11*, 127–153.

Dumas, M. B. (2013). *Diving into the bitstream: Information technology meets society in a digital world*. UK: Routledge.

Gefen, D., Karahanna, E., & Straub, D. W. (2003). Trust and TAM in online shopping: An integrated model. *MIS Quarterly, 27*(1), 51–90.

Gregor, S., & Benbasat, I. (1999). Explanations from intelligent systems: Theoretical foundations and implications for practice. *MIS Quarterly, 23*(4).

Han, W., Serkan, A., Sharman, R., & Raoet, R. (2015). Campus emergency notification systems: An examination of factors affecting compliance with alerts. *MIS Quarterly, 39*(4).

Hollenbaugh, E. E., & Ferris, A. L. (2014). Facebook self-disclosure: Examining the role of traits, social cohesion, and motives. *Computers in Human Behavior, 30*, 50–58. https://doi.org/10.1016/j.chb.2013.07.055.

Kim, C., & Yang, S.-U. (2017). Like, comment, and share on Facebook: How each behavior differs from the other. *Public Relations Review, 43*(2), 441–449. https://doi.org/10.1016/j.pubrev.2017.02.006.

Komiak, S., & Benbasat, I. (2006). The effects of personalization and familiarity on trust and adoption of recommendation agents. *MIS Quarterly, 30*(4).

Liu, J., Li, C., Ji, Y. G., North, M., & Yang, F. (2017). Like it or not: ThefFortune 500's facebook strategies to generate users' electronic word-of-mouth. *Computers in Human Behavior, 73*, 605–613. https://doi.org/10.1016/j.chb.2017.03.068.

Liu, C., Marchewka, J. T., Lu, J., & Yu, C. S. (2005). Beyond concern – a privacy-trust behavioral intention model of electronic commerce. *Information and Management, 42*(2), 289–304.

Matz, S. C., Kosinski, M., Nave, G., & Stillwell, D. J. (2017). Psychological targeting as an effective approach to digital mass persuasion. *Proceedings of the National Academy of Sciences of the United States of America, 114*(48), 12714–12719. https://doi.org/10.1073/pnas.1710966114.

Mayer, R. C., Davis, J. H., & Schoorman, F. D. (1995). An integrative model of organizational trust. *Academy of Management Review, 20*, 709–734.

Meertens, R. M., & Lion, R. (2008). Measuring an individual's tendency to take risks: The risk propensity Scale. *Journal of Applied Social Psychology, 38*(6), 1506–1520. https://doi.org/10.1111/j.1559-1816.2008.00357.x.

Saridakis, G., Benson, V., Ezingeard, J.-N., & Tennakoon, H. (2015). Individual information security, user behaviour and cyber victimisation: An empirical study of social networking users. *Technological Forecasting and Social Change*. ISSN: 0040-1625, *102*.

Sheppard, B. H., & Sherman, D. M. (1998). The grammars of trust: A model and general implications. *Academy of Management Review* (Vol. 23,, 422–437.

Sitkin, S. B., & Pablo, A. L. (1995). Reconceptualizing the determinants of risk behaviour. *Academy of Management Review, 17*, 9–38.

Söllner, M., Benbasat, I., Gefen, D., Leimeister, J. M., & Pavlou, P. A. (2016). Trust. In A. Bush, & A. Rai (Eds.), *MIS quarterly research curations*. http://misq.org/research-curations.

The Guardian. (March 20, 2018). *Data scandal is huge blow for Facebook – and efforts to study its impact on society*. The Guardian. Available at https://www.theguardian.com/news/2018/mar/18/data-scandal-is-huge-blow-for-facebook-and-efforts-to-study-its-impact-on-society.

Timberg, C. (2017). *Russian propaganda may have been shared hundreds of millions of times, new research says*. Retrieved 25th March, 2017 from https://www.washingtonpost.com/news/the-switch/wp/2017/10/05/russian-propaganda-may-have-been-shared-hundreds-of-millions-of-times-new-research-says/?utm_term=.15912b814dc0.

Watson- Manheim, M., & Belanger, F. (2007). Communication media repertoires: Dealing with the multiplicity of media choices. *MIS Quarterly, 31*(2).

Whittle, H., Hamilton-Giachritsis, C., Beech, A., & Collings, G. (2013). A review of young people's vulnerabilities to online grooming. *Aggression and Violent Behavior, 18*(1), 135–146. https://doi.org/10.1016/j.avb.2012.11.008.

Williams, E. J., Beardmore, A., & Joinson, A. N. (2017). Individual differences in susceptibility to online influence: A theoretical review. *Computers in Human Behavior, 72*, 412–421. https://doi.org/10.1016/j.chb.2017.03.002.

Xiao, B., & Benbasat, I. (2007). E-commerce product recommendation agents: Use, characteristics, and impact. *MIS Quarterly, 31*(1).

Xiao, B., & Benbasat, I. (2011). Product-related deception in e-commerce: A theoretical perspective. *MIS Quarterly, 35*(1).

YouGov. (July 2017). *Security trumps privacy.* YouGov.co.uk. Available at: https://yougov.co.uk/news/2017/06/12/Security-Trumps-Privacy/.

## Further reading

Benson, V., & Turksen, U. (2017). Privacy, security and politics: Current issues and future prospects. *Communications Law Journal of Computer, Media and Telecommunications Law, 22*(4).

CHAPTER

# 9

# The impact of sentiment on content post popularity through emoji and text on social platforms

*Wei-Lun Chang*[1], *Hsiao-Chiao Tseng*[2]

[1] Department of Business Management, National Taipei University of Technology, Taipei City, Taiwan; [2] Department of Business Administration, Tamkang University, New Taipei City, Taiwan

OUTLINE



*Cyber Influence and Cognitive Threats*
https://doi.org/10.1016/B978-0-12-819204-7.00009-9

## Introduction

Social media and instant messaging apps are driving factors of network usage. As recent data show, social media use contributes to 80% of the mobile devices usage. Despite the relative consolidation of social media platforms, their growth was reported at nearly 10% per year (Rosen, 2016). The intuitive use and convenience of social platforms provide connectivity for billions of users and facilitate their expression of preferences, emotions and sentiment (Benson & Filippaios, 2015). Emotive functionality, in the form of emoticons and later emojis, has been widely enabled on social platforms (Duan, Xia, & Van Swol, 2018; Garrison, Remley, Thomas, & Wierszewski, 2011; Kaye, Wall, & Malone, 2016). Emojis are also pictorial symbols for communication (Marengo, Giannotta, & Settanni, 2017). Since before the United States presidential election, emojis were integrated into live streaming service, allowing users across the world show their support for a candidate using emojis. With instant online counting, users could easily see which candidate had higher popularity.

Extant literature shows significant research interest in gaining understanding of emotive communications and sentiment analysis using emoticons (Aoki & Uchida, 2011; Chen & Siu, 2017; Dresner & Herring, 2010; Manganari & Dimara, 2017; Rodrigues, Lopes, Prada, Thompson, & Garrido, 2017; Thompson & Filik, 2016). While emoticons convey emotions via text-only facial representation, e.g. :-), invented in late 90s by NTT, emojis use picture characters or pictographs drawing their name from e and moji, which translates from Japanese to pictograph (Miller et al., 2016). By 2016, usage of emoji characters in email, iOS systems and Android systems increased by 7123%, 662% and 1070%, respectively (according to Instagram Engineering). Moschini (2016) found that almost half of social media comments and titles in 2015 contained emoji characters. The emoji usage rate in media messages grew by 777% between 2015 and 2016, indicative of the increasing popularity of this form of emotive communication. It has been suggested that emojis are a form of visual language that can express emotions (Alshenqeeti, 2016). Research shows that when emojis are excluded from tweets, messages can be easily misunderstood, demonstrating that some emojis can help express cross-cultural intentions and emotions. In person-to-person communication, psychologists argue that words account only for 7%, while the voice tone and body language represent 38% and 55% of meaning (Ali & Chan, 2016). Therefore, in computer-mediated communication, meaning of the messages can be misunderstood or misinterpreted without the reliance on alternative methods to expressing emotions and sentiment through the body language.

Tauch and Kanjo (2016) show that text messages fail to express emotions when compared to face-to-face communication. Their research results demonstrate that emojis are frequently used in social messages as modifiers for amplifying message sentiment. A message enhanced with emojis is viewed as having a higher sentiment value. In their discussion on the emotions expressed in microblog text, Wu, Huang, Song, and Liu (2016) suggested that existing sentiment analysis methods fail to grasp sentiments of microblog text due to the large number of new popular expressions. They proposed the concept of text sentiment for microblog text by considering text distribution in messages and users. Niu, Zhu, Pang, and El Saddik (2016) found that textual Twitter posts lacked in expressing of user emotions and posts used significantly different styles, contents and vocabularies leading to wide misinterpretations. In their study of images and videos included in tweets, new sentiment analysis data sets were constructed. The analysis of the perceived meaning of messages indicated a high level of images being negatively correlated to the author's original intention.

Since the 'Like' emoji was first enabled on Facebook (in 2009), a new set of five emojis have been added in 2015. Wang and Castanon (2015) found that unlike plain text, content posts with emojis express individual emotions more clearly as they contain complex sentiments and can represent strong emotions with high reliability. Emojis were also employed to predict food choice from the research of Schouteten, Verwaeren, Lagast, Gellynck, and De Steur (2018). According to Peirce's semiotic theory, signs are determined under the impact of social culture and group conventions. It has been shown that users' interpretations of visual signs are dependent on their personal experiences and social context. That is, without clear definitions or interpretations from other communication media, it is difficult for users to grasp the meaning of a certain sign, potentially leading to inaccurate reading of expressions. In this study, emojis are explored as crucial elements for sentiment expression in computer-mediated text communication. Drawing from the theory of semiotics (Peirce, 1965) and earlier studies on sentiment extraction and emotion expression through pictographs on social platforms, an emoji-sentiment model is proposed based on the consideration of emoji and text sentiment factors.

Naveed, Gottron, Kunegis, and Alhadi (2011) found that Twitter users spread received information onto others, and bad news is shared at a much faster speed than good news. By considering information propagation on social networks, researchers established that shares characterize influence (Romero, Galuba, Asur, & Huberman, 2011; Wang, Lei, & Xu, 2015). According to Moschini (2016) digital discourse offers a distinctly sociolinguistic perspective on the transformative effect of digital technologies on the nature of language. This encompasses increasingly popularized electronic communication through emojis and text, where emojis convey sentiment and meaning is expressed in text. Previous studies investigated the relationship between shares and influence or popularity drivers on social platforms (Niu et al., 2016; Wu et al., 2016). We assume that sentiments contained in emojis and text have more significant implications than driving shares. We sought to find the ratio between textual sentiment factors and emoji sentiment factors through sentiment analysis. Drawing from the social platform content quality framework by Chen, Cheng, He, and Jiang (2012) for articles (content posts) and the sentiment analysis in Linguistic Inquiry and Word Count (LIWC), this study has the following objectives:

**1)** An article popularity analysis model based on emojis and textual sentiment is proposed and empirical evidence is used to test it.
**2)** The implications for practice of emojis and text combination strategies to express sentiment on social networks are presented.

The study explores the use of emojis as sentiment expressions alongside text comments in analysis of the 2017 US election campaign articles. We conclude the paper with the open research questions inviting further studies in post polarity and sentiment communication on social platforms combining text with emojis.

## Sentiment analysis using emojis

### Sentiment and popularity model

Current researchers have explored textual sentiment in detail (Chan & Chong, 2017; Kavanagh, 2016; Komrsková, 2015; Settanni & Marengo, 2015; Soranaka & Matsushita, 2012). Settanni and Marengo (2015) found that individuals' textual content posted on social networks is determined by their behavioural and psychological characteristics. Khatua, Khatua, Ghosh, and Chaki (2015), examining previous studies, showed that Twitter trends can capture electoral sentiment, i.e. election results can be predicted from the sentiment of tweets. Smailović, Kranjc, Grčar, Žnidaršič, and Mozetič (2015) collected tweets about Bulgarian parliament during the Bulgarian election. The results indicated that tweets with negative sentiments prevailed before and after the election, and the negative and positive sentiments of tweets had a close relationship with the election results.

Researchers have also explored emoji sentiment (Cui, Zhang, Liu, & Ma, 2011; Yeole, Chavan, & Nikose, 2015). Casper Grathwohl, the president of Oxford Dictionaries, said that 'emoji are becoming an increasingly rich form of communication, one that transcends linguistic borders, and the characters capture a sense of playfulness and intimacy that embodies emoji culture itself'. Skiba (2016) indicated that emojis are a simple method for expressing emotions and fill a gap in textual sentiment expression, even across linguistic barriers. Wang and Castanon (2015) analysed emoji characters in tweets, focusing on the relationship between emojis and the contexts where they were used. The research results showed that some emoticons are strong and reliable signals of sentiment polarity, whereas a large number of emoticons convey complicated sentiments that should be treated with extreme caution.

It is known from the existing studies on emojis that expression of sentiment with emotions is related to both emojis and text (Mahajan & Mulay, 2015; Thompson & Filik, 2016). Emojis are able to fill the gap in textual sentiment expressions, playing a significant role in communication. Research simultaneously considering emoji sentiment factors and textual sentiment factors is rarely seen. In this study, the influences of both emoji sentiment factors and textual sentiment factors are taken into consideration based on the research of Bahri, Bahri, and Lal (2018) and Mahajan and Mulay (2015). The main concept is shown in Eq. (9.1), where $i$ stands for the $i$th article, $Popularity_i$ for the popularity of the $i$th article, $Emoji_i$ for the positive−negative sentiment ratio of emoji for the $i$th article, and $Comment_i$ for the positive−negative sentiment ratio of text for the $i$th article. Emotion expression in text is relatively limited, as shown in sentiment analysis, whereas emojis are drawing more attention and allow for a wider range of expressions. In this study emojis are viewed as a weighted element and text is analysed as a supplementary dimension. In the context of Facebook users are adapting to the new functionality of the six emojis. In order to avoid habitual clicking the 'Like' button for an article, textual sentiment is introduced as an equilibrating mechanism. In other words, the concept of emoji is equal to weight logic, which makes the existence of emoji a significant compensation for textual content. Here, emoji and text are multiplied for achieving the product effect of sentiment. Therefore, a popular article will exhibit a high positive sentiment of emoji and text, where $Comment_i$ and $Emoji_i$ represent the concepts of the textual sentiment factor and emoji sentiment factor, respectively.

$$Popularity_i = Comment_i * Emoji_i \tag{9.1}$$

## Emoji sentiment expression

In 2009, Facebook launched the 'Like' emoji for user convenience, allowing them to simply express agreement with or favour towards an article, instead of expressing their preference through textual comments. In October 2015, Facebook launched an additional five emojis. As Facebook user base is truly global exhibiting certain differences in both culture and cognition, two major design principles were set to reduce the differences: (1) new emojis needed to be ones that could be understood globally; and (2) new emojis needed to be ones that could be extensively used and reflect ideas about real life. After some modifications, five new emojis were added to Facebook, viz., 'Love', 'HaHa', 'Wow', 'Sad' and 'Angry'. In terms of their literal implications, these emojis can be divided into two categories: positive sentiment emoji and negative sentiment emoji. By classifying the textual sentiments using the software SentiStrength, we established that 'Like', 'Love', 'HaHa' and 'Wow' are positive emojis, and 'Sad' and 'Angry' are negative emojis. Users can respond to certain articles with appropriate emojis corresponding to their sentiment. Based on the total number of each emoji in an article, symbols for the six emojis were set as 'Like' $= L_e$, 'Love' $= L_o$, 'HaHa' $= H$, 'Wow' $= W$, 'Sad' $= S_a$ and 'Angry' $= A$, as shown in Table 9.1.

$$E_p = \left(\frac{L_e}{E} * W_K\right) + \left(\frac{L_o}{E} * W_v\right) + \left(\frac{H}{E} * W_a\right) + \left(\frac{W}{E} * W_o\right) \tag{9.2}$$

Emojis are one sentiment factor, and sentiments can be categorized as positive or negative, where a positive sentiment is expressed using 'Like', 'Love', 'HaHa' and 'Wow'. In order to integrate the values of positive sentiments, the concept shown in Eq. (9.2) is proposed in this paper, where $E_p$ (positive emoji) denotes the score of positive sentiment for

TABLE 9.1 Emoji classification.

| Emoji concept | Like | Love | HaHa | Wow | Sad | Angry |
|---|---|---|---|---|---|---|
| Symbol | $L_e$ | $L_o$ | H | W | $S_a$ | A |
| Definition | Total number of 'Like' | Total number of 'Love' | Total number of 'HaHa' | Total number of 'Wow' | Total number of 'Sad' | Total number of 'Angry' |
| Weight | $W_k$ | $W_v$ | $W_a$ | $W_o$ | $W_s$ | $W_g$ |
| Emoji sentiment | Positive sentiment | | | | Negative sentiment | |

positive emojis in a single article, $E$ (emoji) denotes the total number of emojis in the article, $W_k$ is the weight of 'Like', $W_v$ is the weight of 'Love', $W_a$ is the weight of 'HaHa', $W_o$ is the weight of 'Wow' and $L_e$, $L_o$, $H$ and $W$ stand for the total numbers of 'Like', 'Love', 'HaHa' and 'Wow', respectively.

$\frac{L_e}{\mathrm{E}}$, $\frac{L_o}{\mathrm{E}}$, $\frac{\mathrm{H}}{\mathrm{E}}$ and $\frac{\mathrm{W}}{\mathrm{E}}$, respectively, denote the ratios of 'Like', 'Love', 'HaHa' and 'Wow' to all emojis in a single article, $\left(\frac{L_e}{\mathrm{E}} * W_K\right)$, $\left(\frac{L_o}{\mathrm{E}} * W_v\right)$, $\left(\frac{\mathrm{H}}{\mathrm{E}} * W_a\right)$ and $\left(\frac{\mathrm{W}}{\mathrm{E}} * W_o\right)$ are products of the proportion of each positive emoji and its corresponding weight ($W_k$, $W_v$, $W_a$ and $W_o$), aiming to equilibrate the scores of positive sentiment emojis and negative sentiment emojis. This is because four emojis express positive emotions, but only two express negative ones. The concept of weight is proposed here to eliminate the substantial number difference between positive and negative sentiment emojis and therefore equilibrate the two. The scores of all positive sentiment emojis were respectively calculated and added together to serve as the total score of positive sentiment emojis, $E_p$, for the comparison of positive and negative sentiment emojis.

$$E_n = \left(\frac{\mathrm{Sa}}{\mathrm{E}} * W_s\right) + \left(\frac{\mathrm{A}}{\mathrm{E}} * W_g\right) \tag{9.3}$$

Apart from positive sentiments, emojis also express negative sentiments ('Sad' and 'Angry'). In order to integrate the values of negative sentiments, the concept expressed in Eq. (9.3) is proposed. In the equation, $E_n$ (negative emoji) stands for the score of emoji negative sentiment, $W_s$ is the weight of 'Sad', $W_g$ is the weight of 'Angry', and $S_a$ and $A$ stand for the total number of 'Sad' and 'Angry', respectively. $\frac{\mathrm{Sa}}{\mathrm{E}}$ and $\frac{\mathrm{A}}{\mathrm{E}}$, respectively, denote the ratio of 'Sad' and 'Angry' to all emojis in a single article. $\left(\frac{\mathrm{Sa}}{\mathrm{E}} \times W_s\right)$ and $\left(\frac{\mathrm{A}}{\mathrm{E}} \times W_g\right)$ are products of the proportions of 'Sad' and 'Angry', respectively, and their corresponding weights ($W_s$ and $W_g$), aiming to equilibrate the scores of positive sentiment emojis and negative sentiment emojis. The concept of weight is proposed here to equilibrate the two. The scores of the negative sentiment emojis were respectively calculated and added together to serve as the total score of negative sentiment emojis, $E_n$, for the comparison of positive and negative sentiment emojis.

$$Emoji = \left|\frac{E_p}{E_N}\right| \leq 1 \tag{9.4}$$

where, if $\left|\frac{E_p}{E_N}\right| < 1$, negative sentiment of emoji is dominant; if $\left|\frac{E_p}{E_N}\right| = 1$, negative and positive sentiments of emoji are balanced; if $\left|\frac{E_p}{E_N}\right| > 1$, positive sentiment of emoji is dominant.

The unbiased sentimental tendency of emoji cannot be fully determined, even using the given positive and negative sentiment concepts.

Therefore, a discriminant concept shown in Eq. (9.4) that was derived from the concept of weight (Eq. 9.1) was developed, from which the positive−negative sentiment ratio of emoji can be obtained. In the equation, $\left|\frac{E_p}{E_N}\right|$ represents the positive−negative sentiment ratio of emoji in a single article. In order to make the ratio a positive number even under the negative value for negative sentiment, the absolute value of the ratio was adopted. A ratio less than 1 indicated a value of emoji's negative sentiment higher than that of positive sentiment; a ratio equal to 1 demonstrated an equilibrium of positive and negative sentiment of emoji; and a ratio greater than 1 presented a value of emoji's positive sentiment higher than that of negative sentiment. That is, the larger the negative impact, the lower the ratio; the larger the positive impact, the higher the ratio. Positive−negative sentiment ratio of emoji can be found by calculating the ratio of positive sentiment value (computed using Eq. 9.2) to negative sentiment value (computed using Eq. 9.3). Therefore, positive or negative sentiment tendency can be determined based on the emoji's positive sentiment value and negative sentiment value using Eq. (9.4).

## Textual sentiment factor

Ravi and Ravi (2015) pointed out that many electronic commerce networks rely on users' comments as indicator for market analysis so as to improve the quality and standard of their products and services. Mittal, Goel, and Jain (2016) suggested that online comments help consumers learn about products or services and make objective choices. Roy and Zeng (2014) studied data gathered from social media and multimedia websites and found that comments posted on various social media had a significant effect on the prediction of movie popularity. In this work, textual sentiment of comments on articles posted on Facebook was analysed based on the characteristic described above to investigate the sentiment of the public towards the article. Textual positive and negative sentiment values can be acquired through the sentiment analysis system. In order to obtain the positive−negative sentiment ratio of a given text, the concept shown in Eq. (9.5) is proposed, where $C_p$ (positive comment) represents the total number of words expressing positive sentiment that appear in one comment, and $C_n$ (negative comment) represents the total number of words expressing negative sentiment in one comment. In Eq. (9.5), the total number of negative sentiment words is taken as the denominator and that of positive sentiment words as the numerator. The positive−negative sentiment ratio of textual comments is calculated by dividing the total number of positive sentiments by that of negative sentiments, which are derived from the concept of *Comment* expressed in Eq. (9.1). The absolute value of the ratio is adopted since the negative sentiment is a minus. A ratio less than or equal to 1 indicates a value of comment's negative sentiment higher than that of its positive sentiment; a ratio greater than 1 represents a value of a comment's positive sentiment higher than that of its negative sentiment. That is, the larger the negative impact, the lower the ratio; the larger the positive impact, the higher the ratio. Therefore, positive or negative sentiment tendency can be determined based on the comment's positive sentiment value and negative sentiment value using Eq. (9.5).

$$Comment = \frac{C_p}{C_n} \leq 1 \tag{9.5}$$

where, if $\frac{C_p}{C_n} \leq 1$, negative sentiment of textual comment is dominant; if $\frac{C_p}{C_n} > 1$, positive sentiment of textual comment is dominant.

## Article popularity

Chen et al. (2012) highlight that on Twitter a larger number of retweets of and comments on an article denoted stronger attention to the article, indicating higher impact, whereas a smaller number denoted a poor-quality article with low public participation. The latter type of article has less impact. The concept of Eq. (9.6) proposed in this paper was derived from the 'tweet quality' model proposed by Chen et al. (2012). In the equation for tweet quality, $v$ stands for a node in the microblog (a user), $Q_v$ for the tweet quality of the node in the microblog, *Retweeted (v)* for the number of retweets of the article posted by the node, *Comments (v)* for the number of comments on the article posted by the node, and *Tweets (v)* for the total number of articles posted by the node in a certain period. The sum of retweets and comments, *Retweeted* $(v)$ + *Comments* $(v)$, represents the activity of the article. By dividing this sum by *Tweets (v)*, we were able to find articles with a certain quality from a designated period. Since this study was mainly conducted based on Facebook, *Retweeted (v)* and *Tweets (v)* were replaced by *Shares* and *Total Posts,* corresponding to the terms used in the Facebook interface. However, the sentiment factor is not mentioned in the tweet quality concept, making it impossible to use the revised equation to determine whether the influence is positive or negative. Therefore, based on our revised tweet quality concept, the sentiment factor is introduced for assessment.

$$Q = \frac{\text{Shares} + \text{Comments}}{\text{Total posts}} \tag{9.6}$$

### *Individual article popularity model*

Stieglitz and Dang-Xuan (2012) explored the relationship between influential people on Twitter and retweets of their tweets, discovering that retweets are a simple operation for functional information propagation. Generally, a retweet demonstrates the reaction of a user to an article or evaluates the article's attraction to the user. In order to analyse the situation of an influential individual, apart from the number of retweets, information such as textual sentiment and follower number and age should also be taken into account. In terms of textual sentiment, the software Linguistic Inquiry and Word Count (LIWC) was used for the textual sentiment analysis. Research shows that the words expressing positive and negative sentiment included in a political party's or politician's articles are positively correlated with the retweets of the articles (Stieglitz & Dang-Xuan, 2012). On Twitter, the retweet rate is in direct proportion to the number of relevant words. Intensive discussions and communications can exert certain impacts. Based on the existing studies, Eq. (9.7) is proposed as a way to determine the relationship between sentiment factors and article popularity from the perspective of the sentiment factor.

$$\mathrm{Ind}_i = \sum \left\{ \left[ \frac{S_i + \left( \frac{C_p}{C_{ni}} * C_i \right)}{\mathrm{P}} \right] * \left| \frac{E_p}{E_n} \right|_i \right\} \tag{9.7}$$

In Eq. (9.7), $Ind_i$ represents the $i$th individual article with relatively high popularity, $S_i$ (share) represents the sharing number of the $i$th article, and $\frac{C_p}{C_{ni}}$ stands for the positive–negative sentiment ratio of text in the $i$th article. When the ratio is less than 1, negative sentiment is dominant in the article; when the ratio is greater than 1, positive sentiment is dominant. $C_i$ (total comments) denotes the total number of comments on the $i$th article, and $\left|\frac{E_p}{E_n}\right|_i$ denotes the positive–negative sentiment ratio of emoji in the $i$th article. When the ratio is less than 1, negative sentiment is dominant in the article; when the ratio is equal to 1, positive sentiment and negative sentiment are balanced; when the ratio is greater than 1, positive sentiment is dominant. $P$ (total posts) stands for the total posts of an individual during a designated period.

Eq. (9.7), on article popularity, was derived based on the tweet quality concept expressed by Eq. (9.6). For the purpose of assessing emoji and text sentiment, the discriminant concepts of Eqs. (9.4) and (9.5) were adopted, achieving the ratio of emoji sentiment factor to text sentiment factor. $S_i+C_i$ demonstrates the activity of an article, which determines the popularity of the article from the perspective of the public by taking the numbers of shares and comments as the measuring indices. Because $S_i$ and $C_i$ can be regarded as homogeneous measuring factors, the sum of the two factors was adopted to assess the activity of the article. However, it is impossible to determine whether the influence of an article is positive or negative based solely on the article's activity. As indicated by Eq. (9.1), popularity is the product of the weights of the positive–negative sentiment ratios of text and emoji. Therefore, *Comment*, the positive–negative sentiment ratio, was introduced for determination. $\frac{C_p}{C_{ni}} * C_i$, the product of the text sentiment ratio and total number of comments on a single article, presents the positive–negative sentiment ratio of comments on the article. $\frac{S_i + \left(\frac{C_p}{C_{ni}} * C_i\right)}{P}$ denotes the popularity of individual articles on the same topic in terms of the text sentiment factor. By dividing $S_i + \left(\frac{C_p}{C_{ni}} * C_i\right)$ by $P$, we were able to detect relatively popular articles with different topics in a designated period. It is known from Eq. (9.1) that $\left|\frac{E_p}{E_n}\right|_i$ in $\left[\frac{S_i + \left(\frac{C_p}{C_{ni}} * C_i\right)}{P}\right] * \left|\frac{E_p}{E_n}\right|_i$ expresses the *Emoji* in the equation, i.e., emoji weight, which demonstrates the article sentiment as a positive or negative one via sentiment multiplication.

### *Topic popularity model*

Eq. (9.8) was developed to explore the popularity of different articles on the same topic, where $Topic_i$ stands for the popularity of each topic of individual articles based on the emoji sentiment factor supplemented by the text sentiment factor, $\left|\frac{E_p}{E_n}\right|_i$ for the positive–negative sentiment ratio of the emoji, and $\frac{C_p}{C_{n_i}}$ for the positive–negative sentiment ratio of the text. The numbers of followers have been shown to effectively compare the popularity of articles on the same topic:

$$\text{Topic}_i = \sum\left\{\left[\frac{S_i + \left(\frac{C_p}{C_{ni}} * C_i\right)}{F}\right] * \left|\frac{E_p}{E_n}\right|_i\right\} \tag{9.8}$$

In Eq. (9.8), $Topic_i$ represents the individual's $i$th article on a designated topic, which was designed to compare the article popularities of different people, $S_i$ (share) the number of shares for the $i$th article, and $\frac{C_p}{C_{ni}}$ the positive–negative sentiment ratio of text for the $i$th article. When $\frac{C_p}{C_{ni}} < 1$, negative sentiment is dominant; when $\frac{C_p}{C_{ni}} > 1$, positive sentiment is dominant. $C_i$ (total comment) is the number of comments on the $i$th article, and $\left|\frac{E_p}{E_n}\right|_i$ the positive–negative sentiment ratio of emoji for the $i$th article. When $\left|\frac{E_p}{E_n}\right|_i < 1$, negative sentiment is dominant; when $\left|\frac{E_p}{E_n}\right|_i = 1$, positive sentiment and negative sentiment are balanced; when $\left|\frac{E_p}{E_n}\right|_i > 1$, positive sentiment is dominant. $F$ (follower) denotes the total number of followers for the research object.

Eq. (9.8) expresses article popularity derived from the tweet quality concept shown in Eq. (9.6). In order to consider emoji and text sentiment, discriminant concepts of Eqs. (9.4) and (9.5) were introduced to obtain the ratio of emoji sentiment factor to text sentiment factor. Although Eqs. (9.7) and (9.8) share the same pattern of calculation, they have different denominators. Here, $S_i + \left(\frac{C_p}{C_{ni}} * C_i\right)$ is divided by $F$ because different research objects have diversified numbers of followers on Facebook, making it impossible to compare popular articles on the same level, where their respective follower numbers are applied as the denominator for the equilibrium and thus a comparison of popular articles can be done on the same level.

# Methodological approach

## Data collection

In our study, two candidates from the 2016 United States presidential election, Hillary Clinton and Donald Trump, were taken as research objects. We collected social platform footprint information, including their numbers of Facebook followers, comments to their posted articles, comment contents, number of comments, number of shares, number of each emoji, and total number of all emojis. Due to the large volume of comments, those with at least 10 'Likes' were considered for investigation. Information collection took place in sync with the presidential election period, from September 2016 to November 8, 2016. Since the categories of articles posted during this period were diverse, we used Clinton's and Trump's articles on topics related to the election, i.e., articles representing election activities, such as those for campaign matters and get-out-the-vote movements, articles discussing issues associated with their opponent, articles on social topics (e.g. human rights and military affairs), articles mentioning their personal history and relevant reports and other articles involving at least two of the topics mentioned above.

From September 2016 to 8 November 2016 Clinton campaign posted 46 articles about personal topics, 58 about her opponent, 62 about the election, 28 on other topics related to the election and 24 other articles, totalling 242 articles. Trump campaign posted 4 articles on personal topics, 31 about his opponent, 79 about the election, 25 on other topics related to the election and 9 other articles, totalling 148 articles. In the collected articles, Clinton received 16,316 comments while Trump received 54,009. The number of followers for Clinton and Trump was 10,131,628 and 21,111,235, respectively. Among the articles covering personal topics, Clinton's articles reached peak quantity (26) in October, exceeding Trump's articles in terms of comment and share numbers. Although Trump posted fewer articles than Clinton, his campaign obtained a higher average number of emoji and a higher average number of 'Likes' in September and October. The largest average numbers of 'Sad' and 'Angry' were both observed in Clinton's Facebook feed in October and November.

Regarding articles aimed at their opponent, Trump posted as many as 26 articles in October, substantially exceeding Clinton with respect to comment number, share number, total mean emoji number, average number of 'Likes', average number of 'Loves', average number of 'HaHas' and average number of 'Angrys', although with only a narrow gap in article number (4; Clinton posted 22 articles in October in this category). In this month, the average number of 'Wows' and 'Sads' for Clinton were higher than those for Trump. It can be seen that the public approved more of Trump's articles than Clinton's. Among the articles by the candidates discussing the election, Trump's article number hit a peak of 43 in October, leading to a higher number of comments than that of Clinton. In November, although Trump only posted 26 articles about the election, 13 fewer than Clinton, he exceeded Clinton in share number, comment number, total mean emoji number, average number of 'Likes', average number of 'Loves', average number of 'HaHas', average number of 'Wows' and average number of 'Angrys', achieving more enthusiastic responses from the public. This was potentially caused by the difference in follower number, as well as the fact that these topics attracted more attention from people as the presidential election approached. For the discussion of topics such as current affairs and political ideas, Trump posted 17 articles in October, reaching the peak article number. In September and October, Trump achieved higher scores in aspects including share number, total mean emoji number, average number of 'Likes', average number of 'HaHas', average number of 'Wows' and average number of 'Angrys', whereas Clinton obtained a higher comment number, total mean comment number, average number of 'Loves', and average number of 'Sads'.

## Sentiment analysis

In this study, text and emojis were used in sentiment analysis. Text sentiment was analysed using LIWC based on 218 articles by Clinton and 148 articles by Trump obtained from their Facebook accounts. The articles were divided into four types in terms of content, including articles on personal topics, articles on topics related to the opponent, articles on topics related to the election, and articles on other topics. A total of 16,316 and 54,099 comments were, respectively, obtained from the 218 (Clinton) and 148 (Trump) articles and input into LIWC for analysis to extract useful information, such as the positive–negative sentiment ratio of the text (*Comment*). Emoji sentiment was analysed, and the weights of six Facebook emoji—'Like', 'Love', 'HaHa', 'Wow', 'Sad' and 'Angry'—were respectively determined as 2, 3, 2, 3, −4, and −4 using SentiStrength. The calculation was conducted by taking one single article as the unit. We divided the number of each emoji by the total number of emojis, multiplied by their corresponding weights. The sum of the results for the four positive emojis divided by the sum of the results for the two negative emojis was then the positive–negative sentiment ratio of emoji (*Emoji*). The positive–negative sentiment ratio of the text (*Comment*) was obtained by dividing the number of positive sentiment words ($C_p$) by the number of negative sentiment words ($C_n$) using LIWC.

Averages of emoji and text sentiment for the various articles posted by Clinton and Trump can be seen in Table 9.2, which shows that both Clinton's and Trump's emoji sentiment tendencies were positive. Clinton's negative sentiment score for the articles on Trump-associated topics was as high as 2.8, pulling down the positive–negative sentiment ratio of emoji (*Emoji*), as well as the positive–negative sentiment ratio of text (*Comment*), to 1.28. Trump's positive–negative sentiment ratios of emoji (*Emoji*) for articles on personal topics, Clinton-associated topics and other relevant topics were all higher than Clinton's. Clinton beat Trump on the positive–negative sentiment ratio of text (Clinton's *Comment*, 1.97; Trump's *Comment*, 1.92) for election-related articles only, by a narrow margin of 0.05. Although the relative rankings of the textual positive–negative sentiment ratio (*Comment*) and emoji positive–negative sentiment ratio (*Emoji*) were not necessarily the same, the textual positive–negative sentiment ratio (*Comment*) could be used to adjust the sentiment error of users who were accustomed to clicking 'Like', which does not represent that the relative rankings of the textual positive–negative sentiment ratio (*Comment*) and emoji positive–negative sentiment ratio (*Emoji*) were not consistent, i.e. denying the analysis value of the sentiment factors. According to the idea that influence on social networks needs to be constructed based on articles of a high quality by Chen et al. (2012), the results of the research model were compared with theirs by using the share number and comment number as the measuring index of qualified articles. The concept of individual article popularity (Individual) was constructed by taking emoji and textual sentiment factors into consideration based on article quality popularity (Q).

TABLE 9.2 Comparison of average emoji and text sentiment between Hillary Clinton's and Donald Trump's articles.

| **Hillary Clinton** | **Average score** | | | | | |
|---|---|---|---|---|---|---|
| **Topic** | **Positive sentiment score (Ep)** | **Negative sentiment score (En)** | **Positive–negative sentiment ratio of emoji (*Emoji*)** | **Total number of positive sentiment words** | **Total number of negative sentiment words** | **Positive–negative sentiment ratio of text (*Comment*)** |
| Personal | 4.23 | 0.22 | 95.00 | 1.77 | 1.39 | 1.36 |
| Opponent-associated | 13.12 | 2.80 | 26.18 | 1.65 | 1.67 | 1.01 |
| Related to the election | 3.84 | 0.13 | 83.34 | 1.93 | 1.32 | 1.92 |
| Other topics | 1.99 | 0.05 | 92.97 | 1.74 | 1.33 | 1.63 |
| **Donald Trump** | **Average score** | | | | | |
| **Article Topic** | **Positive sentiment score (Ep)** | **Negative sentiment score (En)** | **Positive–negative sentiment ratio of emoji (*Emoji*)** | **Total number of positive sentiment words** | **Total number of negative sentiment words** | **Positive–negative sentiment ratio of text (*Comment*)** |
| Personal | 3.21 | 0.03 | 298.32 | 1.97 | 1.32 | 1.78 |
| Opponent-associated | 7.87 | 0.94 | 70.51 | 1.82 | 1.51 | 1.28 |
| Related to the election | 4.54 | 0.20 | 63.87 | 1.49 | 0.78 | 1.97 |
| Other topics | 2.71 | 0.05 | 193.96 | 1.92 | 1.32 | 1.74 |

## Popularity of individual topics and joint-topic articles

It can be observed from Fig. 9.1 that the ranking in terms of article quality popularity (Q) was as follows: articles on topics related to the election, articles where Clinton discusses topics associated with Trump, articles on topics associated with Clinton and articles on other topics. The ranking for individual article popularity (Individual) considering sentiment factors is as follows: articles on topics related to the election, articles on topics associated with Clinton, articles on other topics and articles by Clinton discussing topics associated with Trump.

Articles by Clinton discussing topics associated with Trump experienced the most significant change; they were ranked second in terms of article quality popularity (Q) before sentiment factors were considered, but ranked last in terms of individual article popularity (Individual) after the sentiment factors were taken into account. This indicates that articles with high article quality popularity (Q) were not necessarily popular with the public.

It can be seen from Fig. 9.2 that the article ranking in terms of article quality popularity (Q) was as follows: articles on topics related to the election, articles with Trump discussing topics associated with Clinton, articles on other topics and articles on topics associated with Trump. The ranking of individual article popularity (Individual) in consideration of sentiment factors was as follows: articles with Trump discussing topics associated with Clinton, articles on topics related to the election, articles on topics associated with Trump and articles on other topics. Trump's articles discussing topics associated with Clinton experienced the most

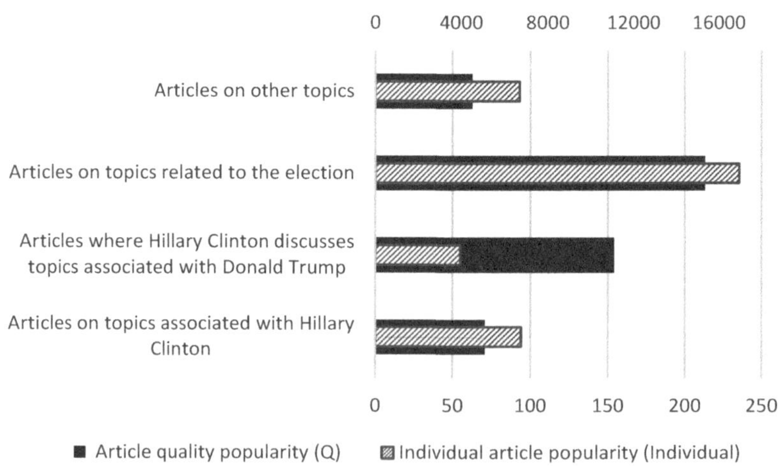


FIGURE 9.1 Mean comparison of article quality popularity and individual article popularity for Hillary clinton's articles.

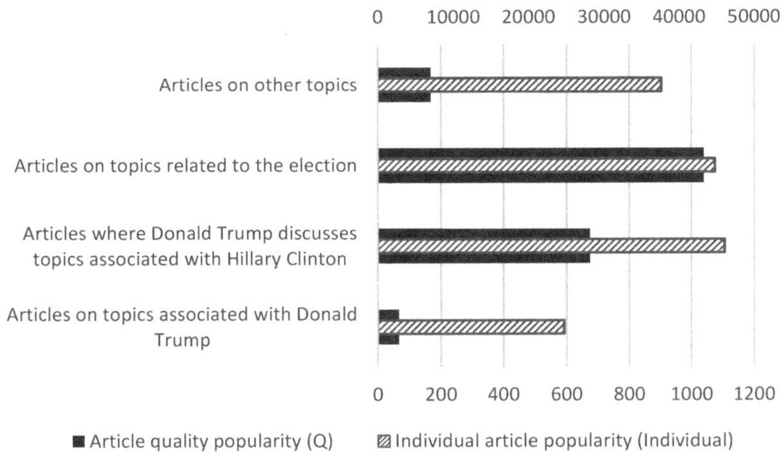


**FIGURE 9.2** Mean comparison of article quality popularity and individual article popularity for Donald Trump's articles.

significant change; they were ranked second in terms of article quality popularity (Q) before the sentiment factors were considered, but ranked first in terms of individual article popularity (Individual) after those factors were taken into account. It was found by further analysing the article content that people demonstrated positive sentiment towards Trump's articles criticizing Clinton, but negative sentiment towards his articles denying Clinton's efforts over the past 30 years, showing that people gave Clinton credit for her efforts, but this did not manifest as support for her. The sentiment tendency of a single article could be clearly determined through individual article popularity (Individual), which helped us obtain results closer to people's real thoughts, instead of a simple article popularity discussion.

As shown in Fig. 9.3, in terms of article quality popularity (Q), Trump exceeded Clinton in articles on other topics, articles on topics related to the election and articles discussing topics associated with his opponent, whereas Clinton was superior to Trump in articles on personal topics. After the sentiment factors are considered, in terms of joint-topic article popularity (Joint topic), Trump achieved higher scores in articles on other topics, articles on personal topics and articles discussing topics associated with his opponent, whereas Clinton exceeded Trump in articles on topics related to the election. Significant changes were observed in articles on personal topics and election-associated topics, where articles on topics related to the election saw the most obvious variation. This was potentially because of Clinton's background as a politician. In social networks for recreation, users' motivation to follow politicians will generally make them express support for the politicians or be interested in political topics.

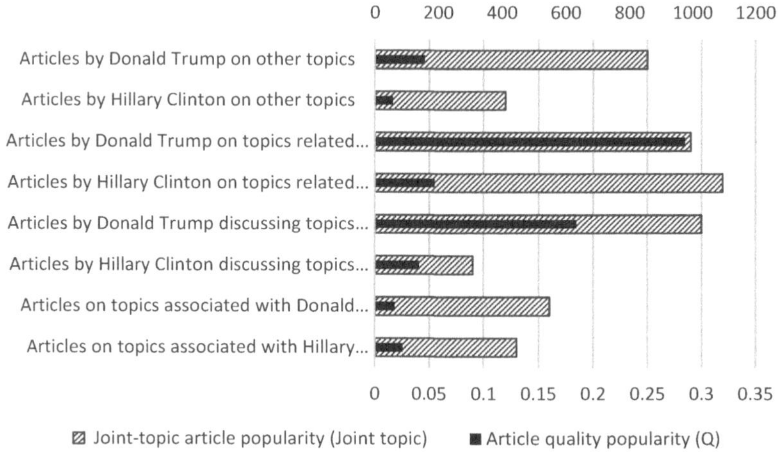


**FIGURE 9.3** Mean comparison of article quality popularity and joint-topic article popularity for Hillary clinton's and Donald trump's articles.

Therefore, discussing election-related topics will resonate with users. Trump drew great attention from the public in these articles, which was closely related to his number of followers on Facebook, because a larger number of followers will produce a high exposure rate, leading to innate advantages in total emoji number, share number and comment number.

## Influence of emoji and textual sentiments

Factors of social influence on social platforms include follower number, shares and comments (Romero et al., 2011; Wang et al., 2015). As indicated by Lahuerta-Otero and Cordero-Gutiérrez (2016), shares are one of the characteristics of influence on social networks, and sentiment and attitudes are commonly expressed with emoji. Due to the sentiment differences in six Facebook emojis, their emoji positive–negative sentiment ratio (*Emoji*) has a higher explanatory power, yielding an effective expression of sentiment and social influence through emoji and shares. Tables 9.3 and 9.4 demonstrate the correlation coefficients of emoji and share number for Clinton's and Trump's articles. It can be seen from Table 9.2 that emoji and share number were correlated for Clinton's articles. 'Like' and 'Love' had the highest correlation with the number of shares for articles on personal topics and election-associated topics. 'Like' and 'Wow' had the highest correlation with the number of shares for articles on other topics. However, although they were directly correlated in the articles mentioned above, the correlation was not at a high level of intensity. In Clinton's articles discussing topics associated with her

TABLE 9.3 Correlation coefficients of emoji and share number for Hillary Clinton's articles.

| | Hillary Clinton | Like | Love | HaHa | Wow | Sad | Angry |
|---|---|---|---|---|---|---|---|
| Correlation coefficient | Articles on personal topics | 0.6295 | 0.5673 | 0.4766 | 0.2014 | 0.2465 | 0.1108 |
| | Articles discussing topics associated with opponent | 0.8989 | 0.5063 | 0.1176 | 0.3908 | 0.9432 | 0.9044 |
| | Articles on topics related to the election | 0.6913 | 0.6123 | 0.3327 | 0.4218 | 0.5577 | 0.4252 |
| | Articles on other topics | 0.6227 | 0.4392 | 0.2569 | 0.6482 | 0.2797 | 0.2572 |

opponent, 'Like', 'Sad' and 'Angry' were most directly correlated with the number of shares at a strong level.

In these articles, two of the top three with the highest individual article popularity (*Individual*) were about Trump discriminating against women and about his view of war, which explains the obvious negative sentiment of the emoji and the extremely large number of shares. Considering the direct correlation of emoji and share number, these results further prove that the public will provide positive feedback to favoured articles, and they will significantly share the articles they do not like, except for providing negative feedback.

Table 9.4 shows the correlation coefficients of emoji and share number for Trump's articles. 'Like' and 'Love' had the highest correlation with the number of shares for articles on personal topics, whereas 'HaHa' and 'Angry' had the lowest negative correlation. In his articles on topics associated with his opponent, 'Like' and 'HaHa' had the highest correlation with the number of shares. In his articles on other topics, 'Like', 'HaHa' and 'Love' had the highest correlation with the number of shares. In his articles on topics related to the election, emoji and share number were highly correlated.

The correlations of emoji and share number for Trump's articles were all higher than those for Clinton's, which may be because the phenomenon is related to the number of followers. Trump had a larger group of followers, making the total number of emoji appearing in these articles as high as 90,000+. For Clinton, the total number of emoji was only 50,000+.

TABLE 9.4 Correlation coefficients of emoji and share number for Donald Trump's articles.

| | Donald Trump | Like | Love | HaHa | Wow | Sad | Angry |
|---|---|---|---|---|---|---|---|
| Correlation coefficientrowhead | Hillary Clinton | 0.9880 | 0.9953 | −0.0782 | 0.8475 | 0.7787 | −0.1736 |
| | Articles on personal topics | 0.7673 | 0.4268 | 0.9455 | 0.2072 | 0.0584 | 0.0431 |
| | Articles discussing topics associated with opponent | 0.8852 | 0.9346 | 0.8098 | 0.7886 | 0.8273 | 0.8790 |
| | Articles on topics related to the election | 0.8320 | 0.7091 | 0.7576 | 0.5882 | 0.3905 | 0.1826 |

This can also be explained by the fact that Trump has a stronger influence than Clinton on Facebook, considering that influential factors of social networks include follower number, shares, and comments, which are closely associated with each other.

Our results highlight that emoji and the number of shares were directly correlated, where 'Like' and 'Love' were the most representative emoji for this relationship. The correlation of emoji and share number essentially varied based on the article content and sentiment feedback of the public on the article. If a link existed between 'Like' and 'Love' and the number of shares, the public liked the article and their sharing behaviour indicated approval. On the contrary, if 'Sad' and 'Angry' had an intense direct correlation with the number of shares, the public hated the article and their sharing behaviour demonstrated strong disapproval. Hence, the sentiment tendency of an article could be determined via the relation between emoji and the share number of the article. Moreover, considering that shares are one of the characteristics and factors of social network influence, it was found that sentiment factors are directly correlated with the influence of social media.

## Discussion

Emojis can be used to express emotions and fill the gap in textual expressions of sentiment (Kaye et al., 2016; Marengo et al., 2017). Since the popularization of social software, emojis have developed into one of the major media for sentiment expression. Facebook has incorporated emoji into its post comment system to meet user needs because 90% of users used emoticons and 15 emoticons represented 99.6% of all emoticons posted (Oleszkiewicz et al., 2017). Based on emoji's characteristic of intensive sentiment, this study explored the relationship of emoji and social network influence by analysing sentiment feedback. A model of sentiment-based article popularity was established to quantify the six emojis and text on Facebook using SentiStrength and LIWC software (Fig. 9.4). In the model, emojis were quantified as weights supplemented by textual sentiment to reduce the error of sentiment factors. Through introducing the concept of sentiment factors into high-quality articles, an article popularity model and a joint-topic article popularity model was developed. Using the models, Hillary Clinton's and Donald Trump's Facebook articles were explored.

In terms of article popularity, to emphasize the impact of sentiment on this factor, we used an equation describing how influence on a social network is constructed based on high-quality articles; the equation was proposed by Chen et al. (2012), i.e. article quality popularity (Q). Article quality popularity (Q) was compared to individual article popularity (*Individual*) and joint-topic article popularity (*Joint topic*). Article quality popularity (Q) simply involves the number of shares, total number of comment words and number of articles, whereas the article popularity model also considers emoji and textual sentiment besides article quality popularity (Q). Through article quality popularity (Q), we could only obtain the discussion intensity of an article, not the sentiment tendency (positive or negative) of people who participated in the discussion. Via individual article popularity (*Individual*), article quality popularity (Q) could be magnified or reduced under the action of sentiment factors, showing the sentiment tendency of an article. For example, for Clinton's articles, the highest article quality popularity (Q) was 55%, which was achieved by an article trying to clarify the candidate's email scandal. From the perspective of article quality popularity (Q), this high value showed a fairly high popularity of discussion and influence. However, when the emoji positive–negative sentiment ratio (*Emoji*) and textual positive–negative sentiment ratio (*Comment*) were considered, an individual article popularity (*Individual*) of only 18% was acquired, demonstrating that the public did not accept Clinton's clarification on the email controversy. Average values of article quality popularity (Q) and individual article popularity (*Individual*) for Clinton's and Trump's articles were compared as well as their average values of article quality popularity (Q) and joint-topic article popularity (*Joint topic*).

From the perspective of emoji and textual influence, the emoji 'Sad' and the number of shares for Clinton's articles discussing topics associated with her opponent exhibited an intense direct correlation. It was found from the individual article popularity (*Individual*) of her articles discussing opponent-associated topics that the public showed feedback with negative sentiments to her articles discussing Trump's women- and war-related topics and made a large number of shares, which is in agreement with

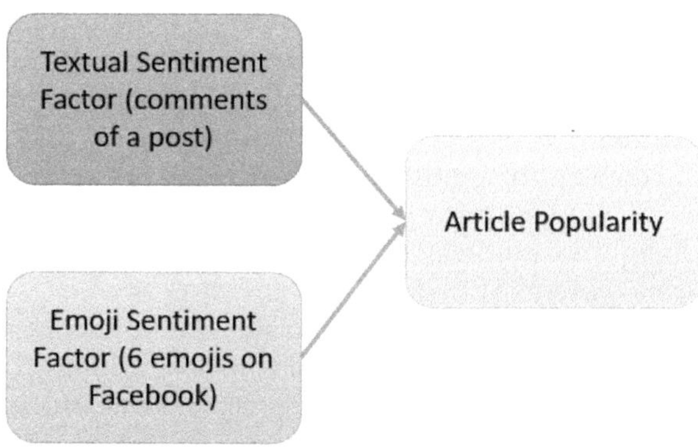


FIGURE 9.4 A conceptual model.

the relation between emoji and share number proposed in this study. The emoji 'HaHa' and share number of Trump's articles discussing opponent-associated topics showed an intense direct correlation. It was discovered by considering the individual article popularity (*Individual*) of these articles that the feedback consisted of positive sentiments, where the emoji 'HaHa' and the number of shares demonstrated a strong direct correlation. This is potentially because of Trump's use of America humour and satire, as expressed in his articles discussing Clinton. Public opinion on the articles was obtained from the direct correlation of emoji and share number.

Moreover, since shares are one of the characteristics and factors of social network influence, it was found that sentiment factors were directly correlated with influence on a social network. Therefore, compared with the existing single index of article quality popularity (Q), the individual article popularity (*Individual*) and joint-topic article popularity (*Joint topic*) concepts developed in this study more accurately reflect public sentiment, based on which the influence power of articles could be enhanced. The results demonstrated the sentiment significance of emoji and text, which are in accordance with the results of Mahajan and Mulay (2015). By matching to the Peirce's semiotic model to our findings, this research proposes two propositions as follows:

**Proposition 1:** Sentiment factors were directly correlated with influence on a social network.
**Proposition 2:** Emoji sentiment factor has more influence than textual sentiment factor on article popularity.

## Implications for practice

Social media has become inseparable from our daily lives, used as much for leisure activities as for commercial and political purposes. From bloggers to Internet celebrities, social influencers leverage social revenue streams via placement marketing, click-through rates and exposure rates. For politicians, higher social influence may lead to election success. In this study, we explored article popularity. The proposed article popularity model uses the sentiment properties of emoji as well as textual sentiment. The model helps better understand social influence obtained from articles on a range of topics, both single and joint. Social influencers with strong influence could be effectively identified and selected as appropriate cooperative actors so as to magnify the publicity effect, exposure rate and advertising effectiveness. We designed an equation by adopting the six emojis used on Facebook as a form of public sentiment feedback and taking the influential factors of social network—*viz.*, number of followers, shares and comments (Naveed et al., 2011)—as the basis, transforming the articles into indicators of market trends based on public feedback and providing companies with more commercial opportunities.

## Limitations

Data for this study were obtained from articles in multiple categories posted on Hillary Clinton's and Donald Trump's Facebook pages, and each article had an average comment number in the tens of thousands. By using comments with a threshold of 'Likes' a portion of articles fell outside of the scope of this study. Comments on Facebook are ranked based on their popularity or correlation with the topic of the article instead of the number of 'Likes'. In addition, the diversified articles by Clinton and Trump were categorized into five groups, *viz.*, articles on personal topics, articles discussing topics associated with the opponent, articles on topics related to the election and articles on other topics. The process of determining the article category was other studies using different thematic categorization approaches may yield a different outcome. Hence, in future work, we would welcome further empirical testing of the proposed model with appropriate measures, such as comparing differences via certain thresholds of 'Likes', comments and shares, so as to establish article categories in different fields.

## References


Ali, A., & Chan, E. C. (2016). *The key to coaching. Learning, application and practice.* Lulu. com.

Alshenqeeti, H. (2016). Are emojis creating a new or old visual language for new generations? A socio-semiotic study. *Advances in Language and Literary Studies, 7*(6), 56–69.

Aoki, S., & Uchida, O. (2011, March). A method for automatically generating the emotional vectors of emoticons using weblog articles. In *Proceedings of the 10th WSEAS international conference on applied computer and applied computational science* (pp. 132–136). World Scientific and Engineering Academy and Society (WSEAS).

Bahri, S., Bahri, P., & Lal, S. (2018). A novel approach of sentiment classification using emoticons. *Procedia Computer Science, 132*, 669–678.

Benson, V., & Filippaios, F. (2015). Collaborative competencies in professional social networking: Are students short changed by curriculum in business education? *Computers in Human Behavior* 51 (part B), 1331–1339. https://doi.org/10.1016/j.chb.2014.11.031.

Chan, S. W., & Chong, M. W. (2017). Sentiment analysis in financial texts. *Decision Support Systems, 94*, 53–64.

Chen, W., Cheng, S., He, X., & Jiang, F. (November 2012). Influencerank: An efficient social influence measurement for millions of users in microblog. In *Cloud and green computing (CGC), 2012 second international conference on* (pp. 563–570). IEEE.

Chen, X., & Siu, K. W. M. (2017). Exploring user behaviour of emoticon use among Chinese youth. *Behaviour and Information Technology, 36*(6), 637–649.

Cui, A., Zhang, M., Liu, Y., & Ma, S. (December 2011). Emotion tokens: Bridging the gap among multilingual twitter sentiment analysis. In *Asia information retrieval symposium* (pp. 238–249). Berlin, Heidelberg: Springer.

Dresner, E., & Herring, S. C. (2010). Functions of the nonverbal in CMC: Emoticons and illocutionary force. *Communication Theory, 20*(3), 249–268.

Duan, J., Xia, X., & Van Swol, L. M. (2018). Emoticons' influence on advice taking. *Computers in Human Behavior, 79*, 53–58.

Garrison, A., Remley, D., Thomas, P., & Wierszewski, E. (2011). Conventional faces: Emoticons in instant messaging discourse. *Computers and Composition, 28*(2), 112–125.

Kavanagh, B. (2016). Emoticons as a medium for channeling politeness within American and Japanese online blogging communities. *Language and Communication, 48*, 53–65.

Kaye, L. K., Wall, H. J., & Malone, S. A. (2016). "Turn that frown upside-down": A contextual account of emoticon usage on different virtual platforms. *Computers in Human Behavior, 60*, 463–467.

Khatua, A., Khatua, A., Ghosh, K., & Chaki, N. (January 2015). Can# twitter_trends predict election results? Evidence from 2014 indian general election. In *System sciences (HICSS), 2015 48th Hawaii international conference on* (pp. 1676–1685). IEEE.

Komrsková, Z. (2015). The use of emoticons in polite phrases of greetings and thanks. *International Journal of Social, Behavioral, Educational, Economic, Business and Industrial Engineering, 9*(4), 1309–1312.

Lahuerta-Otero, E., & Cordero-Gutiérrez, R. (2016). Looking for the perfect tweet. The use of data mining techniques to find influencers on Twitter. *Computers in Human Behavior, 64*, 575–583.

Mahajan, C., & Mulay, P. (2015). E3: Effective emoticon extractor for behavior analysis from social media. *Procedia Computer Science, 50*, 610–616.

Manganari, E. E., & Dimara, E. (2017). Enhancing the impact of online hotel reviews through the use of emoticons. *Behaviour and Information Technology, 36*(7), 674–686.

Marengo, D., Giannotta, F., & Settanni, M. (2017). Assessing personality using emoji: An exploratory study. *Personality and Individual Differences, 112*, 74–78.

Miller, H., Thebault-Spieker, J., Chang, S., Johnson, I., Terveen, L., & Hecht, B. (2016). Blissfully happy" or "ready to fight": Varying interpretations of emoji. In *Proceedings of ICWSM, 2016*.

Mittal, S., Goel, A., & Jain, R. (March 2016). Sentiment analysis of E-commerce and social networking sites. In *Computing for sustainable global development (INDIACom), 2016 3rd international conference on* (pp. 2300–2305). IEEE.

Moschini, I. (2016). The" face with tears of joy" emoji. A socio-semiotic and multimodal insight into a Japan-America mash-up. *HERMES-Journal of Language and Communication in Business*, (55), 11–25.

Naveed, N., Gottron, T., Kunegis, J., & Alhadi, A. C. (June 2011). Bad news travel fast: A content-based analysis of interestingness on twitter. In *Proceedings of the 3rd international web science conference* (p. 8). ACM.

Niu, T., Zhu, S., Pang, L., & El Saddik, A. (January 2016). Sentiment analysis on multi-view social data. In *International conference on multimedia modeling* (pp. 15–27). Cham: Springer.

Oleszkiewicz, A., Karwowski, M., Pisanski, K., Sorokowski, P., Sobrado, B., & Sorokowska, A. (2017). Who uses emoticons? Data from 86 702 facebook users. *Personality and Individual Differences, 119*, 289–295.

Peirce, C. P. (1965). *Basic concepts of peirce: An sign theory.* London: Sage Publications.

Ravi, K., & Ravi, V. (2015). A survey on opinion mining and sentiment analysis: Tasks, approaches and applications. *Knowledge-Based Systems, 89*, 14–46.

Rodrigues, D., Lopes, D., Prada, M., Thompson, D., & Garrido, M. V. (2017). A frown emoji can be worth a thousand words: Perceptions of emoji use in text messages exchanged between romantic partners. *Telematics and Informatics, 34*(8), 1532–1543.

Romero, D. M., Galuba, W., Asur, S., & Huberman, B. A. (September 2011). Influence and passivity in social media. In *Joint European conference on machine learning and knowledge discovery in databases* (pp. 18–33). Berlin, Heidelberg: Springer.

Rosen, J. (2016). *Social media growth statistics*. Business2Community. http://www.business2community.com/social-media/social-media-growth-statistics-01545217#qXFAbHMgZeAMJHKH.97.

Roy, S. D., & Zeng, W. (July 2014). Influence of social media on performance of movies. In *Multimedia and expo workshops (ICMEW), 2014 IEEE international conference on* (pp. 1–6). IEEE.

Schouteten, J. J., Verwaeren, J., Lagast, S., Gellynck, X., & De Steur, H. (2018). Emoji as a tool for measuring children's emotions when tasting food. *Food Quality and Preference, 68*, 322–331.

Settanni, M., & Marengo, D. (2015). Sharing feelings online: Studying emotional well-being via automated text analysis of facebook posts. *Frontiers in Psychology, 6*, 1045.

Skiba, D. J. (2016). Face with tears of joy is word of the year: Are emoji a sign of things to come in health care? *Nursing Education Perspectives, 37*(1), 56–57.

Smailović, J., Kranjc, J., Grčar, M., Žnidaršič, M., & Mozetič, I. (October 2015). Monitoring the twitter sentiment during the Bulgarian elections. In *Data science and advanced analytics (DSAA), 2015. 36678 2015. IEEE international conference on* (pp. 1–10). IEEE.

Soranaka, K., & Matsushita, M. (November 2012). Relationship between emotional words and emoticons in tweets. In *Technologies and applications of artificial intelligence (TAAI), 2012 conference on* (pp. 262–265). IEEE.

Stieglitz, S., & Dang-Xuan, L. (January 2012). Political communication and influence through microblogging – An empirical analysis of sentiment in twitter messages and retweet behavior. In *System science (HICSS), 2012 45th Hawaii international conference on* (pp. 3500–3509). IEEE.

Tauch, C., & Kanjo, E. (September 2016). The roles of emojis in mobile phone notifications. In *Proceedings of the 2016 ACM international joint conference on pervasive and ubiquitous computing: Adjunct* (pp. 1560–1565). ACM.

Thompson, D., & Filik, R. (2016). Sarcasm in written communication: Emoticons are efficient markers of intention. *Journal of Computer-Mediated Communication, 21*(2), 105–120.

Wang, H., & Castanon, J. A. (2015). Sentiment expression via emoticons on social media. In *Big data (big data), 2015 IEEE international conference on* (pp. 2404–2408). IEEE.

Wang, H., Lei, K., & Xu, K. (June 2015). Profiling the followers of the most influential and verified users on sina weibo. In *Communications (ICC), 2015 IEEE international conference on* (pp. 1158–1163). IEEE.

Wu, F., Huang, Y., Song, Y., & Liu, S. (2016). Towards building a high-quality microblog-specific Chinese sentiment lexicon. *Decision Support Systems, 87*, 39–49.

Yeole, A. V., Chavan, P. V., & Nikose, M. C. (March 2015). Opinion mining for emotions determination. In *Innovations in information, embedded and communication systems (ICIIECS), 2015 international conference on* (pp. 1–5). IEEE.

CHAPTER

# 10

# Risk and social influence in sustainable smart home technologies: a persuasive systems design model

*Nataliya Shevchuk*[1], *Harri Oinas-Kukkonen*[2], *Vladlena Benson*[3]

[1] Oulu Advanced Research on Service and Information Systems (OASIS), Faculty of Information Technology and Electrical Engineering, University of Oulu, Oulu, Finland; [2] Oulu Advanced Research on Service and Information Systems (OASIS), Faculty of Information Technology and Electrical Engineering, University of Oulu, Oulu, Finland; [3] Professor of Information Systems, Aston Business School, Aston University, Birmingham, United Kingdom

OUTLINE



*Cyber Influence and Cognitive Threats*
https://doi.org/10.1016/B978-0-12-819204-7.00010-5

## Introduction

Environmental sustainability has become a central theme in development and social change activities. Sustainable interventions in economic, environmental, social, and cultural spheres of life are necessary to ensure a world worth living in for future generations. Discussion on the emergent need to take care of the environment has been brought up in various research disciplines, including information systems (IS) that have often been praised for their intrinsic capacities to promote social integration and social change. Finite resources, increasing electricity consumption, rising environmental consciousness, rapid technological advancements, engineering a sustainable energy supply and electricity grid have attracted the attention of public policy, firms, and media. Several initiatives aimed to enhance energy efficiency, secure supply and mitigate climate change were introduced (Wunderlich, Veit, & Sarker, 2012, pp. 1–17). However, these initiatives need to be supplemented with the IS solutions to ensure that people's daily behaviour incorporates sustainable practises. Thus, a facilitating persuasive framework for encouraging sustainable behaviours is necessary.

The use of IS to influence people's behaviour in IS research predominantly takes place in the domains of residential energy consumption and the mobility sector (Brauer, Eisel, & Kolbe, 2015) and still requires more attention. In the energy domain, the IS are used to monitor household energy consumption and provide feedback to the user (Graml, Loock, Baeriswyl, & Staake, 2011; Loock, Staake, & Thiesse, 2013; Oppong-Tawiah et al., 2014; Weiss, Staake, Mattern, & Fleisch, 2012). Smart metering technology (SMT) combined with presentation layers for user interaction have become a frequently addressed area in Green IS research (Brauer et al., 2016). Because the research has not yet addressed encouraging environmentally conscious behaviour with the use of smart thermostats at homes, we are looking into this topic. We consider persuasive systems design (Oinas-Kukkonen & Harjumaa, 2009) as a strategic approach to convincing people to change behaviour with the help of technologies. While the impact of persuasive systems design has been studied in health, well-being, and social platforms contexts, research in the context of smart homes and smart metres is scarce. For example, with the recent surge in mobile app adoption, numerous health apps (e.g., Fitbit or Waterlogged) have been successful in encouraging people to stay healthy and fit by exercising or taking water regularly (Morreale et al., 2015). Thus, mobile applications have the potential to be also effective in promoting sustainable behaviour. Based on the findings from the health domain, people favour apps that provide convenient tools, such as feedback, to help them monitor, track, and review attempts to change or improve health behaviours. However, after a certain period, the users ignore or discontinue using the applications. Until the postadoption usage of the IT can be confirmed, it is premature to classify an IT adoption as a success because the ultimate viability of an IT is dependent on individuals' continued usage of the IT (Bhattacherjee, 2001; Karahanna, Straub, & Chervany, 1999). If the enthusiasm over the initial adoption of an IT diminishes after individuals gain experience from using it, then the IT will suffer from decreased usage and may even subsequently fall into disuse (Thong, Hong, & Tam, 2006). Therefore, it is crucial not only to convince people to adopt a certain application but also to ensure that the usage of it is continuous. Thus, the first research question of the our study is

*RQ1: How does persuasive systems design influence intention to continue using a smart metering system?*

Furthermore, interconnectedness of devices brings convenience and benefits. However, with the positive aspects of it, numerous disadvantages including privacy and trust are often mentioned in IS literature. Nevertheless, the closely related concepts of self-disclosure and perceived risk are much less often discussed. With the increased human–computer interaction, we believe it is important to understand how the need of self-disclosure and the perceived risk impact people's relationship with technologies, specifically persuasive mobile applications. Thus, the second research question of this chapter is

*RQ2: How do risk and self-disclosure alter impact of the persuasive design of a smart metering system?*

To answer the research questions, we will examine persuasive factors affecting continued use of a smart home heating system. Among examples of the smart thermostat tools on the UK market (Hive Multizone, Nest, Tado, Netatmo, Devolo, Heat Genius and Honeywell EvoHome), we will use Hive smart heating thermostat (SHT) controlled by mobile app referred to as Hive or SHT app henceforth.

The rest of the chapter is structured as follows. First, theoretical background of the relevant concepts is provided. Next, the research model and the hypotheses are introduced. After that, the research methodology is presented followed by discussion of the findings. Finally, conclusions are drawn and the summary is presented.

# Theoretical background

## Proenvironmental behaviour research in IS

Because environmental sustainability is 'the issue of the day' (Pitt, Parent, Junglas, Chan, & Spyropoulou, 2011) and 'one of the most important global challenges of the 21st century' (Melville, 2010, p. 14), the IS discipline has both a responsibility and an opportunity to contribute to solving this challenge (Watson, Boudreau, & Chen, 2010). Because individuals are able to contribute to solving the problems of their societies (El Idrissi & Corbett, 2016), an important role of individuals' participation in addressing sustainability issues appeared in Green IS research. To achieve improvements in environmental sustainability, changes in human behaviour are believed to be needed because technical efficiency gains resulting from, for example, energy-efficient appliances, home insulation, and water-saving devices tend to be overtaken by consumption growth (Midden et al., 2007). Moreover, physical and technical innovations imply behaviour changes as well because individuals need to accept and understand them, buy them and use them in proper ways (Steg and Vlek 2009). Therefore, Green IS research initiated consideration of user-centric solutions for sustainable improvements and development that encourage individuals to choose more sustainable behaviours in their day-to-day routines (Ijab, Molla, Kassahun, & Teoh, 2010). In addition to the developing theme of the SMT (Brauer, Ebermann, & Kolbe, 2016), a range of artifacts was designed to monitor and influence people's daily behaviour related to household energy consumption (Graml et al., 2011; Loock et al., 2013, Loock, Staake and Landwehr, 2011; Oppong-Tawiah et al. 2014; Weiss et al., 2012), driving (Tulusan, Staake, & Fleisch, 2012), and resource consumption (Khansari et al. 2013). Nevertheless, the overall amount of research is still low despite its vast potential (Brauer et al., 2015; Malhotra, Melville, & Watson, 2013) because only a few studies investigate how environmental behaviour and decisions of individual systems users can be improved with Green IS (Degirmenci & Recker, 2016). Pitt et al. (2011) noted that research of smartphone applications related to the pursuit of green and sustainable agendas is needed because it provides implications not only for academics in marketing or social sciences but also for IS strategy scholars.

## Smart metering

Smart metres have the potential to not only increase the energy efficiency of the residential and industrial sector but also to radically alter the way energy is produced and consumed (Potter, Archambault, & Westrick, 2009). Smart metre systems comprise an electronic box, just like a regular digital electricity metre, and a communications link. Not only does a smart metre electronically measure the consumption, and possibly other parameters in a certain interval of time, but it also transmits measurements over a communication network to the utility or other actor responsible for metering. This information can be shared with end-use devices informing the customers about energy consumption and related costs. Many smart metre systems comprise enhanced user interfaces like home displays, Internet platforms, Internet widgets and smartphone apps that detach the smart metre user interface from the smart metre and its physical location and often provide supplementary information and dedicated functions for consumption analysis (Uribe-Pérez, Hernández, de la Vega, & Angulo, 2016). Smart thermostat is a type of an enhanced smart metre that replaces a regular home thermostat and lets the users control heating remotely from their smartphones, tablets or computers. As a result, it largely impacts people's habits, home lives, and consumption behaviour.

Nachreihner et al. (2015) posed a claim that the existing smart metres on the market do not satisfactorily exhaust the possibilities inherent in these systems to optimally support customers or to tap into the reduction potential in household electricity consumption. Currently, feedback is the only most commonly used way to control electricity consumption that can be a powerful intervention capable of motivating consumption reduction (Abrahamse, Steg, Vlek, & Rothengatter, 2005; Allcott, 2011; Fischer, 2008; Vine, Buys, & Morris, 2013). However, merely providing the users with the energy usage data is not enough to change the users' behaviour based on a simple cause—effect relationship (Hargreaves et al., 2010). To have a stronger impact on interventions effectiveness, feedback should be combined with other motivational intervention techniques like goal setting/ commitment and action-relevant information. Previous studies suggest that the combination of measures proves to be more effective than using each measure on its own (Hargreaves et al., 2010). With reference to computerized interfaces (in-home displays, web portals, apps), both Erhardt-Martinez et al. (2010) and Fischer (2008) emphasize that the most effective designs incorporate multiple feedback and analysis options, including historical comparisons, as well as motivational techniques and information related to electricity saving. Nechreicher et al. (2015) proposed incorporating the following features: presenting action and problem-related information, showing the relevance of consumption figures, offering socially comparative feedback or social norms, encouraging the setting of goals, initiating competitions, collecting points and giving incentives, providing general and tailored action-related information, providing reminders after commitment to a particular behaviour intention and information supporting an implementation plan. To extend this list and to provide a more thorough theoretical background for these examples, we suggest referring to Persuasive Systems Design model (PSD). We propose that implementing its features is likely to equip smart metres with the full range of behaviour-changing characteristics.

Furthermore, Hargreaves et al. (2010) suggest that having users reduce electricity usage and sustain the low consumption levels is complicated and requires accounting for various aspects. This leads to significant challenges related to the adoption by consumers. Additionally, Fox-Penner (2010) noted that energy suppliers seldom engage in programs informing their customers about the specifics of smart metres. Wundelich et al. (2012, pp. 1–17) noted that despite several challenges associated with the smart metre usage and adoption, this topic has found little attention amongst academic researchers. Wunderlich et al. (2012, pp. 1–17) contributed to research by studying the determinants of consumers' intention to continue using SMT and encouraged to provide further insights into factors of continuing intention to use smart metres. Perceived privacy risk was assumed to directly impact consumers' SMT continuance intention (Wunderlich et al., 2012, pp. 1–17); however, findings have shown no direct influence. Possibly, this is due to a trade-off consumers make between privacy concerns and benefits (Malhotra, Kim, & Agarwal, 2004) or due to the users' certainty about effectiveness of privacy protection. The 'privacy paradox' can also arise from the users' perceptions regarding the sensitivity of information disclosed (Mothersbaugh et al., 2012). In any case, self-disclosure is a mandatory component related to the use of smart metres which so far has not received required attention in literature, and thus its impact on continuance intention needs to be investigated. Moreover, because user perceptions may alter over time due to changing societal values or contemporary incidents (Wunderlich et al., 2012, pp. 1–17), we suggest further research of the relationship of perceived risk and the use of smart metres.

## Persuasive systems design

The omnipresent social web and extensive use of mobile applications made creating, accessing, and sharing information easier than ever before because the users of interactive IS can be reached in a matter of seconds.

Therefore, influencing users with various IS, such as the web, the Internet, mobile, and other ambient systems, creates opportunities for persuasive interaction. Combining attributes of interpersonal and mass communication, web and mobile systems are ideal for persuasion (Cassell, Jackson, & Cheuvront, 1998; Oinas-Kukkonen & Harjumaa, 2009). Such interactive IS designed for changing users' attitudes or behaviour are known as persuasive systems (Fogg, 2003). Behaviour Change Support Systems (BCSSs) are, in essence, persuasive systems and can be defined as 'sociotechnical information system(s) with psychological and behavioural outcomes designed to form, alter or reinforce attitudes, behaviours or an act of complying without using coercion or deception' (Oinas-Kukkonen, 2013, p 1225). PSD model is as a tool developed for designing and evaluating BCSSs (Oinas-Kukkonen, 2013). PSD process consists of three steps (Oinas-Kukkonen & Harjumaa, 2009).

The first step of the PSD process involves addressing seven postulates related to the users' perspectives, persuasion in general, and features of IS (Oinas-Kukkonen & Harjumaa, 2009). First, information technologies are never neutral but rather always influences the users; thus, persuasion should be considered as a process rather than a single act. Second, based on the concept of commitment and cognitive consistency (Cialdini, Petty, & Cacioppo, 1981), people like their views about the world to be organized and consistent. Third, persuasion is often incremental, meaning that it is easier to persuade people not with a single one-time suggestion but rather with several suggestions over a period of time. Fourth, the direct and indirect routes are the key persuasion strategies, which require users to either carefully evaluate the content of a persuasive message or to use cues or cognitive shorthands. Fifth, to ensure a voluntary change of attitude or behaviour, persuasive systems should be transparent, i.e., reveal the designer's bias. Sixth, persuasive systems should be unobtrusive, avoiding interference with the performance of the primary task by users. Seventh, persuasive systems should be both useful and easy to use, which is a general software requirement.

Next is the analysis of the persuasion context. This step includes recognizing the intent of the persuasion, understanding the persuasion event, and defining the strategies. After determining who the persuader is and whether persuasion will aim at attitude and/or behaviour change, the problem domain, user and technology-dependent features are considered. Then, the message and the route for its delivery are defined.

The final step of the PSD process is designing specifications of a system based on a wide range of software features classified in four categories: primary task support, computer–human dialogue support, perceived system credibility support, and social support. Design principles of the primary task category, such as reduction, tailoring, tunnelling, personalization, self-monitoring, simulation, and rehearsal, focus on providing support for achieving primary goals of the user. Design principles related to computer–human dialogue, e.g., rewards, praise, suggestions, reminders, similarity, liking, and social role, facilitate accomplishing established goals. Credibility support design principles, namely, trustworthiness, expertise, surface credibility, real-world feel, authority, third-party endorsements, and verifiability, aim to increase persuasiveness of the system by making it more credible. Design principles in the social support category introduce system features that motivate users by leveraging social behaviours, such as recognition, competition, cooperation, normative influence, social learning, social comparison, and social facilitation. It is assumed that persuasive system features enhance participation and engagement with the interventions (Kelders, Kok, Ossebaard, & Van Gemert-Pijnen, 2012). However, all possible software features do not have to be present in a BCSS because additional persuasive features may lead to decreased overall persuasiveness (Oinas-Kukkonen, 2013).

Up-to-date, fostering improved health and healthier lifestyles have been the dominant areas of application of persuasive systems. Positive results of persuasive systems were observed in management of smoking cessation, hazardous drinking, obesity, diabetes, asthma, tinnitus, stress, anxiety and depression, complicated grief, insomnia, and exercise behaviours (Oinas-Kukkonen, 2013). Persuasive systems design has already been used to evaluate and create systems supporting sustainable behaviour. (e.g., Brauer et al., 2016; Corbett, 2013; Shevchuk & Oinas-Kukkonen, 2016); however, this area of research remains less investigated compared with the others and requires more attention.

## Self-disclosure

Self-disclosure involves 'the act of revealing personal information about oneself to another' (Collins & Miller, 1994, p. 457), i.e., by an individual to another individual, an organization or a group. Personal information handling and self-disclosure online, including mobile apps, are areas of major concern and are interconnected. Self-disclosure is voluntary and purposeful and refers to what individuals voluntarily and intentionally reveal about themselves to others (Pearce & Sharp, 1973). Factors, such as the target audience, how well they are known to the person disclosing information, etc., could influence the quantity and quality of information disclosed (Jourard & Richman, 1963). It is generally agreed that there are two types of self-disclosure: factual disclosure that reveals personal facts and data, and emotional disclosure that reveals private feelings, opinions, and judgements (Laurenceau, Barrett, & Pietrornonaco, 2004, pp. 241–257). The first type is discussed here as this is the type relevant to the substance of the study.

The phenomenon of self-disclosure has been widely studied in social psychology, sociology, interpersonal communication as well as in marketing, social media, and e-commerce research (Kim, 2015). Sharma and Crossler (2014) found out that self-disclose in social commerce is affected by the fairness of information exchange, privacy benefits, and privacy apathy. Fairness of information exchange is important in an online setting particularly when customers lose control over the information once it has been disclosed. Online vendors can misuse such information disclosed by customers for nontransactional purposes including targeted advertising or sale to data aggregators (Balough, 2011). Although the essence of the self-disclosure concept for the smart metre users is slightly different, the users are likely to have an experience with sharing information similar to the abovementioned scenarios related to online shopping or social networks. Even if smart metre users are recognized as the owners of their data, this does not ensure full control over personal data. Assuming that the users are empowered to authorize or refuse disclosure to third parties, the data remain subject to security breaches, inadvertent disclosure by the utility, and unknowingly authorized releases by the consumer to third parties – all of which would result in personal data reaching possibly unsecured areas on the Internet, where it may remain residing permanently (Balough, 2011).

## Perceived risk

Originally, the concept of perceived risk was introduced by Bauer (1960) who defined it in terms of the uncertainty and consequences associated with consumer's actions. It is crucial in decision-making and can also be understood as 'a combination of uncertainty plus seriousness of outcome involved' (Bauer, 1960). Logically, perceived risk increases with the magnitude of consumers' perceptions of the uncertainty, probability of loss, and adverse consequences associated with buying a product (or service) (Cunningham, 1967). Perceived risk is often treated as a multidimensional construct, which encompasses several types of risk, including financial, physical, functional, social, and time-loss risk (Jacoby & Kaplan, 1972; Kaplan, Szybillo, & Jacoby, 1974; Roselius, 1971). Overall, the two major components perceived risk are the probability of a loss and the subjective feeling of unfavourable consequences (Ross, 1975).

From a perspective of IS, the notion of perceived privacy risk requires attention. It is the perception of the possible exposure or potential violation of a user's private information (Featherman & Pavlou, 2003) which includes service providers intentionally collecting, disclosing, transmitting or selling personal data without a consumer's knowledge or permission, or hackers intercepting such information (Yang, Liu, Li, & Yu,

2015). Privacy risk beliefs are 'the expectation that a high potential for loss is associated with the release of personal information' to others in their online communities (Malhotra et al., 2004, p. 341).

Furthermore, perceived risk is relevant in IS usage decisions when users experience feelings of doubt, discomfort, anxiety (Dowling & Staelin, 1994) or conflict (Bettman, 1973), which often occurs when personal information is transferred via vulnerable communication infrastructures, e.g., the Internet. In relation to the Internet use, these concerns are found to be significant barriers (Hoffman, Novak, & Peralta, 1999) because online transactions involve more perceived risk than traditional, face-to-face ones. Making decisions to use online applications under security threats, individuals are becoming increasingly accustomed to considering the risks associated with transacting online. Because the data gathered by smart metres involves data transmission over the Internet and allows service providers to identify users' lifestyle, perceived risk is indeed a relevant concern. In this context, perceived risk constitutes the presence of a degree of uncertainty related to the use of the smart metres and presents a possibility of suffering a loss while using the systems.

## Adaptation level theory

Helson's (1964) adaptation level theory suggests that individuals perceive new stimuli or experiences as deviations from the existing cognitions. New cognitions are viewed as a shift from their prior baseline or reference levels (adaptation levels). Hence, new cognitions tend to remain in the general vicinity of prior cognitions (homeostasis), adjusted appropriately for any new positive or negative stimuli. Considering this, later-stage cognitions can be viewed as an additive function of prior cognitions plus the deviation or discrepancy from those levels due to actual experience (Bhattacherjee & Premkumar, 2004).

This theory is relevant in this study in two ways. First, it relates to the incrementality postulate included in the PSD model, and thus, it provides a clarification that the level of incrementality depends on how different the user's existing cognition(s) from the new ones triggered by the process of persuasion. Second, the theory explains that the smart metre users' beliefs related to risk perception and self-disclosure may be to some extent predetermined by existing cognitions and depend on a combination of factors, ranging from internal (e.g., personal convictions, abilities, etc.) to external stimuli that affect personal cognitions. Therefore, this provides a proof of the need to focus on perceived risk and self-disclosure – the aspects associated with the use of majority IS and IT systems connected to the web.

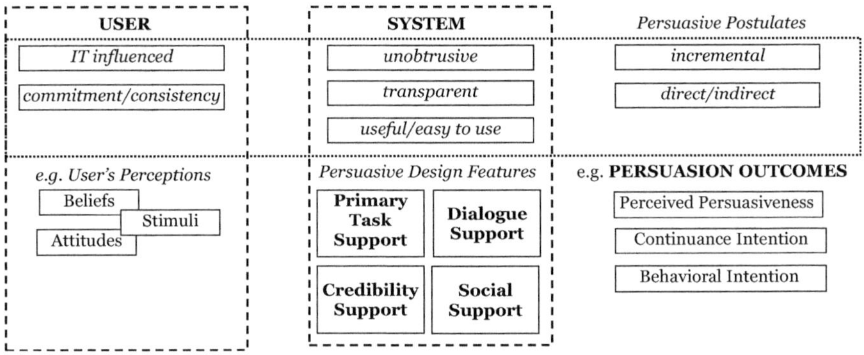


FIGURE 10.1 Persuasion process framework.

## Theoretical framework

The framework is based on understanding the key parts of the persuasion process, which involves the user, the system, and, if persuasion is successful, the desired outcomes. In our case, the desired outcomes are perceived persuasiveness, continuance intention, and, consequentially, sustainable behaviour. According to the PSD model (Oinas-Kukkonen & Harjumaa, 2009), seven persuasive postulates hold true for the process of persuasion, the user, and the system. According to the Adaptation Level Theory (Helson, 1964), the user's persuasion process depends on presystem usage beliefs and attitudes which determine the 'reference level', a certain behaviour that needs to be changed in the course of persuasion. The presence of adaptation means that persuasion is more effective when incremental and behaviour change should be achieved via either a direct or indirect route – whichever one can provide a better fit for adapting to a different behaviour. The system used for persuasion should be transparent, unobtrusive, useful, and easy to use while incorporating persuasive features (i.e., primary task support, dialog support, credibility support, and social support). The graphical summary of the framework is presented in Fig. 10.1.

## Research model and hypotheses

Based on the theoretical background and the developed framework, presented in the previous chapter, we propose the following research model (Fig. 10.2) and hypotheses.

Dialogue support assists with keeping the user active and motivated to use the system, helping the users to perform a target behaviour. Ideally, dialogue support promotes users' positive effect, which will likely

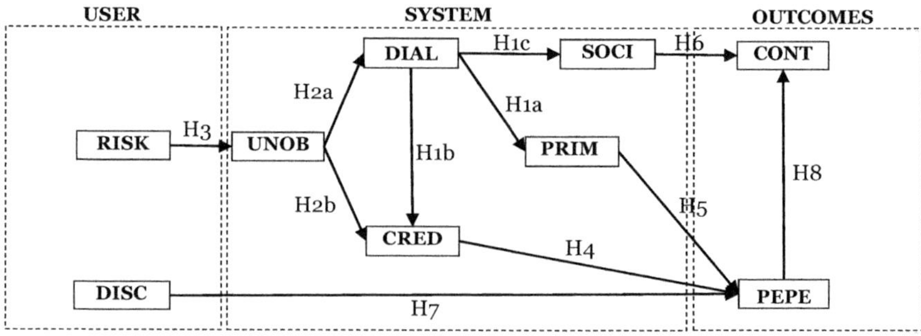


FIGURE 10.2 Research model.

influence the user's confidence in the source (credibility) (Kahn & Isen, 1993; Lehto, Oinas-Kukkonen & Drozd, 2012, pp. 1–15, Lehto, Oinas-Kukkonen, Pätiälä & Saarelma, 2012, p. 154). Moreover, people tend to react to IT artefacts as if they are interacting in social situations (Al-Natour & Benbasat, 2009; Lee, 2009). Additionally, because people's social relationships are increasingly maintained through technology-mediated communications, dialogue support is likely to influence social support.

*H1a: Dialogue support (DIAL) has a positive impact on primary task support (PRIM)*
*H1b: Dialogue support (DIAL) has a positive impact on credibility support (CRED)*
*H1c: Dialogue support (DIAL) has a positive impact on social support (SOCI)*

Unobtrusiveness is one of the key PSD postulates (Oinas-Kukkonen & Harjumaa, 2009), defined as a contextual construct that reflects whether the system fits in the user's environment in which the system is used (Lehto, Drozd et al., 2012, pp. 1–15). Goodhue and Thompson (1995) emphasized the importance of the fit between technology and its users on individual performance. Therefore, we hypothesize that both the dialogue support and credibility support are influenced by unobtrusiveness.

*H2a: Unobtrusiveness (UNOB) has a positive impact on dialogue support (DIAL)*
*H2b: Unobtrusiveness (UNOB) has a positive impact on credibility support (CRED)*

As discussed earlier, the major components that define perceived risk are the probability of a loss and/or the subjective feeling of unfavourable consequences. The presence of perceived risk and the negative perceptions it evokes constitutes a disturbance that prevents the application from fulfilling the user's positive expectations including assistance with carrying out the primary task. The amount of the perceived risk will define how much of the adverse impact the system has on the user's routines. Thus, the following hypothesis states that the more perceived risk is associated with using the system, the more obtrusive the system will be considered by its users.

*H3: Perceived risk (RISK) has a negative impact on unobtrusiveness (UNOB)*

Credibility and trust are important related constructs. According to Everard and Galletta (2006, p 60), the apparent difference between trust and credibility is that 'trust is an attribute of an observer (to have trust), whereas credibility is an attribute of another person or an object of interest (to be credible)'. Moreover, trust is a manifestation of credibility, which could be considered to be trustworthiness (Everard & Galletta, 2006). A highly credible source is usually perceived as more persuasive than a low-credibility one (Pornpitakpan, 2004).

*H4: Credibility support (CRED) has a positive impact on perceived persuasiveness (PEPE)*

Primary task support refers to the means provided by the system to aid the user in performing the primary task (Oinas-Kukkonen & Harjumaa, 2009). Primary task support is related to cognitive fit (Vessey & Galletta, 1991), task-technology fit (Goodhue & Thompson, 1995), and person–artefact–task fit (Finneran & Zhang, 2003). Primary task support enables reflection on one's behaviour, personal goal setting and tracking progress towards the goals (cf. Locke & Latham, 2002). Lehto, Drozd et al. (2012), Lehto, Pätiälä et al. (2012, p. 154) found that primary task support has a positive and direct impact on perceived persuasiveness.

*H5: Primary task support (PRIM) has a positive impact on perceived persuasiveness (PEPE)*

According to Uchino (2006), social support may be connected to social networks (groups, familial ties), specific behaviours (e.g., emotional or informational support) or to the perceived availability of support resources. Shumaker and Brownell (1984, p. 11) defined social support as 'an exchange of resources between two individuals perceived by the provider or the recipient to be intended to enhance the well-being of the recipient'. Social support design principles motivate users by leveraging social influence that is fundamental for proenvironmental mindset and behaviour (Gifford, 2011; Siero, Bakker, Dekker, & Van Den Burg, 1996; Stern, Dietz, & Guagnano, 1995). Social activities and interaction with like-minded people with similar interests or personal goals can promote the users' favourable perception of the Green IS and increase willingness to engage in sustainable behaviour (Ebermann & Brauer, 2016; Lindenberg & Steg, 2013).

*H6: Social support (SOCI) has a positive impact on continuance intention (CONT)*

The increasingly social nature of smartphone applications and other web-based software (e.g., social network sites) places a privacy cost on users due to a heightened requirement for disclosure of personal information as a part of the functionality of the system (Joinson, 2008). Self-disclosure is most of the time a prerequisite to access services, make online purchases (Metzger, 2006) or is requested for the services to be personalized (e.g., in the form of recommendations or 'one-click' purchasing) (Joinson, Reips, Buchanan, & Schofield, 2010). Additionally, the development of ambient and ubiquitous technologies that easily store information in cross-reference databases increase likelihood that devices will communicate, or even broadcast, personal information without the user's approval (Bellotti & Sellen, 1993). Therefore, we hypothesize that the requirement to self-disclose and potential negative consequences associated with it are likely to diminish perceived persuasiveness of the system.

*H7: Self-disclosure (DISC) has a negative impact on perceived persuasiveness (PEPE)*

Perceived persuasiveness in this study is defined as an individual's favourable impressions of the system. According to Crano and Prislin (2011), a central aspect that must be taken into account when reflecting on persuasion involves the fundamental construct of attitude. Previous studies have shown that perceived persuasiveness has a moderate but significant impact on intention to adopt the system (Lehto, Drozd et al., 2012, p. 1–15, Lehto, Pätiälä et al., 2012, p. 154). However, the success or failure of an IS artefact depends on whether consumers resist to use it or are willing to adopt and engage with it (Anda & Temmen, 2014; Kupfer, Ableitner, Schöb, & Tiefenbeck, 2016, pp. 1–10). IS research has developed various models to understand the factors that drive consumers either to resist a technology (e.g., Kim & Kankanhalli, 2009) or to adopt (e.g., Venkatesh, Morris, Davis, & Davis, 2003) and continuously use it (e.g., Bhattacherjee & Lin, 2015). We predict that the users will be prone to continue using the system if it makes a positive impression on them.

*H8: Perceived persuasiveness (PEPE) has a positive impact on continuance intention (CONT)*

# Research methodology

## Instrument development and measurement of constructs

Hive Active Heating 2 is a schedule-based heating system used for illustrating a case of persuasive features in smart thermostats. Hive, produced by British Gas, is the system widely known in the United Kingdom, where data were collected. The smart thermostat provides control of heating and water, lets users set schedules, enables holiday mode, and adjusts the zone temperatures. Although the thermostat can be installed in a house to be used as the sole control system, most people install the Hive app on their smartphones or use the Hive website from a PC or laptop to tweak the heating settings. Hive uses the phone's GPS to monitor the user's location and alert the user turn off and on the heating when leaving and returning home. The user can set up app or text message notifications that alert when the temperature reaches a specified level. The user can set the dates of leaving and coming back for the 'holiday mode', which automatically lowers the temperature in the house for the time the user is away, and increases it back upon arrival. Thus, with the comfort of controlling the climate and energy use, the smart thermostat requires users to experience self-disclosure and perceived risk when using the system. Because the persuasive features are currently not implemented in Hive, we created enhanced graphical interfaces that incorporate into the system all four categories of persuasive features.

To validate and improve the questionnaire, a paper-based pilot survey session was conducted. Participants of the session watched an animated PowerPoint presentation showing implementation of the new features in Hive (enhanced interfaces were displayed) and were asked to fill out the survey afterwards. Based on this session, the survey was improved by restructuring order of the questions to keep participants focused as well as by modifying the introduction description of the study, in which participants were informed that they will see new features added to Hive. In the actual survey, implemented in an online software tool Webropol 2.0 and distributed via email, the users were shown images of the enhanced interface and were asked questions regarding the researched constructs and the demographics. The items were measured using a 7-point Likert scale ranging from 'Strongly disagree' to 'Strongly agree' to determinethe extent to which a participant agrees with the statements. In total, 50 complete answers were obtained, one was omitted from the data analyses due to uniform responses to all items. There were no missing responses because all of the questions were set as mandatory. Descriptive statistics of the sample are provided in Table 10.1.

TABLE 10.1 Descriptive statistics of the sample.

| Demographics | Value | Frequency | Percent (%) |
|---|---|---|---|
| Age | 18–24 | 6 | 12 |
| | 25–34 | 16 | 33 |
| | 35–44 | 7 | 14 |
| | 45–54 | 9 | 18 |
| | 55–64 | 6 | 12 |
| | 65–74 | 4 | 8 |
| | 75 or older | 1 | 2 |
| Gender | Female | 27 | 55 |
| | Male | 22 | 45 |
| Education | Middle school | 1 | 2 |
| | High school | 18 | 37 |
| | Bachelor's degree | 15 | 31 |
| | Master's degree | 11 | 22 |
| | Doctorate/ professional/advanced degree | 4 | 8 |
| Employment | Employed full time | 24 | 49 |
| | Employed part time | 5 | 10 |
| | Self-employed | 2 | 4 |
| | Student | 10 | 20 |
| | Retired | 4 | 8 |
| | Unemployed | 4 | 8 |

# Data analysis and results

SmartPLS is a software with graphical user interface for variance-based structural equation modelling using the partial least squares path modelling method. PLS-SEM is a good fit for this study because it is appropriate when the purpose of the model is to predict, rather than to test established theory (Hair, Ringle, & Sarstedt, 2011). According to Gefen, Rigdon, and Straub (2011), PLS-SEM suits well for exploratory research. Moreover, PLS-SEM is reasonably robust to deviations from a multivariate distribution. The statistical objective of PLS-SEM is similar to that of linear regression: to demonstrate explained variance in the latent variable with the $R^2$ values, to indicate the strength of the relationship between latent variables and to test the significance of the relationship between latent variables by estimating t-values and reporting their corresponding *P*-values (Gefen et al., 2011; Hair et al., 2011). Overall, testing the PLS-SEM model is carried out in two steps: (1) assessment of the reliability and validity of the measurement model and (2) assessment of the structural model. The measurement model includes the relationships between the constructs (Table 10.2). The convergent and discriminant validity of the measurement instrument is examined to verify that the measures of the constructs are valid and reliable before attempting to draw conclusions regarding relationships among constructs (i.e., structural model).

According to Hair et al. (2011), PLS-SEM minimum sample size should be equal to the larger of 10 times the largest number of structural paths directed at a particular latent construct in the structural model. Our sample size meets this requirement. As most of the variables were measured using the same instrument, common method variance (CMV) or common method bias (CMB) poses a potential threat to the validity of the results. To minimize CMV ex ante, the respondents were assured of the anonymity and confidentiality of the study, and they were encouraged to answer as honestly as possible. For the ex post test and possible control for CMV, several measures were taken. A correlation matrix of the constructs was inspected to determine if any of the correlations were above 0.90, which would serve as evidence that CMB may exist (Pavlou, Liang, & Xue, 2007). In our case, none of the constructs correlated so highly. Additionally, full collinearity (VIFs $< 5$) indicates that CMV should not cause a detrimental effect. Items that had VIFs significantly about the given criterion were deleted not to contaminate the corresponding variables they belong to.

## Assessment of measurement model

The indicators of the measurement instrument employed were derived from several sources to operationalize the constructs (Appendix A). Similar and identical items for measuring the researched constructs have already been tested in previous studies (Lehto, Drozd et al., 2012, pp. 1–15, Lehto, Pätiälä et al., 2012, p. 154; Stibe, Oinas-Kukkonen, Bērziņa, & Pahnila, 2011; Stibe and Oinas-Kukkonen 2014a, 2014b, pp. 1–17, pp. 224–235). Boudreau, Gefen, and Straub (2001) emphasize that the use of previously validated instruments is efficient, especially since the fast pace of technological change poses a challenge to allocate time for development of novel instruments. Before the study, the survey items were carefully analyzed to ensure that the items suit the context of the study and demonstrate good face and expert validity.

TABLE 10.2 Latent variables properties.

| | CRA | COR | AVE | CONT | CRED | DIAL | DISC | PEPE | PRIM | RISK | SOCI | UNOB |
|---|---|---|---|---|---|---|---|---|---|---|---|---|
| CONT | 0.929 | 0.965 | 0.933 | **0.966** | | | | | | | | |
| CRED | 0.919 | 0.949 | 0.861 | 0.787 | **0.928** | | | | | | | |
| DIAL | 0.933 | 0.953 | 0.834 | 0.655 | 0.642 | **0.913** | | | | | | |
| DISC | 0.925 | 0.945 | 0.853 | 0.340 | 0.358 | 0.388 | **0.923** | | | | | |
| PEPE | 0.916 | 0.947 | 0.857 | 0.725 | 0.759 | 0.714 | 0.203 | **0.926** | | | | |
| PRIM | 0.890 | 0.948 | 0.901 | 0.759 | 0.753 | 0.840 | 0.388 | 0.829 | **0.949** | | | |
| RISK | 0.797 | 0.878 | 0.705 | −0.245 | −0.331 | −0.228 | −0.017 | −0.342 | −0.228 | **0.840** | | |
| SOCI | 0.921 | 0.950 | 0.863 | 0.683 | 0.697 | 0.594 | 0.165 | 0.712 | 0.693 | −0.179 | **0.929** | |
| UNOB | 0.855 | 0.911 | 0.774 | 0.571 | 0.618 | 0.583 | 0.078 | 0.620 | 0.508 | −0.399 | 0.326 | **0.880** |

*AVE*, Average variance extracted; Bolded cells, Square root of AVE; *COR*, Composite reliability; *CRA*, Cronbach's alpha.

The properties of the scales are assessed in terms of item loadings, discriminant validity and internal consistency. Item loadings and internal consistencies greater than 0.70 are considered acceptable (Fornell & Larcker, 1981) (Appendix A). The constructs in the model display good internal consistency, as evidenced by their composite reliability scores, which range from 0.878 to 0.965. Item cross loadings ranged from 0.812 to 0.969. Inspection of the latent variable correlations and square root of the average variance extracted (AVE) in Table 10.2 demonstrates that all constructs share more variance with their own indicators than with other constructs. In addition, AVE values of all the constructs were well above the suggested minimum of 0.50 (Fornell & Larcker, 1981), thus demonstrating adequate internal consistency.

## Structural model and hypotheses testing

For nomological validity, the research model was tested by applying parametric bootstrapping with 5000 subsamples (parallel processing, no sign changes). The path coefficients and explained variances for the model were obtained. All constructs were modelled as reflective and included in the model with corresponding indicators (Appendix A). The results of the PLS analysis provide substantial support for the proposed research model since all of the hypotheses were supported (Fig. 10.3).

In the structural model, perceived risk (RISK) explains 16% of the variance in system unobtrusiveness (UNOB), which in turn explains 34% of the variance in dialogue support (DIAL). Together, unobtrusiveness and dialogue support explain half of the variance in system credibility (CRED). Additionally, dialogue support explains 35% of the variance in social support (SOCI) and almost 71% in primary task support (PRIM). Consequentially, credibility support, primary task support and

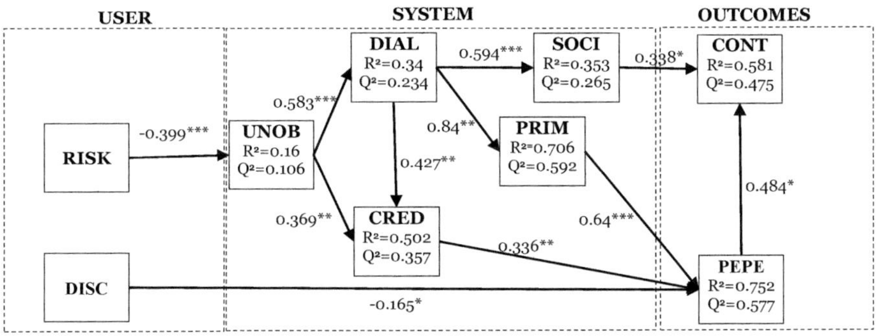


**FIGURE 10.3** Results of the PLS-SEM analysis (***$P < .001$, **$P < .01$, *$P < .05$).

self-disclosure (DISC) explain 75% of the variance in perceived persuasiveness (PEPE). Finally, social support together with perceived persuasiveness explains 58% of the variance in continuance intention (CONT).

The total effects and effect sizes for total effects are examined in Table 10.3. Effect sizes ($f^2$) determine whether the effects indicated by path coefficients are small (0.02), medium (0.15) or large (0.35) (Cohen, 1988, p. 567). Effect sizes below 0.02 are considered to be too weak to be relevant. All effect sizes for total effects are above the 0.02 level, thus providing support for their practical relevance. A blindfolding procedure was used to observe the predictive validity of the model. The Stone-Geisser cross-validated redundancy value ($Q^2$) was considered to observe predictive validity of endogenous constructs. All endogenous constructs demonstrate $Q^2 > 0$ and thus indicate adequate predictive validity of the path model in connection with endogenous latent variables. $Q^2$ is similar to $R^2$ but is generally viewed as a more reliable measure.

## Discussion

We constructed and tested a theoretical research model predicting perceived persuasiveness and continuance intention of a persuasive smart thermostat system. Results of the PLS-SEM analysis support all of the hypotheses about factors affecting perceived persuasiveness and continuance intention. Most importantly, as expected, the persuasive system categories presented in the PSD model (Oinas-Kukkonen & Harjumaa, 2009) seem to have a significant impact on perceived persuasiveness, which consequently influences continuance intention.

Primary task support refers to whether the persuasive features of the SHT app provide the means to aid the user in performing the primary task. We found out that primary task support has a significant effect on perceived persuasiveness. Through dialogue support, the users of the system receive appropriate feedback, which keeps them motivated in their endeavours. The results show that dialogue support has significant connections to primary task support, perceived credibility, and social support. This is a sign of technologies being proactive devices instead of being merely reactive tools optimized to respond to users' requests (Lyytinen, 2010). The current technological advances allow novel dialogue support solutions for establishing and maintaining long-term human computer relationships (Bickmore & Picard, 2005). Additionally, social support plays a vital role in the model as it has a direct and statistically significant connection to continuance intention. This indicates that the engagement with the other users of the system is important for the user's continuous engagement with the system, which ultimately is likely to have a larger impact on the user's overall behaviour change.

TABLE 10.3 Total effects and effect sizes (Cohen's $f^2$).

| | PRIM | DIAL | CRED | SOCI | UNOB | PEPE | RISK | DISC | CONT |
|---|---|---|---|---|---|---|---|---|---|
| PRIM | | | | | | 0.640*** | | | 0.310** (0.690) |
| DIAL | 0.840*** (2.404) | | 0.427** (0.241) | 0.594*** (0.545) | | 0.681*** | | | 0.531*** |
| CRED | | | | | | 0.336** (0.195) | | | 0.163 |
| SOCI | | | | | | | | | 0.338* (0.135) |
| UNOB | 0.490*** | 0.583*** (0.516) | 0.618*** (0.180) | 0.347*** | | 0.521*** | | | 0.369*** |
| PEPE | | | | | | | | | 0.484** (0.276) |
| RISK | −0.196** | −0.233** | −0.247** | −0.138* | −0.399*** | −0.208** | | | −0.148** (0.190) |
| DISC | | | | | | −0.165* (0.092) | | | −0.080* |
| CONT | | | | | | | | | |

***$P < .001$; **$P < .02$; *$P < .05$.

By definition (Lehto, Drozd et al., 2012, pp. 1–15), perceived credibility support encompasses trust, believability, reliability, and credibility. Logically, if the users do not perceive the system as credible, especially in a highly sensitive domain dealing with personal information, they are more likely to abandon it or not adopt it at all (Sillence, Briggs, Harris, & Fishwick, 2006). Our findings proved that perceived credibility has a significant relationship to perceived persuasiveness. Both credibility support and dialogue support are influenced by unobtrusiveness, a construct based on one of the persuasive postulates (Oinas-Kukkonen & Harjumaa, 2009). In this study, unobtrusiveness is operationalized as a contextual construct that reflects whether the system fits within the user's daily routine. Interestingly, perceived risk has an impact on unobtrusiveness, i.e., the higher is the user's perception of risk, the more obtrusive the user finds the system.

One of the key contributions of this study is the introduction of the perceived risk and information self-disclosure constructs in the context of the persuasive smart thermostat system. As expected, self-disclosure decreases perceived persuasiveness. Therefore, the higher level of self-disclosure to the app is associated with the individuals' lower favourable impression of the system. These findings support previous research about self-disclosure: people do not automatically self-disclose important information about themselves, despite the innate desire for acceptance and relational formation (Altman & Taylor, 1973). Therefore, in the context of using a persuasive smart thermostat system which controls an individual's home environment, the need of high self-disclosure might lead to negative consequences in terms of the user–application interaction.

Overall, the contributions of this study facilitate the further theory development regarding factors related to perceived persuasiveness and continuance intention of BCSSs. The presented framework is complex and requires further studies. Future research should take into account the other persuasive postulates as well as the aspects that form the users' perceptions. From a practical perspective, it is beneficial to recognize which constructs are valuable and can lead to perceived persuasiveness and, in turn, to prolonged use of the system. This knowledge will help guiding the design and development processes of enhanced applications that encourage sustainable behaviour.

Nevertheless, there are limitations to this study that need to be tackled in the further research. For instance, the research participants in this study were from one country (United Kingdom), so the results may not be generalizable to other settings and contexts, as the cultural aspects might have had an impact on the obtained results. Additionally, although the sample was rather diverse in terms of age, education, and employment status, a bigger sample is required to be investigated. As a consequence, the theoretical model should be tested further with various participants and in different settings. In any case, it is always important to keep in mind that all consumers or users are not the same, and therefore, the effect of the persuasive features will not be completely universal for all.

## Conclusion

The power of technologies lies in its ability to both harm and help the environment. After all, the consequences of technological impact on the environment largely depend on the users' behaviours. In this study, we considered a scenario of using a persuasive SHT system for encouraging proenvironmental behaviour. The main contribution of the study includes compiling a theoretical framework suitable for the investigated context, which was translated in the research model. We developed a theoretical framework of the persuasion process based on the PSD model and Adaptation Level Theory. Testing of the measurement instrument augmented existing knowledge of using persuasive system features for encouraging proenvironmental behaviour.

Specifically, this study looked at enhancing the design of the smart metering devices by adding persuasive features. The empirical findings of the study showed that such modifications have positive impact on persuasive outcomes, such as perceived persuasiveness and, even more important, on continuance intention which ultimately leads to behaviour change. Essentially, the proposed theoretical framework and the design of particular persuasive features are likely to have application in multiple contexts beyond the SHT scenario. In future research, it is necessary to develop the framework further and conduct more testing of the constructs applicable to the persuasion process with BCSSs. Larger and more diverse samples will be able to provide deeper insights into the potential outcomes of the persuasive process, for instance, the individuals' perceived persuasiveness, continuance intention, and the actual behaviour change.

## Appendix A survey

| Construct | Items | Loading | VIF | Source |
|---|---|---|---|---|
| Primary task support (PRIM) | *The SHT app makes it easier for me to reach my sustainability goals.* | – | – | Oinas-Kukkonen & Harjumaa, 2009 |

*Continued*

—cont'd

| Construct | Items | Loading | VIF | Source |
|---|---|---|---|---|
| | The SHT app helps me in reaching my sustainability goals. | 0.947 | 2.796 | |
| | *The SHT app helps me keep track of my progress.* | – | – | |
| | The SHT app should guide me in reaching my goals through a process or experience. | 0.951 | 2.796 | |
| Dialogue support (DIAL) | The SHT app encourages me to reach my sustainability goals. | 0.884 | 2.951 | Oinas-Kukkonen & Harjumaa, 2009 |
| | The SHT app rewards me for reaching my sustainability goals. | 0.924 | 4.127 | |
| | The SHT app provides me with appropriate feedback. | 0.922 | 4.074 | |
| | The SHT app service provides me with reminders for reaching my sustainability goals. | 0.921 | 4.250 | |
| Credibility support (CRED) | The SHT app is trustworthy. | 0.935 | 4.290 | Oinas-Kukkonen & Harjumaa, 2009 |
| | The SHT app is reliable. | 0.953 | 5.034 | |
| | *The SHT app shows expertise.* | – | – | |
| | The SHT app instils confidence in me. | 0.895 | 2.566 | |

—cont'd

| Construct | Items | Loading | VIF | Source |
|---|---|---|---|---|
| Social support (SOCI) | The SHT app allows me to observe actions and outcomes of other people's sustainable behaviour. | 0.907 | 3.324 | Oinas-Kukkonen & Harjumaa, 2009 |
| | *The SHT app allows me to compare my sustainable behaviour with the others.* | – | – | |
| | The SHT app shows me who and to what extent other people perform sustainable behaviour. | 0.954 | 5.043 | |
| | The SHT app gives me public recognition about my sustainable behaviour. | 0.925 | 3.207 | |
| Unobtrusiveness (UNOB) | Using the SHT app fits into my daily life. | 0.859 | 1.828 | Lehto, Drozd et al., 2012 |
| | *I find that using the SHT app is convenient.* | – | – | |
| | I always find time to adjust the SHT app settings. | 0.873 | 2.414 | |
| | Using the SHT app does not interfere with my daily routine. | 0.907 | 2.420 | |
| Perceived persuasiveness (PEPE) | *The SHT app has an influence on me.* | – | – | Oinas-Kukkonen, 2013; Lehto, Drozd et al., 2012 |
| | The SHT app is personally relevant for me. | 0.898 | 2.909 | |
| | The SHT app makes me reconsider my habits. | 0.954 | 5.015 | |

*Continued*

—cont'd

| Construct | Items | Loading | VIF | Source |
|---|---|---|---|---|
| | The SHT app persuades me to adopt desirable sustainable behaviour. | 0.924 | 3.436 | |
| Perceived risk (RISK) | In general, it would be risky to give information to the SHT app. | 0.854 | 2.633 | Benson, Saridakis, & Tennakoon, 2015; Malhotra et al. 2004 |
| | There would be high potential for loss associated with giving information to the SHT app. | 0.853 | 2.729 | |
| | *There would be too much uncertainty associated with giving information to the SHT app.* | – | – | |
| | It is safe to provide information to the SHT app (reverse scaled). | 0.812 | 1.311 | |
| Self-disclosure (DISC) | It usually bothers me when mobile apps ask me for personal information. | 0.831 | 2.699 | Posey, Lowry, Roberts, & Ellis, 2010; Benson et al. 2015 |
| | When mobile apps ask me for personal information, I sometimes think twice before providing it. | 0.969 | 4.635 | |
| | It bothers me to give personal information to so many mobile apps. | 0.963 | 4.873 | |
| | *Usually, I feel certain providing personal information to mobile apps (reverse scaled).* | – | – | |

—cont'd

| Construct | Items | Loading | VIF | Source |
|---|---|---|---|---|
| Continuance intention (CONT) | I will be using the SHT app in the future. | 0.968 | 4.016 | Bhattacherjee, 2001 |
| | I Intend to continue using the SHT app. | 0.964 | 4.016 | |
| | *I am considering discontinuing using the SHT app (reverse scaled).* | – | – | |
| | *I am not going to use the SHT app from now on (reverse scaled).* | – | – | |

Items in *italics* were deleted due to high collinearity (VIF significantly >5).

# References


Abrahamse, W., Steg, L., Vlek, C., & Rothengatter, T. (2005). A review of intervention studies aimed at household energy conservation. *Journal of Environmental Psychology, 25*(3), 273–291.

Al-Natour, S., & Benbasat, I. (2009). The adoption and use of it artifacts: A new interaction-centric model for the study of user-artifact relationships. *Journal of the Association for Information Systems, 10*(9), 661–685.

Allcott, H. (2011). Social norms and energy conservation. *Journal of Public Economics, 95*(9–10), 1082–1095.

Altman, I., & Taylor, D. A. (1973). *Social penetration: The development of interpersonal relationships.* Holt, Rinehart & Winston.

Anda, M., & Temmen, J. (2014). Smart metering for residential energy efficiency: The use of community based social marketing for behavioural change and smart grid introduction. *Renewable Energy, 67*, 119–127.

Balough, C. D. (2011). Privacy implications of smart meters. *Chicago Kent Law Review, 86*, 161.

Bauer, R. A. (1960). Consumer behavior as risk taking. In *Risk taking and information handling in consumer behavior* (pp. 389–398).

Bellotti, V., & Sellen, A. (1993). Design for privacy in ubiquitous computing environments. In *Proceedings of the european Conference on computer-supported cooperative work* (pp. 77–92).

Benson, V., Saridakis, G., & Tennakoon, H. (2015). Information disclosure of social media users: Does control over personal information, user awareness and security notices matter? *Information Technology & People, 28*(3), 426–441.

Bettman, J. R. (1973). Perceived risk and its components: A model and empirical test. *Journal of Marketing, 10*(2), 184–190.

Bhattacherjee, A. (2001). Understanding information systems continuance: An expectation-confirmation model. *MIS Quarterly, 25*(3), 351.

Bhattacherjee, A., & Lin, C. P. (2015). A unified model of IT continuance: Three complementary perspectives and crossover effects. *European Journal of Information Systems, 24*(4), 364–373.

Bhattacherjee, A., & Premkuma, G. (2004). Understanding changes in belief and attitude toward information tech nology usage: A theoretical model and longitudinal test. *MIS Quarterly, 28*(2), 229–254.

Bickmore, T. W., & Picard, R. W. (2005). Establishing and maintaining long-term human-computer relationships. *ACM Transactions on Computer-Human Interaction, 12*(2), 293–327.

Boudreau, M.-C., Gefen, D., & Straub, D. W. (2001). Validation in information systems research: A state-of-the-art assessment. *MIS Quarterly, 25*(1), 1.

Brauer, B., Ebermann, C., & Kolbe, L. M. (2016). An acceptance model for user-centric persuasive environmental sustainable IS. In *Proceedings of the international Conference on information systems* (pp. 1–22).

Brauer, B., Eisel, M., & Kolbe, L. M. (2015). The state of the art in smart city research - a literature analysis on green IS solutions to foster environmental sustainability. In *Proceedings of the Pacific Asia conference on information systems* (p. 74).

Cassell, M. M., Jackson, C., & Cheuvront, B. (1998). Health communication on the internet: An effective channel for health behavior change? *Journal of Health Communication, 3*(1), 71–79.

Cialdini, R. B., Petty, R. E., & Cacioppo, J. T. (1981). Attitude and attitude change. *Annual Review of Psychology, 32*(1), 357–404.

Cohen, J. (1988). *Statistical power analysis for the behavioral sciences* (2nd ed.). Hillsdale, NJ: Erlbaum.

Collins, N. L., & Miller, L. C. (1994). Self-disclosure and liking: A meta-analytic review. *Psychological Bulletin, 116*(3), 457–475.

Corbett, J. (2013). Designing and using carbon management systems to promote ecologically responsible behaviors. *Journal of the Association for Information Systems, 14*(7), 339–378.

Crano, W. D., & Prislin, R. (2011). *Attitudes and attitude change*. Psychology Press.

Cunningham, S. M. (1967). The major dimensions of perceived risk. In D. F. Cox (Ed.), *Risk taking and information handling in consumer behavior* (pp. 82–108). Cambridge, Mass: Harvard University Press.

Degirmenci, K., & Recker, J. (2016). Boosting green behaviors through information systems that enable environmental sensemaking. In *Proceedings of the international conference on information systems* (pp. 1–11).

Dowling, G. R., & Staelin, R. (1994). A model of perceived risk and intended risk-handling activity. *Journal of Consumer Research, 21*(1), 119.

Ebermann, C., & Brauer, B. (2016). The role of goal frames regarding the impact of gamified persuasive systems on sustainable mobility behavior. In *Proceedings of the European conference on information systems* (pp. 1–18).

Ehrhardt-Martinez, K., Donnelly, K. A., & Laitner, S. (2010, June). *Advanced metering initiatives and residential feedback programs: a meta-review for household electricity-saving opportunities*. Washington, DC: American Council for an Energy-Efficient Economy. Report Number E105.

El Idrissi, S. C., & Corbett, J. (2016). Green IS research: A modernity perspective. *Communications of the Association for Information Systems, 38*(1), 596–623.

Everard, A., & Galletta, D. F. (2006). How presentation flaws affect perceived site quality, trust, and intention to purchase from an online store. *Journal of Management Information Systems, 22*(3), 56–95.

Featherman, M. S., & Pavlou, P. A. (2003). Predicting E-services adoption: A perceived risk facets perspective. *International Journal of Human-Computer Studies, 59*(4), 451–474.

Finneran, C. M., & Zhang, P. (2003). A person-artefact-task (PAT) model of flow antecedents in computer-mediated environments. *International Journal of Human-Computer Studies, 59*(4), 475–496.

Fischer, C. (2008). Feedback on household electricity consumption: A tool for saving energy? *Energy Efficiency, 1*(1), 79–104.

Fogg, B. J. (2003). *Persuasive technology: Using computers to change what we think and do.* San Francisco: Morgan Kaufmann Publishers.

Fornell, C., & Larcker, D. (1981). Evaluating structural equation models with unobservable variables and measurement error. *Journal of Marketing Research, 18*(3), 39–50.

Fox-Penner, P. (October 4, 2010). The smart meter backslide. *Harvard Business Review Blog.*

Gefen, D., Rigdon, E. E., & Straub, D. (2011). Editor's comments: An update and extension to SEM guidelines for administrative and social science research. *MIS Quarterly, 35*(2), III–XIV.

Gifford, R. (2011). The dragons of inaction: Psychological barriers that limit climate change mitigation and adaptation. *American Psychologist, 66*(4), 290–302.

Goodhue, D. L., & Thompson, R. L. (1995). Task-technology fit and individual performance. *MIS Quarterly, 19*(2), 213.

Graml, T., Loock, C.-M., Baeriswyl, M., & Staake, T. (2011). Improving residential energy consumption at large using persuasive systems. In *Proceedings of the european conference on information systems* (pp. 1–15).

Hair, J. F., Ringle, C. M., & Sarstedt, M. (2011). PLS-SEM: Indeed a silver bullet. *Journal of Marketing Theory and Practice, 19*(2), 139–152.

Hargreavesn, T., Nye, M., & Burgess, J. (2010). Making energy visible: A qualitative field study of how householders interact with feedback from smart energy monitors. *Energy Policy, 38*(10), 6111–6119.

Helson, H. (1964). *Adaptation-level theory: An experimental and systematic approach to behavior.* New York: Harper and Row.

Hoffman, D. L., Novak, T. P., & Peralta, M. (1999). Building consumer trust online. *Communications of the ACM, 42*(4), 80–85.

Ijab, M. T., Molla, A., Kassahun, A. E., & Teoh, S. Y. (2010). Seeking the 'green' in 'green IS': A spirit, practice and impact perspective. In *Proceedings of the Pacific Asia conference on information systems* (p. 46).

Jacoby, J., & Kaplan, L. B. (1972). The components of perceived risk. In M. Venkatesan (Ed.), *SV - proceedings of the annual conference of the association for consumer research* (pp. 382–393). Chicago, IL.

Joinson, A. N. (2008). 'Looking at', 'looking up' or 'keeping up with' people? Motives and uses of facebook. In *CHI proceedings: Online social networks* (pp. 1027–1036).

Joinson, A. N., Reips, U. D., Buchanan, T., & Schofield, C. B. P. (2010). Privacy, trust, and self-disclosure online. *Human-Computer Interaction, 25*(1), 1–24.

Jourard, S. M., & Richman, P. (1963). Factors in the self-disclosure inputs of college students. *Merrill Palmer Quarterly of Behavior and Development, 9*(2), 141–148.

Kahn, B. E., & Isen, A. M. (1993). The influence of positive affect on variety seeking among safe, enjoyable products. *Journal of Consumer Research, 20*(2), 257.

Kaplan, L. B., Szybillo, G. J., & Jacoby, J. (1974). Components of perceived risk in product purchase: A cross-validation. *Journal of Applied Psychology, 59*(3), 287–291.

Karahanna, E., Straub, D. W., & Chervany, N. L. (1999). Information technology adoption across time: A cross-sectional comparison of pre-adoption and post-adoption beliefs. *MIS Quarterly, 23*(2), 183.

Kelders, S. M., Kok, R. N., Ossebaard, H. C., & Van Gemert-Pijnen, J. E. W. C. (2012). Persuasive system design does matter: A systematic review of adherence to web-based interventions. *Journal of Medical Internet Research, 14*(6), 2–25.

Khansari, N., Mostashari, A., & Mansouri, M. (2013). Impacting sustainable behavior and planning in smart city. *International journal of sustainable land Use and Urban planning, 1*(2), 46–61.

Kim, S. (2015). Can you persuade 100,000 strangers on social media? The effect of self-disclosure on persuasion. In *Dissertation abstracts international section A: Humanities and social sciences*. Boston University.

Kim, H.-W., & Kankanhalli, A. (2009). Investigating user resistance to information systems implementation: A status quo bias perspective. *MIS Quarterly, 33*(3), 567–582.

Kupfer, A., Ableitner, L., Schöb, S., & Tiefenbeck, V. (2016). Technology adoption vs. Continuous usage intention: Do decision criteria change when using a technology?. In *Twenty-second Americas Conference on information systems.*

Laurenceau, J. P., Barrett, L. F., & Pietrornonaco, P. R. (2004). Intimacy as an interpersonal process: The importance of self-disclosure, partner disclosure, and perceived partner responsiveness in interpersonal exchanges. In *Close relationships: Key readings.*

Lee, E. J. (2009). I like you, but I won't listen to you: Effects of rationality on affective and behavioral responses to computers that flatter. *International Journal of Human-Computer Studies, 67*(8), 628–638.

Lehto, T., Oinas-Kukkonen, H., & Drozd, F. (2012). Factors affecting perceived persuasiveness of a behavior change support system. In *Proceedings of the international Conference on information systems* (pp. 1–15).

Lehto, T., Oinas-Kukkonen, H., Pätiälä, T., & Saarelma, O. (2012). "Consumer's perceptions of a virtual health check: An empirical investigation. In *Proceedings of the european Conference on information systems* (p. 154).

Lindenberg, S., & Steg, L. (2013). Goal-framing theory and norm-guided environmental behavior. In H. C. M. van Trijp (Ed.), *Encouraging sustainable behavior: Psychology and the environment* (pp. 37–54). New York: Psychology Press.

Locke, E. A., & Latham, G. P. (2002). Building a practically useful theory of goal setting and task motivation: A 35-year odyssey. *American Psychologist, 57*(9), 705–717.

Loock, C.-M., Staake, T., & Landwehr, J. (2011). Green IS design and energy conservation: An empirical investigation of social normative feedback. In *Proceedings of the international Conference on information systems* (pp. 1–15).

Loock, C.-M., Staake, T., & Thiesse, F. (2013). Motivating energy-efficient behavior with green is: An investigation of goal setting and the role of defaults. *MIS Quarterly, 37*(4). 1313-A5.

Lyytinen, K. (2010). HCI research: Future directions that matter. *AIS Transactions on Human-Computer Interaction, 2*(2), 22–25.

Malhotra, N. K., Kim, S. S., & Agarwal, J. (2004). Internet users' information privacy concerns (IUIPC): The construct, the scale, and a causal model. *Information Systems Research,* 336–355.

Malhotra, A., Melville, N. P., & Watson, R. T. (2013). Spurring impactful research on information systems for environmental sustainability. *MIS Quarterly, 37*(4), 1265–1274.

Melville, N. P. (2010). Information systems innovation for environmental sustainability. *MIS Quarterly, 34*(1), 1–21.

Metzger, M. J. (2006). Effects of site, vendor, and consumer characteristics on web site trust and disclosure. *Communication Research, 33*(3), 155–179.

Midden, C. J. H., Kaiser, F. G., & Mccalley, L. T. (2007). Technology's Four Roles in Understanding Individuals' Conservation of Natural Resources. *Journal of Social Issues, 63*(1), 155–174.

Morreale, P., Li, J. J., McAllister, J., Mishra, S., & Dowluri, T. (2015). Mobile persuasive design for HEMS adaptation. In *Procedia computer science* (Vol. 52, pp. 764–771).

Mothersbaugh, D. L., Foxx, W. K., Beatty, S. E., & Wang, S. (2012). Disclosure antecedents in an online service context: The role of sensitivity of information. *Journal of service research, 15*(1), 76–98.

Nachreiner, M., Mack, B., Matthies, E., & Tampe-Mai, K. (2015). An analysis of smart metering information systems: A psychological model of self-regulated behavioural change. *Energy Research & Social Science,* (9), 85–97.

Oinas-Kukkonen, H. (2013). A foundation for the study of behavior change support systems. *Personal and Ubiquitous Computing, 17*(6), 1223–1235.

Oinas-Kukkonen, H., & Harjumaa, M. (2009). Persuasive systems design: Key issues, process model, and system features. *Communications of the Association for Information Systems, 24*(1), 485–500.

Oppong-Tawiah, D., Webster, J., Staples, D. S., Cameron, A. F., & Guinea, A. O. (2014). Encouraging Sustainable Energy Use in the Office with Persuasive Mobile Information Systems. In *Proceedings of the international conference on information systems* (pp. 1–11).

Pavlou, P. A., Liang, H., & Xue, Y. (2007). Understanding and mitigating uncertainty in online exchange relationships: A principal-agent perspective. *MIS Quarterly, 31*(1), 105–136.

Pearce, W. B., & Sharp, S. M. (1973). Self-disclosing communication. *Journal of Communication, 23*(4), 409–425.

Pitt, L. F., Parent, M., Junglas, I., Chan, A., & Spyropoulou, S. (2011). Integrating the smartphone into a sound environmental information systems strategy: Principles, practices and a research agenda. *The Journal of Strategic Information Systems, 20*(1), 27–37.

Pornpitakpan, C. (2004). The persuasiveness of source credibility: A critical review of five decades' evidence. *Journal of Applied Social Psychology, 34*(2), 243–281.

Posey, C., Lowry, P. B., Roberts, T. L., & Ellis, T. S. (2010). Proposing the online community self-disclosure model: The case of working professionals in France and the U.K. who use online communities. *European Journal of Information Systems, 19*(2), 181–195.

Potter, C. W., Archambault, A., & Westrick, K. (2009). Building a smarter smart grid through better renewable energy information,. In *Proceedings of the IEEE/PES power systems conference and exposition* (pp. 1–5).

Roselius, T. (1971). Consumer rankings of risk reduction methods. *Journal of Marketing, 35*(1), 56.

Ross, I. (1975). Perceived risk and consumer behavior: A critical review. *Advances in Consumer Research*, (2), 1–20.

Sharma, S., & Crossler, R. E. (2014). Disclosing too much? Situational factors affecting information disclosure in social commerce environment. *Electronic Commerce Research and Applications, 13*(5), 305–319.

Shevchuk, N., & Oinas-Kukkonen, H. (2016). Exploring green information systems and technologies as persuasive systems : A systematic review of applications. In *Proceedings of the international conference on information systems* (pp. 1–11).

Shumaker, S. A., & Brownell, A. (1984). Toward a theory of social support: Closing conceptual gaps. *Journal of Social Issues, 40*(4), 11–36.

Siero, F. W., Bakker, A. B., Dekker, G. B., & Van Den Burg, M. T. C. (1996). Changing organizational energy consumption behaviour through comparative feedback. *Journal of Environmental Psychology, 16*(3), 235–246

Sillence, E., Briggs, P., Harris, P., & Fishwick, L. (2006). A framework for understanding trust factors in web-based health advice. *International Journal of Human-Computer Studies, 64*(8), 697–713.

Steg, L., & Vlek, C. (2009). Encouraging pro-Environmental Behaviour: An Integrative Review and Research Agenda. *Journal of Environmental Psychology, 29*(3), 309–317.

Stern, P. C., Dietz, T., & Guagnano, G. A. (1995). The new ecological paradigm in social-psychological context. *Environment and Behavior, 27*(6), 723–743.

Stibe, A., & Oinas-Kukkonen, H. (2014a). Designing persuasive systems for user engagement in collaborative interaction. In *Proceedings of the European conference on information systems* (pp. 1–17).

Stibe, A., & Oinas-Kukkonen, H. (2014b). Using social influence for motivating customers to generate and share feedback. In *Proceedings of the international conference on persuasive technology* (pp. 224–235).

Stibe, A., Oinas-Kukkonen, H., Bērziņa, I., & Pahnila, S. (2011). Incremental persuasion through microblogging,. In *Proceedings of the international conference on persuasive technology* (pp. 1–8).

Thong, J. Y. L., Hong, S. J., & Tam, K. Y. (2006). The effects of post-adoption beliefs on the expectation-confirmation model for information technology continuance. *International Journal of Human-Computer Studies, 64*(9), 799–810.

Tulusan, J., Staake, T., & Fleisch, E. (2012). Providing eco-driving feedback to corporate car drivers: What impact does a smartphone application have on their fuel efficiency?. In *Proceedings of UbiComp* (pp. 212–215).

Uchino, B. N. (2006). Social support and health: A review of physiological processes potentially underlying links to disease outcomes. *Journal of Behavioral Medicine, 29*(4), 377–387.

Uribe-Pérez, N., Hernández, L., de la Vega, D., & Angulo, I. (2016). State of the art and trends review of smart metering in electricity grids. *Applied Sciences, 6*(3), 68.

Venkatesh, V., Morris, M. G., Davis, G. B., & Davis, F. D. (2003). User acceptance of information technology: Toward a unified view. *MIS Quarterly, 27*(3), 425–478.

Vessey, I., & Galletta, D. (1991). Cognitive fit: An empirical study of information acquisition. *Information Systems Research, 2*(1), 63–84.

Vine, D., Buys, L., & Morris, P. (2013). The effectiveness of energy feedback for conservation and peak demand: A literature review. *Open Journal of Energy Efficiency, 2*(1), 7–15.

Watson, R. T., Boudreau, M.-C., & Chen, A. J. (2010). Information systems and environmentally sustainable development: Energy informatics and new directions for the is community. *MIS Quarterly, 34*(1), 23–38.

Weiss, M., Staake, T., Mattern, F., & Fleisch, E. (2012). PowerPedia: Changing energy usage with the help of a community-based smartphone application. *Personal and Ubiquitous Computing, 16*(6), 655–664.

Wunderlich, P., Veit, D., & Sarker, S. (2012). Examination of the determinants of smart meter adoption: An user perspective. In *Proceedings of the international Conference on information systems.*

Yang, Y., Liu, Y., Li, H., & Yu, B. (2015). Understanding perceived risks in mobile payment acceptance. *Industrial Management & Data Systems, 115*(2), 253–269.

# Index

'*Note:* Page numbers followed by "t" indicate tables and "f" indicate figures.'

## J



## K



## L



## M

9780128192047